5-7-80.

PLAYING
TO
WIN

AN INSIDER'S GUIDE TO POLITICS

JEFF GREENFIELD

Simon and Schuster | New York

Library of Congress Cataloging in Publication Data

Greenfield, Jeff.
  Playing to win.

  1. Electioneering—United States. I. Title.
JK1976.G73   324.7'0973   80-229

ISBN 0-671-24762-X

2089510

This book is a product of personal experience, research, and a decade spent listening to political tales told by practitioners and journalists alike. To thank everyone who has shared a memorable, or forgettable, or improbable experience with me would take more time and a better memory than I have. Instead, I want to express my gratitude to the New York Public Library, whose remarkable facilities were made available to me for research purposes. Without this institution, this book would not have been possible. I hope other writers will follow my belated recognition of the library's value by putting their financial resources where their gratitude is.

I also want to thank Mark Wallach, a former student of mine at Columbia Law School, for his help in unearthing fragments of American political folklore.

Finally, I want to thank Carrie Carmichael and Casey Carmichael Greenfield—my wife and daughter—for their patience and fortitude and love.

J.G.

For David Garth

CONTENTS

PLAYING
TO
WIN

CHAPTER I

THE PLEASURES OF POLITICS

We live in a time when the American people are looking inward, when the passionate public issues of another decade have been replaced by the pursuit of private pleasures. Ten years ago, hundreds of thousands of citizens poured into the streets in common cause, marching to secure justice or to end a war. Today, hundreds of thousands of citizens pour into the streets as solitary souls, running to flatten their stomachs and to widen their arteries. In the 1960s, thousands of people packed classrooms and church basements and storefront offices to change American policy by changing the President. Today, thousands pack hotel ballrooms to change themselves through exhortation, inspiration, and insult.

Clearly, the premise that politics can alter the course of our nation is in disrepute. But just as clearly, the political life has lost none of its appeal as an *enterprise*. The sons and daughters of millionaires hunger for careers in public life, or for access to the political world; the widget mogul sells his

factory and plans a campaign for office; high-powered lawyers put aside lucrative careers for jobs that pay a tenth of
what their private practices might bring them. Indeed, in any
campaign season, you can see dozens of successful, affluent
professional people battling to the last for a place in a political campaign. As a twenty-four-year-old innocent, swept up
in the presidential politics of 1968, I watched as lawyers and
businessmen, academics and artists, paid their own way halfway across the country for the privilege of spending sleep-
less nights in dingy campaign headquarters, gulping down
lukewarm coffee from Styrofoam cups, planning the logistics
of an airport rally or downtown motorcade, or stood direct-
ing cars through crowds of frenzied supporters. Today, for
all of the cynicism about the process, the process itself still
attracts thousands of otherwise rational and intelligent people.

Why? What is the lure of the political life, which flourishes
in time of public energy and apathy alike? I spent nearly a
decade in the political world, at the fringes and at the center
(or, at least, an epicenter), and I think I understand its attraction. Put most simply, the political life offers more
chances to fulfill more desires than does almost any other
enterprise. Moreover, these satisfactions can fully substitute
for the impulses that bring many people into the arena in the
first place. Outsiders may be drawn to politics because they
want to stop a war, or to reduce the size and power of the
federal government, or to help end discrimination against
blacks or women, or to fight for cleaner air or against nuclear
power, or for a stronger American commitment to Israel. In
its *substance,* our system may quickly bend or break this
sense of idealism. But the process of politics offers an impressive set of consolations:

Politics is inherently dramatic.   Unlike a typical nine-to-five
job, where the mechanism of an office or factory or store is
more or less predictable and repetitive, the political world is
intensely exciting. In every campaign there is an "opening

night" urgency to the work; nothing can be postponed beyond the first Tuesday after the first Monday in November. Any enterprise with a predetermined, attenuated life-span is emotionally exhilarating—a cruise, summer camp, a convention. Politics offers this exhilaration with a guaranteed climax whose outcome can never be known with any real certainty. And because there is no way to file a crisis away until tomorrow, this dramatic atmosphere forces people to perform at levels they did not know they could attain. If a harried campaign official points to you and says, "Smithers is twenty minutes away from the shopping center and the goddamn sound system's just gone on the blink!" you will probably find a way to repair or replace that sound system in twenty minutes. You have no choice. You cannot delegate; you cannot put off the rally another month. So you fix the sound system. There is no shortage of adrenaline in politics.

Politics is a meritocracy.   You are not required to accept the notion that America is an essentially classless society to recognize that politics offers relatively rapid advancement to competent people. (Incidentally, if you *do* accept the notion that America is essentially classless, I have some beachfront property in Miami I'd like to talk to you about.) As we shall see, money is a valuable commodity in seeking political office or influence, and family ties have been known to help political newcomers, as Senator Edward M. Kennedy, Senator Harry Byrd, Jr., and others can confirm. As of 1980, *at least* 25 percent of the United States Senate is composed of millionaires, and that is a somewhat higher proportion than the national average, even in this age of the inflated dollar.

Nonetheless, if we compare the process of politics with, let us say, the process of advancement in a company like General Motors, the contrast becomes striking. At G.M., you will enter a carefully measured system of advancement, with carefully controlled chances to move up the ladder. If you enter the assembly line, the chance to demonstrate your managerial or design skills will be highly limited. Or join a police force, and you will find your chances to move from patrolman to sergeant to detective will be as frequent as the appearances of total solar eclipses. Or go to work as a blue-collar worker on a college campus and see how easy it is to convince the administration that you have the skill to teach a course in literature.

By contrast, political life is a wide-open field, where ability can be recognized almost instantly. Why? Because political veterans are more compassionate or fair-minded than their colleagues in business or government or academia? No—it is because they are *desperate*. Because politics is so dramatic, because the time to deliver is so short, there will almost inevitably come a time when a crisis is thrown into the lap of an unknown body who is wandering about a campaign office looking for something to do. For example, if it is the middle of the night, and you are asked to find someone's unlisted telephone number in the next fifteen minutes—or to find an all-night tailor, or a statistic which will prove the inaccuracy of an opponent's charge—you will have a chance to demonstrate your competence the way a small boy demonstrates his swimming ability when his father throws him into the water. There is never enough time to "organize" properly a political campaign, and there are no civil service examinations or personnel procedures. So the traditional barriers to advancement do not exist.

Jerry Bruno was a forklift operator at an American Motors plant in Kenosha, Wisconsin, when he volunteered to help William Proxmire in his 1957 Senate campaign. That led to his work as a logistical planner—an "advance man"—for John Kennedy in 1960. John Ehrlichman was a baggage handler for Richard Nixon in 1960; his organizational ability led to his ascension in the Nixon White House as one of the President's two top aides (his subsequent performance is not our concern here). I became a speechwriter in Robert Kennedy's Senate office in 1967—two days after beginning work as a junior-grade assistant—because he needed a speech written and nobody else was available to do the job. In 1974, when I was working with political consultant David Garth, we stumbled upon a nineteen-year-old undergraduate named Phil Friedman working in the catacombs of Hugh Carey's gubernatorial campaign as a $50 a week gofer. We quickly discovered that he was smarter and more competent than almost everyone else in the campaign. Within two weeks, he was being given responsibility for complicated and sensitive campaign matters, and he is today—in his mid-twenties—a formidable political figure. Family breeding, wealth, and the right schools and friends still matter—but they do not count nearly as much as simple energy and ability.

Politics is a rapid route to financial success. In the Gilded Age—the latter quarter of the nineteenth century, and into the first years of the twentieth—it was not unknown for politicians to enrich themselves by stealing. With government put at the service of the expanding industrial and corporate engines of America, people in high places were known to accept large sums of money in order to assure the untrammeled development of railroad lines, trolley franchises, river and harbor projects, and land speculations. While this habit has not been entirely abandoned in recent years—tradition still being a powerful hold on our habits—it has been rendered absolutely unnecessary. Today, the road to affluence through politics is not one path, but a network of superhighways; and they are diverse enough to accommodate a remarkable variety of careers.

In the early twentieth century, New York political power George Washington Plunkett described "honest graft" as the practice of cashing in on information available to political insiders, such as the location of future municipal improvements or the route of a new road. Today, even this kind of ambiguous activity is unnecessary. Indeed, it is possible to gain great financial success in the process of fighting hard for social justice. For example: You are a bright young lawyer. You care about the environment. You join a public-interest law firm to fight for tougher regulation of toxic substances.

You help a political candidate win office who pledges to fight for tougher laws. You join his staff, or the staff of a legislative committee, or a government agency. Two years later, your bill is passed, giving an Environmental Protection Agency power to draw up regulations to keep dangerous chemicals out of the environment. By this time, you have wearied of the battle, and you are looking for some time out in the private sector.

What will you find? You will find businesses—huge, profitable, multibillion-dollar businesses—that are searching for a lawyer to explain to them how to comply with these massive new regulations. You also find that you are one of the only people around who understands the law, because you helped to write it. Suddenly, your time is worth $150 an hour to an institution that can pay it, and that needs your skill. In effect, you began as a trailblazer, seeking a new path through the forest of injustice, and you have now become a tour guide.

This is only one way to do well by doing good. With government now constructing, or subsidizing, everything from housing to convention centers to sports arenas to job centers, insurance must be taken out on property worth hundreds of billions of dollars. Government has the resources to insure itself, of course, but that would clearly run contrary to the Spirit of Private Enterprise Which Made This Country Great—especially when there are public and political party officials who have chosen to widen their activity for the public good by providing such insurance. In New York, the then-Speaker of the Assembly, Stanley Steingut, and the Democratic leader of Kings County, Meade Esposito, were partners in an insurance company which compiled an enviable record of success in winning contracts for public buildings. Similar good fortune befell one of the sons of the late Richard Daley, Mayor of Chicago, although his luck was marred by the unfortunate conviction of a gentleman who took the state insurance examination for Daley the Younger.

Even for those whose principles would recoil at such activity, there are other alternatives. Public service itself has now become a rewarding enterprise for young idealists. When the Carter Administration swept in dozens of public-interest lawyers in second-level positions in 1977—making sure that their superiors were of more prudent views—the activists found their salaries had risen remarkably, in many cases by more than 100 percent. Overnight, $20,000-a-year attorneys, struggling along in privately funded legal clinics, became $47,000-a-year assistants-to, and associates-of. In two-career households with both spouses in government service, some found their family incomes exceeding $100,000, without a whiff of the marketplace to sully their well-gotten gains.

There is more, much more. Politics involves "campaigns," and, as with their military forebears, these campaigns demand an army of camp followers, each of whom can find enrichment. Journalists who cover major campaigns find themselves inundated with book contracts and speaking engagements; onetime workers in successful campaigns hire themselves out as campaign consultants; the Age of Television has provided enough work for camera and sound equipment operators, lighting technicians, studio engineers, and makeup artists to earn the undying gratitude of the technical community. For those who retire from the scene, for rest and rejuvenation, there is a smorgasbord of visiting professorships, adjunct professorships, one-year fellowships, and foundation grants for the study of the political process. Even the worst conceivable outcome—let us say, to take a ludicrous example, imprisonment for participation in a criminal conspiracy—can be financially rewarding. In recent years the MacDowell Colony has been replaced by Allenwood and Lompoc Federal Correctional facilities as an atmosphere for the encouragement of creative writing.

Politics offers the ambience of importance and self-worth. To right-thinking people of our age, the prospect of entering the world of commerce can be a dispiriting one. Even with the return of acquisitiveness as a respectable trait, even with the ability of the Dow Chemical Company to recruit on campuses without the presence of armed guards, the quest for Meaning in Work is still with us. Professions which offer good pay, travel, glamour, and a complete lack of hard labor still induce at times spasms of guilt and doubt. This is why the image of the public-relations specialist, advertising executive, college professor, or salesman, staring blankly into a Scotch glass murmuring about life's purpose, is such a hardy perennial of sensitive journalism and literature.

Politics is a splendid profession for those who care about the meaning of what they do. Its whole sensibility is bound up with the sense of urgency, of life-and-death decisions lurking in every election, every legislative session. Few campaigns are run on the platform espoused by William J. Bular, who ran for—and won—the governorship of South Dakota in 1926 by declaring, "There are no issues. My opponent has a job and I want it. That's what this election is about." Rather, most campaigns are fought in the spirit of Theodore Roosevelt's call to the Bull Moose Republicans in 1912, when he told them, "We stand at Armageddon, and we battle for the Lord."

Every four years, America stands at the crossroads. Each election will determine the destiny of the nation not just for the next four years, no; rather, it will determine the destiny of the nation for the rest of the century, or millennium, or lifetime of us, our children, and theirs. There is, of course, a certain sense of skepticism that can be triggered by exposure to campaign after campaign, each of which is said to be the next century's destiny shaper. As a football player named Duane Thomas once said on the eve of the Super Bowl when asked how it felt to play the Ultimate Game, "If this is the ultimate game, how come they're gonna play it again next year?"

For those working in a campaign, for those who are seeking office, for those covering the campaign, such skepticism is all but unthinkable. To spend eighteen-hour days and seven-day weeks in pursuit of political office is by itself evidence of a campaign's worth; would any sane person put in so much effort for a trivial enterprise? When you arrive at a campaign office at 8:00 A.M. on a brilliant summer morning, with the air conditioning shut off for the weekend, the elevators and corridors deserted by happy weekenders splashing in the surf or sunning themselves high in the mountains, when you spend four hours eating stale Danishes and struggling to find the right answer for a complicated question that is sure to arise in a noon debate in a hot television studio, when you awake at night with your heart pounding as you face the prospect of defeat, the stabilizing realization is that you are going to help Make a Difference. And when the campaign is over, and you are occupying high office, or are working in a Cabinet department, or City Hall, or on the White House staff, everything you do is cloaked in the mantle of the public business. Even if your job is to compose the form letters that are typed on automatic typing machines and signed by robot pens ("Thank you for your interest in S. 1618. I have long believed that federal relief for long-grain-rice jobbers is one of the most critical tasks we as a nation face. I am enclosing remarks I made recently on the Senate floor . . ."), you are part of the greater enterprise.

The substantive accuracy of this sense of importance does not matter. The urgent telephone calls, the late nights and weekends, all suggest the sense of a cause of overriding importance. If the United States will not be different after the Administration of Jimmy Carter than before, that does not change the state of mind that surrounds those laboring in his cause—or against him. It is not only possible, it is commonplace to find someone who has worked in politics for years, with a constantly renewed sense of passion, who would be utterly paralyzed by the task of finding a single act of which he or she was part that measurably altered the public weal for good or ill. This is an achievement of which any profession could be proud.

What gives this impression its vitality is that the political process is, *in fact,* capable of making great changes in our society. Though the labor, civil rights, and environmental movements did not begin inside the political system to be sure, politicians turned those movements into permanent achievements which have altered the way we live. Elected officials, after all, *do* decide who shall pay what taxes, how schools shall be run and financed, what you can build on the property you own, how our waterways shall be used, how the conduct of commerce shall be restricted, who shall operate our radio and television airwaves, and whether your sons—and perhaps daughters—shall go to war. The irony is that the process which proclaims its importance tends to make these decisions within the narrowest possible range of choices. Surrounded by an apathetic electorate—except when it breaks down into specific interest groups passionately committed to defending their narrow turf—the process moves only at the margins, as each proposed change in the operation of the public business triggers outrage and panic from those who fear that they are losing their only beneficial grip on an otherwise indifferent or hostile government. (When President Carter proposed that federal employees pay for parking spaces they had been enjoying free of charge— that is, at taxpayers' expense—the response from public employee unions suggested that Carter had proposed involuntary servitude for life as a condition of federal employment.)

Thus, the way politics is practiced today—and by politics I include the actual governing process—suggests the image of an enormous model railroad, covering the entire floor of a great arena, complete with every imaginable switching device and special effect, which has been turned over to an operator who chooses to run a two-car train around a small circle. Its proud owners can point to a mechanism of remarkable size and sweep, and outsiders can marvel at this great system, even as the little locomotive spins around the little track. And should anyone scoff at the power and complexity of the operation, a simple gesture at the unused track should serve to reassure the operators that they are, indeed, part of a great and worthy enterprise.

Given a profession with such appeal, it is not surprising that there are always more applicants than there are positions in the field of politics. This is true of every level of the operation, from top to bottom, no matter how uninviting the job may seem at first glance. Viewed dispassionately, for example, the Presidency of the United States might seem a job for masochists. In this century, for example, three Presidents—Theodore Roosevelt, Calvin Coolidge, and Dwight Eisenhower—left the White House with health and reputations intact. Everyone else suffered one or another form of an unhappy fate: Taft defeated, Wilson crippled by a stroke, Harding dead, Hoover beaten and discredited, FDR killed by a stroke, Truman and Johnson forced from the field by intraparty strife, John Kennedy murdered, Richard Nixon disgraced into resignation, Gerald Ford defeated. Look at any picture of an incumbent President three years after inauguration; he will have aged a decade. But the lineup begins to form even before the votes are counted from the last election, and in a dozen political heads dance the visions of campaigns four, eight, a dozen years away.

Similarly, the offices of Representatives, Governors, Mayors, and other officeholders are filled with applications from dozens of job-seekers for every available position; at one point, David Garth, my former employer and one of the best-known and most successful media consultants, had résumés from two thousand potential employees; at the time, the office employed eleven people. And between those who dream of covering politicians, and those who dream of uncovering them—between, in other words, would-be top journalists David Broders and R. W. Apples, and would-be Woodwards and Bernsteins, the journalism schools of America are being besieged by people who want to be writing about the words and deeds of those now besieging the law schools of America.

We are looking, then, at an enterprise of great attraction

for a great many people—those who hope to hold office, those who hope to help them hold office, those who hope to turn them out of office. We are talking about an enterprise which stands often at the center of our national hype machine; the device that once made celebrities only of movie stars and athletes now makes celebrities of politicians, political aides, and political journalists. And yet, we are also talking about an enterprise in which newcomers face alien terrain, with not so much as a road map to help them in their first uncertain steps. So surrounded is political life by myth —indeed, by a set of myths which succeed each other—that there is usually no recourse but to learn by trial and error (or, in the case of the Nixon White House, error and trial). Often, however, education comes too late: When a promising political career is in ruins, when a steady ascension up the political ladder is followed by a sudden plummet into defeat, the price of the lesson comes too high. There is no reason why those looking to succeed in politics must bear this burden of self-education. It is the purpose of this book to lighten the load.

It is important to state early on that this is not a book of spells to ensure political victory. I write as one who has helped draft too many concession statements to bring any arrogance into this discussion. The first book I coauthored about politics concluded with a brilliant demonstration of how John Lindsay would be elected President of the United States in 1972 (I also predicted in 1964 that the Beatles would be forgotten in six months). Fundamentally, no one can show you how to succeed in politics, because every political campaign is different; the same plan that led to an upset victory one year will be a sure guarantee of defeat in another.

In fact, sometimes the precise campaign tactic that results in victory one place will be suicidal in another. In 1962, to take a particularly obscure example, Republican Phil Kuehn was considered the odds-on favorite to win the governorship of Wisconsin; not far away, in Indiana (if you live in New York nothing in the Midwest is far away from anything else),

Democrat Birch Bayh was fighting an uphill battle to win a United States Senate seat from veteran Homer Capehart. Both Kuehn and Bayh used the same campaign song—adaptations of "Hey, Look Me Over." Bayh's lyric went, "Hey, look him over / don't pass him by / His first name is Birch and his last name is Bayh." Given Bayh's relatively low recognition in 1962, and the hard-to-figure-how-to-pronounce last name, it was a brilliant way to increase voter recognition. It was also used only in the closing weeks of the campaign. In contrast, Phil Kuehn's campaign used the song over—and over—and over (time has obscured the lyric). By Election Day, domestic violence would break out whenever the song was played.

Birch Bayh won.

Phil Kuehn lost.

Or consider another example. In 1972, during the Wisconsin primary, some of John Lindsay's advisers decided to try to ease his image as a big-city aristocrat. The solution was to have him spend the night at the home of a typical blue-collar worker. Lindsay, accompanied by the press, trudged into the home of the worker, spent an uneasy evening talking about issues, and slept on the family's living-room couch. The press corps treated the exercise as a ludicrously heavy-handed exercise in image-making, and the Lindsay campaign continued on to its ignominious end.

In 1976, unknown candidate Jimmy Carter came into the political season after more than a year on the road. At almost every stop, he had spent the night in the home of a supporter, rising early to make the bed. The network of Carter supporters, their loyalty intensified by the personal visits, was the key to his Iowa caucus and New Hampshire primary victories which in turn put him on the road to the Democratic nomination.

The different outcomes of the same strategy can be explained easily enough: a one-shot visit to an "ordinary" home with press hoopla is very different from a regular pattern of such visits. And the political atmosphere of 1976 was far more favorable to a candidate who sought to identify himself as an anti-imperial, antipolitician than was the 1972 atmosphere.

But it also demonstrates that there *is* no specific strategy whose application will increase the chances of political victory. To suppose that the same tactics will always work, or generally work, in campaign after campaign, is to believe that the same strategy in tennis will work against an aggressive player as will work against a steady, base-line player. You don't play Jimmy Connors with a plan developed against Guillermo Vilas.

Or—to mix the metaphor a little more thoroughly—you can't play two bridge hands alike without running the strong risk of turning your partner into a homicidal maniac. Political campaigns, indeed, are a lot like bridge; they depend on the cards you were dealt and the way you play the hand. Some campaigns—like some bridge hands—are absolutely unwinnable. In 1975, an intelligent, politically skilled Chicago Alderman named William Singer ran for Mayor against Richard Daley. I worked on that campaign, and Bill Singer ran the best campaign possible. He was beaten by a 2–1 margin not because he made any mistakes, but because the Daley legend and the Daley machine were impregnable—only had Daley marched naked down North Michigan Avenue would Singer have had a chance (and Daley would probably have called the pictures a media distortion). Some campaigns, by contrast, cannot be lost. When Brendan Byrne ran for Governor of New Jersey in 1973, he faced a corpulent, highly conservative Republican Congressman who had defeated the liberal Republican Governor in a bitter primary. Further, in the midst of the Watergate scandal, Byrne had a reputation for total integrity. Everyone connected with that campaign kept warning one another of the danger of complacency. The truth was that the only rational mood in that campaign was complacency. Byrne couldn't lose; and in fact he won by more than a 2–1 margin.

What I intend to do, then, is not to write an infallible

handbook on politics, but to pass along some useful lessons to the would-be candidate or active participant, and the interested observer. If most of my remarks are addressed to you as if you were running for office, it is because that is the best way to think about politics. This identity with the figure alone at the podium helps to get a fix on the emotional state in which political life operates. For the ambitious young man or woman, the political field offers a wealth of pleasures, among which wealth is but one. If you would make of this career your life, you must be able to do two apparently contradictory things at once: You must be able to understand the all-consuming passion that envelops political men and women, and you must be able to understand that the political life is not the measure of the universe. You must understand what drives otherwise sensible people to abandon occupations and families for nothing more than the chance to participate in political life, and you must guard against these impulses when they threaten to dominate your own life. You must recognize that for political candidates a campaign is often a matter of emotional survival, and, unless you are seeking office yourself, you must remember the world of family and friends and quieter pleasures which will keep you sane in the days before Election Day.

You must, finally, learn to distinguish between the myths of political life and the realities. Much of this book is devoted to the simple premise that most of what you have been taught about politics just isn't so. You have been taught that politicians must learn to shade the truth. I will argue here that, properly moderated by prudence, candor is one of the greatest weapons in the political arsenal. You have been taught that politicians must always please an audience. I believe that a measured dose of direct confrontation with an audience is a highly desirable electoral device. You have been taught that the Age of Television has fundamentally changed our political system. I believe that the changes in the conduct of American politics are dwarfed by the consistent patterns in that conduct. You have been taught that we live in an age

of personality politics. I argue that the overwhelming majority of campaigns are decided by issues, although those issues
are sometimes disguised as personality politics. Finally, I
believe that the political process cannot be understood in a
vacuum, that the coverage of political mechanics and maneu-
verings that was triggered by Theodore White's fascinating
book *The Making of the President: 1960* has both over-
informed and misinformed the American voter. We know
more than we need to about the memoranda from media
advisers and political consultants, and much less than we
need to about what candidates stand for and what they intend to do with the power they seek.

Although I intend to take you through the deepest laby-
rinths of campaign tactics, strategies, and mechanisms, I
urge you to keep in mind that none of these devices are
worth anything without an understanding of one fundamental
premise: *political campaigns, and the skill to keep political
support while governing, are inseparable from the reality of
what you say and what you do.* Whenever a defeated incumbent, or his aide, explains that "Smithers did an excellent
job, but we failed to communicate his achievements properly," you can take it as almost certainly true that Smithers
did a very bad job, and that the voters understood that fact.
Of course it is possible for bad people to get elected to office,
and for bad incumbents to win reelection, and for good incumbents to lose. But usually—not always, but usually—
this means that good incumbents either did things that the
citizenry did not want them to do, and could not persuade
the citizenry otherwise, or else that the incumbents did such
a bad job of teaching thier constituency that they quite properly lost trust in their stewardship.

I have drawn here both on my own experiences and obser-
vations, and on the rich political lore that has grown out of
more than 150 years of political campaigning in the United
States (which was begun in earnest by Andrew Jackson in
1828). I believe, with all due modesty, that if you take these
lessons to heart, you will come away from this book power-

fully armed to take your rightful place among the political movers and shakers of this country if you so desire. Perhaps four years from now, as you rest from your labors on some Caribbean island, frosty cold drink in your hand, luxuriating over the prospect of the high political office you have just won, or the line of clients massing outside your door upon your return home, or on the book and lecture offers that will be coming your way, you will pause and raise your glass to the source from which you drew your political skills.

That—and an occasional invitation to an intimate White House dinner—is all I ask.

CHAPTER II

UNDERSTANDING THE POLITICAL TERRAIN—AND THE ETERNAL PRINCIPLES OF POLITICS

Every political campaign is wholly different from every other political campaign, and every campaign is fundamentally identical to every other political campaign.

This is not an exercise in Zen philosophy, nor a plank from Jerry Brown's political handbook. It is, instead, an attempt to bring you gently into the political world by distinguishing political phenomena from those eternal political principles which constantly apply. If you try to run one campaign by the tactics you have adopted in another, you are asking for trouble, but if you fail to recognize the principles that remain true from year to year, from decade to decade, you will find yourself wasting enormous amounts of time and money rediscovering what you did not realize you knew.

32

The "rules" that govern political life change so frequently, so fundamentally, that the most useful thing to do with a rule is either to ignore it, or to violate it with impunity. Thirty years ago, when political parties were essentially state parties which came together in convention to choose presidential candidates, it was said that presidential candidates only came from big state governorships, that there was no constituency in Washington. For much of the twentieth century this was true. Except for Ohio Senator Warren Harding, and Missouri Senator Harry Truman (whom no one expected to see in the White House), Capitol Hill was a graveyard for presidential hopes. By contrast, Woodrow Wilson, Calvin Coolidge, Al Smith, Franklin D. Roosevelt, Alf Landon, Thomas Dewey, Adlai Stevenson, all went from governorships to become presidential nominees. Then, with the concentration of power in Washington and with television making national figures of important Washington personalities, the rules changed. In 1960, Nixon, Lodge, Kennedy, and Johnson all came, directly or indirectly, from the United States Senate; none had any links back to their home states. And from 1960 to 1972, of the sixteen major party nominees, only one—Spiro Agnew, Governor of Maryland—came from a governorship. Twelve had Senate backgrounds, and one more was a member of the House of Representatives.

Now we had a new rule: With television and Washington as power centers, only those who could capture the national limelight by way of the capital could hope to win a presidential nomination. This was a splendid rule, to be engraved in bronze and incanted through every primary night—until Jimmy Carter, a former Governor of a middling state, swept the Democratic nomination from his Washington rivals, challenged effectively only by another Governor, California's Jerry Brown, and until former California Governor Ronald Reagan almost wrested the Republican nomination from incumbent President Ford.

Once it was a basic rule of American politics that "the presidential election doesn't start until after the World Series." (This was in an era when the World Series began in early October, before the combined avarice of major-league baseball and the American television networks combined to stretch the baseball season out between something like Washington's Birthday and Thanksgiving.) The idea was that the electorate would not become interested in the election until the last month or so, and that any activity before this was essentially a waste of time.

Now the situation has been stood completely on its head. The national press has been burned repeatedly by the unexpected successes of candidates who got into the race early, and who built constituencies that were all but invisible until it was too late. Barry Goldwater was a candidate for the 1964 Republican nomination as early as the 1960 campaign, when he told that national convention that if conservatives wanted to control the party, "go to work." Eugene McCarthy began his running for 1968 in October of 1967; George McGovern announced for the Presidency two years before the 1972 election; Jimmy Carter began his race *more* than two years before 1976's Election Day. To combat this early activity, the press no longer covers a campaign; it smothers it. One of the consequences is that by mid-October, the public has become stupefied; indeed, most of the reporting in the last weeks of the 1976 campaign—one of the cleanest, least vitriolic in presidential history—was how boring the campaign was, how it had turned off the American people. The "rule" is now better rendered as: "The American Presidential election doesn't *stop* until the World Series is over."

Collecting discarded political rules is about as difficult as collecting soda cans from Coney Island after the Fourth of July. For example:

RULE: A DIVORCÉ CANNOT WIN HIGH POLITICAL OFFICE. Remember how badly Adlai Stevenson was hurt in 1952, and how Nelson Rockefeller's remarriage and subsequent fatherhood just before the 1964 California primary hurt him in that race?

Such flaming hedonists as Ronald Reagan and Texas Senator John Tower won their races after their divorces. Indeed, given Jerry Brown's political successes in light of his romance with singer Linda Ronstadt, it is safe to say that the public is essentially indifferent to the private (heterosexual) conduct among consenting adults. One of the unacknowledged events in our changing rules of political morality occurred after the 1978 election, when Brown and New York Governor Hugh Carey each celebrated reelection by going off with their respective great and good friends—Brown with Ronstadt and Carey with Anne Ford.   **2089510**

RULE: A CATHOLIC CANNOT BE ELECTED PRESIDENT OF THE UNITED STATES. Not only did John Kennedy's election shatter this convention, it is now evident that a Democratic presidential nominee who is not a Catholic had better have a compelling reason for not choosing a Catholic running mate.

RULE: PRESIDENTIAL CANDIDATES ARE NEVER CHOSEN BY PRIMARIES. As late as 1968, it was possible for a candidate to ignore the primaries and still have a fighting chance for a nomination, provided the major power blocs within a party supported him. Indeed, entering primaries was sometimes seen as an affront to the power brokers—a sure way to guarantee that you would *not* be their choice. When Estes Kefauver entered New Hampshire in 1952, and defeated President Truman, he earned himself the enmity of Truman and big-state bosses, who delivered the nomination to Adlai Stevenson. When Hubert Humphrey declared for President in 1968, he did not win a single contested primary; but in the wake of Robert Kennedy's death, and the then-existing convention rules, he was able to win enough big-state votes—Pennsylvania, Illinois, Ohio, Texas, and Michigan among them—to win the nomination.

Now, this rule, too, has been completely reversed. It is now impossible to win a presidential nomination except through the primary path. In one form or another, thirty-six states will have primaries in 1980; in most of these states, delegates are bound to the candidate they represent through one or two ballots. And this trend will grow in coming years. For any incumbent President to ignore the primaries on the ground that it is an insult to his office is to guarantee that he will be hiring a moving van for the January 19 after leap year. This rule, as with all the others, is immutable—until a campaign comes along where major states send uncommitted delegations to the convention in order to increase their respective bargaining positions—and a new rule will be born.

RULE: A SENATE SEAT IS FAR SAFER THAN A HOUSE OF REPRESENTATIVES SEAT. It was and is a virtual rule of physics that the first act of a newly elected member of the House of Representatives is to maneuver for election to the United States Senate. Under the Constitution, Representatives serve for two years, Senators for six. This was to balance the Congress: one house would, presumably, be in close touch with voter sentiment, while the upper chamber, the Senate, would be more insulated from the passions of the moment, more able to reflect on legislation and policies.

The Senate still has great appeal for Representatives. The offices are bigger, the desks are nicer, there are only 100 Senators—as opposed to 435 Congressmen—so the attention given by the national press corps is greater. But in terms of political vulnerability, the job of Representative has become much safer. In the last two Congressional elections, *a third* of all Senators seeking reelection—sixteen of forty-seven—were defeated. By contrast, 96 percent of House members running again held on to their jobs. Thus, if your interest is simply in keeping your job, rather than looking toward higher office, it makes much more sense to keep running for reelection every two years than to fight for a Senate seat. (See chapter 12 for an explanation).

These are some examples of the kinds of rules that cannot be relied upon from year to year. They demonstrate in part why every campaign is completely different from every other campaign. But these rules are like the weather conditions in a region. In contrast, the political *terrain*, where electoral battles are fought out, is, in my judgment, remarkably unchanging. It is shaped not by changing conditions, but by movements almost geologic in the lace of change. It is not too much to say that, with regard to American politics, there are principles so fundamental as to be eternal. One can search the history of our political life in vain for any shift in the applicability of these principles. They are not always easy to apply. But that does not make them invalid. Indeed, to the readers who angrily demand to know how they will help them win election to high office, or to manipulate their candidate to victory, I would respond in the spirit of Will Rogers, who once announced a foolproof plan to end submarine warfare. All that needs to be done, he said, is to heat the oceans underwater to the boiling point. Then, any nation launching a submarine attack would find its crew boiled to death, and thus submarine warfare would end.

"But, Will," a skeptic asked, "how do you heat the oceans?"

"Look," Rogers answered impatiently, "that's a technical problem."

The understanding of these principles, then, will not by itself bring you one step closer to success in politics. But they will enable you to grasp the nature of the political terrain in which you will be fighting your dramatic, rewarding, vital battles over the coming years and decades:

There is no such thing as a fair-minded political campaign. Remember the literal meaning of campaign: a military operation carried out in pursuit of a specific objective. As I suggested earlier, for anyone working full-time in a campaign, the months or years of work represent an enormous personal gamble. Regardless of whether participation is fueled by pecuniary lust, personal ambition, or deep moral imperatives, the commitment to the "specific objective"—

victory—is total. When Walter Mondale pulled out of the 1976 presidential race because, he said, he did not want to spend two years of his life in Holiday Inns, he was expressing more than an admirable sense of aesthetics. He was reflecting the level of personal drive required to compete for political office.

Sometimes the sacrifice is tangible. When Dan Walker entered the race for Governor of Illinois in 1971—a race considered hopeless—he gave up a six-figure job as Montgomery Ward's general counsel, and mortgaged his home to pay for his campaign. Unsuccessful New York candidates such as would-be governor Howard Samuels and Senatorial aspirant Richard Ottinger committed personal or family funds in excess of a million dollars, as did the brother of New York Governor Hugh Carey in 1974. And even where the financial commitment does not represent sacrifice, or where others supply the funds, a campaign involves an emotional risk of frightening proportions. Which of us would be willing to ask our colleagues, our friends, and total strangers, to vote on whether they trust us, or like us, or believe in us more than someone else? Thus, for a candidate, a campaign is not an enterprise designed to produce a casual indifference toward opposition. The same intensity holds true for campaign managers, advance operators, schedulers, speechwriters, researchers, drivers, mail-room clerks, and messengers. Here, too, the motive doesn't matter. Whether people hope for a cushy job, or a step toward a better world, they are working for the clearly defined goal of victory.

Moreover, the same fact of a predetermined end to the enterprise—the fact which makes political life so dramatic —also gives the process an unnatural sense of urgency. Imagine how much more intensely you would lead your life if you knew it would end on a given date in the not-too-distant future, and you have some idea of how obsessive a political campaign can be, and how deeply those inside a campaign resent any outside force that stands between them and victory. Remember, too: unlike paranoids, politicians always have real enemies. Like Yossarian in *Catch-22*, who knew there were people out there trying to kill him, politicians know there are people out there working night and day against them. Politics is always either a zero-sum game or a minus-sum game: there are always more people disappointed by an Election Day result than pleased by it, at least inside the world of politics.

This means that within a campaign there is no such thing as objectivity. In 1972, veteran journalists working for George McGovern found themselves raging at press coverage of the campaign; given Richard Nixon's insularity, and the McGovern camp's accessibility, they found that reporters could more easily write stories about conflicts and stumblings inside the McGovern camp. In effect, these honest reports became assets to the Nixon camp. Similarly, the Nixon campaign complained that CBS's extended coverage of Watergate on one broadcast was harmful *whether or not it was fair,* because it could only sway voters against Nixon. In political terms, both camps were right in their complaints. If you plan to succeed in politics, you must borrow the standard of the old immigrant, whose grandson raced home to exclaim, "Babe Ruth hit three home runs today!" Replied the grandfather, "Is it good for the Jews?"

This attitude has two consequences. First, you will applaud every damaging attack on your opponent, no matter how petty or unfair; second, you will protest vehemently over every slight against yourself, or your principal, no matter how insignificant. In 1974, during the New York gubernatorial primary between Hugh Carey and Howard Samuels, one New York newspaper headlined a Samuels interview this way: SAMUELS: I'LL RUN THINGS FROM ALBANY. All he'd meant was that he would spend full-time in the capital, instead of in New York City. The implication, however, was that Samuels was arrogant and autocratic. Those of us working for Hugh Carey were delighted.

Some weeks later, before the general election, a local TV station interviewed the candidates for a week-long series of answers on the issues. The camera happened to catch Carey on his way to a formal dinner in white tie and tails. There was no malice whatever intended by the station, but we were furious, because—with the interview presented in five segments—for five straight nights New Yorkers saw this "FDR Democrat" looking like a belted earl.

The intensity of the campaign atmosphere, and the win-at-all-costs outlook it breeds, accounts in large measure for the consistent pattern of outrageous attacks on political rivals that always seems to occur in our campaigns. This is as certain a sign of normal campaign fever as the frost upon the pumpkin or the running of the polls. Anyone emotionally committed to a political cause will sooner or later view the triumph of his opponent not as a disappointment, but as a threat to the survival of mankind. Look back to 1804, and you find Timothy Dwight, the president of Yale, warning that Thomas Jefferson's reelection "would make our wives and daughters the victims of legalized prostitution" (he was accusing Jefferson of a permissive attitude toward sex). Look back to 1896, and you find *The New York Times* printing a letter from an "alienist" who, after analyzing William Jennings Bryan, concluded that he was a "maltoid" suffering from "megalomania." Move ahead to 1964, and you find *Fact* magazine publishing a distorted survey of psychiatrists who concluded that Barry Goldwater was emotionally unfit to be President of the United States. Slide back to 1936, and you discover the *Chicago Tribune* printing pictures of people with dog tags around their necks, explaining that this is what would happen if Social Security went into effect. Move back in time a few years earlier, to 1928, and you find widespread distribution of a photograph of Alfred E. Smith standing next to the then newly dedicated Holland Tunnel. A caption explained that this was a photo of the underground tunnel between the White House and the Vatican that would be opened if Smith became the first Catholic President. Move forward to the more enlightened era of 1960, and you find that a Lutheran lay preacher "composed" an alleged Kennedy plea that went: "Elect Kennedy so our Blessed Lady Ever-Virgin Mary will be the First Lady of the Land."

Indeed, it is not too much to say that most people who have worked in political campaigns had some kind of empathy, however fleeting, for the tactics of the Nixon White House. How often do political workers say to themselves wistfully, "I'd sure like to be a fly on the wall over at Dithers' headquarters?" It is not that big a leap from wishing for a fly on the wall to planting a bug in the phone. How often, in preparing for a big speech, does a candidate or speechwriter wish for a flood of letters and telegrams supporting that speech? What could be more natural than for the Nixon White House to buy up thousands of copies of a Washington newspaper with a coupon poll on Nixon's Vietnam policy, clip and fill in the coupons, mail the coupons in, and then claim that the poll proved support for Nixon's policy? Or, on another occasion, what could be more logical than to "encourage" the flooding of the White House with pro-Nixon telegrams, then help draft and send them, then "prove" that the American people backed the President? Deep in their hearts, the Nixon aides believed—no, *knew*— that they were on the right side, the same way people in politics always believe their cause is right.

Issues are almost always decisive in political campaigns. At least as far back as 1952—when the New York advertising firm Batten Barton Durstine & Osborn developed television spots for the Eisenhower-Nixon campaign—we have been battered by political commentators telling us that campaigns have been turned into nothing more than marketing efforts, with candidates being sold like soap. Nothing is more common during election years, for example, than to see a television commentator taking ninety seconds to explain how shallow sixty-second political commercials are as a method of dealing with issues. Over and over, the notion that personality politics dominates today's elections is heard in the land.

As a general proposition, this is almost always false. If

you plan a career in politics, I can think of no advice more important than this: *make sure you—or your principal— knows the issues, knows how to make the most effective case for those issues, and forget about personality.* More often than not, when observers argue that issues are not being discussed in a campaign, they mean that people are not coming down on *their side* of the issues. For example, toward the end of the 1972 presidential campaign, when Nixon was heading toward a landslide victory over George McGovern, playwright Arthur Miller wrote in *The New York Times* that "if the system worked as it is supposed to, [elections] would be decided on the positions taken toward issues, but the issues mean next to nothing, apparently."

But on what was the 1972 election decided? On Nixon's more pleasing personality? Even Peter Dailey, who headed the November Group, the ad hoc agency that prepared Nixon's 1972 advertising, acknowledged that their research showed people believed Nixon to be aloof, cold, and something less than candid (how much less than candid was not that obvious in 1972). Their idea was to link these negative personality traits to *issues*—to argue, for example, that Nixon's very secretiveness was in large measure responsible for the success of the initiative toward China. More significant was the postelection comment of Ben Wattenberg, a conservative Democrat who worked for Senator Henry Jackson.

"The real issue," he said in *The Media and the Nominating Process*, "to the mind of a voter is not trust but what do you trust a candidate to do? There were a lot of people by November 1972 who trusted that Senator McGovern, in point of fact, would be isolationist, would turn over Israel to the Arabs . . ." What happened in 1972, I believe, is that millions of traditional Democrats put aside their long-held, fully justified suspicions about Nixon's personality, and voted for him precisely *because* they believed him closer to their beliefs than was George McGovern on such matters as the vitality of the work ethic, the way to pursue peace, support for traditional social values. They may have been wrong about this belief, but it was on this basis—not personality—that McGovern went down to his historic defeat.

Without making harsh judgments about the personalities of our political figures, a look at the recent past hardly supports the idea that we live in an age of personality politics. Did Jimmy Carter beat Gerald Ford in 1976 because he was more attractive than Ford? I would argue that Carter's precipitous decline in the polls between the Democratic convention and Election Day occurred because voters were increasingly unsure of what Carter would do as President (an uncertainty borne out by his performance); and that the margin of Carter's victory can be explained far more by party ties, Ford's pardon of Nixon, and the levels of unemployment than by Carter's charm. Did Barry Goldwater appear less attractive than Lyndon Johnson in 1964? One of LBJ's close advisers, when asked by the President why he was not well-liked, replied by telling him, "Mr. President, you are not a very likable man." He swamped Goldwater because most Americans disagreed with Goldwater's positions on Social Security, federal aid programs, and the use of nuclear weapons. They believed that by voting for Johnson, they were voting for peace.

The campaign of 1968 does not suggest the triumph of personality politics, either. Hubert Humphrey was, by most accounts, as agreeable and pleasant a figure ever to grace the political system. The general assessment of Richard Nixon, even before the Watergate scandal, was somewhat less charitable. But 1968 was a political maelstrom; the Democratic Party was bitterly divided over the war in Vietnam, and the national convention, with division inside the hall and disorder without, suggested that the party in power was incapable of maintaining order in its own house, or the nation's. Without question, the long-standing suspicion of Nixon contributed to his rapid decline in the polls, leading to a hairbreadth victory in the general election. But the record of the Democratic Administration, which Humphrey had served as Vice

President for four years, was almost certainly the decisive factor in that race.

It is possible to find campaigns where personalities *did* seem to be the essential difference between the candidates. Former Eisenhower speechwriter Emmet John Hughes in his book *The Ordeal of Power,* described the 1960 Kennedy-Nixon race as one where "the difference in substance between these two young veterans of the Senate—whether measured by their views on national defense, their perception of foreign policy, or their passion for civil liberties— were so small as almost to elude expression." It was a campaign where John Kennedy based his notions about defense on the existence of a "missile gap" which disappeared magically at about the time of Kennedy's inaugural, and where a major source of contention was whether American prestige was slipping, as measured by a European public-opinion poll reflecting citizens' ideas about military strength. The voters' choice in this campaign—and given Kennedy's 100,000-vote plurality, smallest in modern presidential election history, and one in which a shift of 20,000 votes in two states would have made Nixon the winner, the word "choice" is used loosely—seems to have been based on a vague sense that John Kennedy was a more appealing figure than Richard Nixon.

Moreover (see below), all candidates *do* seek to envelop themselves in symbols and traits that are appealing to the voter. But this is to miss the point: as a governing proposition, the advice of a longtime Ohio Congressman, the late Michael Kirwan, stands: "Issues decide elections."

The manipulation of symbols is a critical factor in winning elections. To say that issues decide elections is one thing. To say that the average citizen reads fifteen-point position papers on the reform of the Civil Service System is something else. V. O. Key, the great political scientist, probably put it best when he said: "Voters are not fools . . . the electorate behaves about as rationally and responsibly as we should expect, given the clarity of the alternatives presented to it, and the character of the information available to it.''

For example, voters in a given year may be outraged by the tax system: perhaps by the loopholes available to the wealthy; perhaps, as with Proposition 13 in California in 1978, by the rapid increases in the property tax. In this sense, the issue of taxation would probably be decisive. But if a candidate were to give a thirty-minute speech on, say, the depreciation provisions of capital assets as it affects income-averaging, that candidate would be unlikely to enthrall the audience.

In contrast, here is what happened in the race for the United States Senate in Tennessee in 1976. Incumbent Republican William Brock, under pressure from his Democratic opponent James Sasser, released his income tax records; they showed that, through the use of perfectly legal provisions of the tax code, he paid a negligible tax on a six-figure income. Within days, buttons began appearing on the shirts of factory workers all over the state proclaiming, ''I paid more taxes than Brock.'' Brock's substantial loss was due in good measure to the *issue* of unfair tax burdens, but the symbol of thousands of ordinary Tennesseans proclaiming that they paid more taxes than a millionaire Senator was what drove the issue home.

The idea that politicians have seized upon symbols in the Age of Television is understandable; after all, a medium which combines words, sounds, and images in any order a producer chooses makes television a perfect tool for symbol manipulation. Symbols, however, have been with us as long as we have had political campaigns.

When Andrew Jackson lost the 1824 presidential election through Electoral College chicanery, he immediately set out to win the 1828 prize by campaigning throughout the United States. In the course of this three-year-long drive to the White House, thousands of rallies in support of Jackson were held, during which hickory poles were raised—a symbol of Jackson's nickname, ''Old Hickory.'' So pervasive was this symbol that, for twenty years after the election, thousands of hickory poles dotted the landscape of the United States.

A more common form of symbolism is to identify with the "ordinary people." This is almost strong enough to qualify by itself as an "eternal principle" of American politics. The impulse to shade over the trappings of wealth is as old as William Henry Harrison's 1840 campaign, when this aristocrat painted himself as a "born in a log cabin" child, while Harrison campaign supporter Davy Crockett wrote a spurious "biography" of Harrison's opponent, self-made Martin Van Buren, picturing him as being "laced up in corsets such as women in town wear." And it is as recent as Jimmy Carter's 1976 portrait of himself as "a farmer . . . a small businessman," despite the fact that the Carter warehousing business made him one of the most affluent and powerful figures in his community.

Sometimes this effort becomes absurd. A campaign pamphlet for Franklin D. Roosevelt, whose family's roots go far back in New York aristocracy, pictured him as having been born and raised "in the old ancestral farm." And during his tenure as Governor of Illinois, Dan Walker told a citizen of downstate Illinois that he hailed from "a little town up near the Wisconsin border, name of Deerfield"—which is roughly equivalent to calling Bel Air "a little mountain town in California." And, given the reach of television cameras, it would be ludicrous for candidates such as Ted Kennedy, Ronald Reagan, John Connally, or Jay Rockefeller to pretend that their families run struggling grocery stores.

Nonetheless, politicians are constantly looking for devices, gestures, images to demonstrate that they are not part of the arrogant, distant elite into whose ranks they are working so hard to enter. Nelson Rockefeller's first campaign for Governor of New York, in 1958, became famous—or notorious—for the endless stream of photos showing Rockefeller munching knishes, pizza, and other "soul foods" of different New York ethnic groups. The implication: Rocky's a regular guy. Jerry Brown became instantly famous after his election as Governor of California for his refusal to live in the newly constructed governor's mansion, preferring instead to live in a $250-a-month state-owned apartment in Sacramento. This bold, unprecedented symbol actually had its roots in our political past. When former Oklahoma Governor William H. ("Alfalfa Bill") Murray sought a political comeback in 1930, he promised to live in the garage of the governor's mansion, and rent the house out in order to save money. (In fact, Murray went Jerry Brown one better: after his election, he planted potatoes in the front yard of the mansion.) And James Ferguson, the flamboyant Texan who became Governor in 1915, labeled himself "a real dirt farmer," and nicknamed himself "Farmer Jim," even though his spread was worked by hired hands. Eugene Talmadge entered Georgia politics in 1926 with exactly the same approach: "a red dirt farmer," he called himself, and flashed red galluses under his jacket which became the Talmadge symbol. Even Wisconsin's Joseph McCarthy, in the days before he became the champion of anti-Communism, first ran for the Senate saying of himself, "I'm just a farm boy, not a politician."

Given America's love for the Jeffersonian myth—the independent, landowning, land-working citizen—it is not surprising that the family farm should have become so pervasive in our political life. But for an inventive political mind, there is no limit to the source of effective symbols. Here is one example of how a single gesture altered a major political race: In 1965, four Democrats were battling for the New York mayoral nomination. John Lindsay was already the Republican and Liberal Party nominee, and the key question for the Democrats was whether the liberals in the party would stay with their nominee, or desert to Lindsay. The two front-running Democrats were Abe Beame, backed by the party's more conservative elements, and Paul Screvane, backed by the moderates. A third candidate, Congressman William Ryan, was the most liberal candidate in the race, but was considered to have no chance at racking up a substantial vote.

In 1965, New York City was in the grip of a severe water

shortage. About a week before the primary, a Ryan campaign worker discovered a huge break in a city water main underneath Central Park; the break had, in effect, created a small lake. Ryan went to the scene of the break, and waded in, with his trousers rolled halfway up his legs. The front-page photograph on *The New York Times* seemed to symbolize both the city administration's inefficiency, and Ryan's effectiveness in rooting out mistakes. On primary day, Ryan's bigger-than-expected vote total took just enough votes away from Screvane to give the nomination to Beame —which in turn diverted enough liberal Democrats to Lindsay to give him the mayoralty.

And sometimes the symbolic surroundings of a campaign can return to haunt a candidate. In 1972, the first time a Democratic convention had convened under a new, more open, delegate selection process, there were faces at the convention, chosen in primaries and open caucuses, who had never been represented before: far more blacks, Hispanics, women, and young people than had ever been seen at a convention. To McGovern supporters, it was proof that the closed door to political responsibility had been opened. To outsiders, it was proof of something else. To Representative James O'Hara, a Michigan Congressman who chaired the Rules Committee, it was the downfall of the whole campaign.

"I think we lost the election at Miami," he said not long after the Nixon landslide. "It was not . . . anything that McGovern did. But the American people made an association between McGovern and gay lib, and welfare rights, and pot smoking, and black militants, and women's lib, and wise college kids, and everything else they saw as threatening their value system."

There is much deploring of this kind of symbolic politics by people who consider themselves "progressive," or "well informed politically." They deplore the marketing of candidates by advertising on television, and shake their heads over such stunts as candidates who use the flag as a statement of their political beliefs. But it is almost impossible to think of a candidate who does *not* use symbols—the only difference is that we respond well to some symbols, and poorly to others. Adlai Stevenson won the hearts of liberals because of his exceptional rhetorical grace, and his obvious affection for the eloquent phrase (a phrase most likely turned out by one of the members of the biggest ghostwriting staff any presidential candidate ever had). The fact that Stevenson was one of the more conservative Democratic political figures of his time, the fact that his stand on civil rights was markedly less sympathetic to blacks than the stands of his competitors, the fact that he had at least a whiff of country-club anti-Semitism, and was vocally hostile to the influence of labor in the Democratic Party councils, were not sufficient to overcome the affection Stevenson's style instilled in his supporters.

And in 1960, when Minnesota's Eugene McCarthy delivered a brilliant nominating speech for Stevenson at the Democratic convention ("do not reject this man who has made us all proud to be Democrats"), Stevenson's supporters found themselves with a new hero, who inherited much Stevenson support in his own 1968 campaign. The symbolic act —standing against the John Kennedy machine to proclaim devotion to Adlai—concealed the fact that McCarthy's real candidate for President in 1960 was *Lyndon Johnson,* bane of every good liberal. The appeal for Stevenson was designed to deadlock the convention, so that Johnson could emerge the nominee by fiat of the power brokers.

We *do* find some symbols appealing and others appalling. Some gestures are designed to heal divisions while others are designed to intensify them. Indeed, some symbols are better than others. But to deny the prevalence of symbols as a means by which we—all of us—make political choices is to ignore undeniable evidence. Shrewd politicians will make sure their symbols are effective; idealistic politicians will make sure their symbols appeal to our better instincts. The politician who decides to ignore the use of symbols will soon be ringing your doorbell, offering a dandy buy on magazine subscriptions.

A good offense is always better than a good defense. The late Robert Humphreys was for many years a key political analyst and writer for the Republican National Committee. It was his famous "Document X," authored in the 1952 presidential campaign, that has since been recognized as the first coherent plan for the waging of a presidential campaign: with specific goals, methods of implementing those goals, and responsibility for achieving those goals. In 1953, Humphreys wrote a memo to Republican National Chairman Leonard Hall. He wrote:

> Politics is the presentation of a choice to the people. If political party A speaks only of its affirmative actions and does not undertake to characterize the alternatives offered by political party B, then it is doing only half of its job. As in all forms of conflict, attack is the strongest political weapon. It is axiomatic in politics that you must have an enemy.

Given the fact that the Republicans had just won a campaign characterized by widespread accusations that the Democratic Administration had been soft on Communism, with Joseph McCarthy accusing his rivals of "twenty years of treason," we are entitled to take this advice with a grain of salt. But, however ingenuous Humphreys' outlook may have been in the particular, his general proposition survives. It is not only necessary in political life, it is part of your responsibility to make the strongest possible assault on the position of your rivals. In one of those happy mixtures of self-interest and public interest, you will be doing an "objective" good if you fight hard to discredit those running against you.

In part, this impulse to attack is nothing more than a practical application of the philosophy of number ten of *The Fed-*

eralist Papers, in which James Madison notes that in the clash of "factions," the broader interest will prevail. As I suggested earlier, there is no such thing as a fair-minded political campaign. If you are in a political campaign, you will face real enemies, people whose every waking moment is devoted to the thwarting of your most urgent hopes and dreams. The obligation to find the flaws in your opponent's ideas and character is not an obligation that comes hard to the political animal.

In part, this impulse is an accurate reflection of a fundamental fact of political psychology: it is easier to arouse people against something, or someone, than to stir people's passions *for* something. Depending upon your political philosophy, you can always describe a passionate feeling as positive or negative. The riots over busing in Boston can be seen as an explosive antiblack outburst on the part of the white majority, or as a passionate outburst *in favor* of neighborhood tradition and the sense of community. The civil rights marches of the 1960s can be described as a movement for social justice, or as a movement against the laws and customs that consigned black Americans to second-class citizenship. What is fascinating is that no movement, however idealistic or noble it believes itself, is without a clearly defined enemy. Civil rights workers had then Commissioner of Public Safety Eugene ("Bull") Connor of Birmingham, and Sheriff Jim Clark of Selma, Alabama. The Vietnam peace movement had Johnson, Secretary of Defense Robert McNamara, Selective Service Director Lewis Hershey. Even the propaganda of World War II spoke not just of preserving the democratic way of life, or the right to boo the Dodgers, but offered grotesque caricatures of Hitler, Mussolini, Tojo, and buck-toothed "Japs." (One of the more popular war songs of the day was entitled, "We're going to find a fellow who is yellow and beat him red, white, and blue." Another was called: "When those little yellow bellies meet the Cohens and the Kellys." This, presumably, was designed to promote brotherhood.)

In political campaigns, the most certain way to win is to identify your opponent with a viewpoint that is anathema to most voters. At one level of subtlety, the late Mississippi Senator Theodore Bilbo, a notorious racist, anti-Semite, and demagogue of the first order, announced during his 1934 Senate campaign that he stood foursquare against: ". . . farmer murderers, poor-folk haters, shooters of widows and orphans, international well-poisoners, charity hospital destroyers, spitters on our heroic veterans, rich enemies of our public schools, private bankers who ought to come out in the open and let people see what they are doing, European debt-cancellers, unemployment makers, Pacifists, Communists, munitions-manufacturers, and skunks who steal Gideon Bibles."

At another level of subtlety, Richard Nixon constantly sought to put his opponents into vaguely defined camps who held positions—"as is their right to do," Nixon would carefully say—that no sane political figure in the United States would ever have held. He would explain that "there are those who believe the United States should stop trying to be number one," or "there are those who believe we should replace our free-enterprise system with a rigid set of bureaucratic controls." Then, after defending their right to take this position, he would explain why he disagreed with "them" (see chapter 6 for a discussion of speechmaking in general, and Richard Nixon's rhetoric in particular).

Attacks on opponents come in all shapes and sizes. Jimmy Carter, who ran in 1976 on the premise that he was a figure of exceptional integrity and decency, concluded his attack on the Ford Administration during the last Ford-Carter debate by saying, "Gerald Ford is a good and decent man," but then noting that he had served as President almost as long as had John Kennedy, without producing any important results. Anything stronger would have undermined Carter's own personal appeal as a quiet, almost serene political figure, who could restore our trust in government after the trauma of Watergate.

In an earlier time, the Southern political climate was stormier. In 1926, Robert Reynolds defeated Senator Cameron Morrison in the North Carolina Democratic primary by waving a jar of caviar in front of audiences and exclaiming, "Cam eats fish eggs, and Red Russian fish eggs at that, and they cost two dollars. Do you want a Senator who ain't too high and mighty to eat good old North Carolina hen eggs, or don't you?" Nor was this kind of attack confined to areas below the Mason-Dixon line. James Michael Curley, the much-elected and twice-jailed Mayor of Boston, delighted his Irish supporters by demanding of his Yankee Protestant opponent, "And where was my esteemed opponent while [a civic crisis] was going on? He was in the Ritz Hotel in white tie and tails eating a steak dinner—and on Friday!"

Fundamentally, a successful attack on an opponent can decide an election without the attacker having to make the case for himself at all. Particularly when the electorate is choosing a candidate for high office, its first question is whether one or another candidate is fit for the job. In both of our two recent presidential landslides, the electorate was offered a choice between an incumbent President and a rival who represented a distinct ideological wing of his party. In both cases, opponents within that party engaged in strenuous attacks on the eventual nominee: Barry Goldwater was assailed by his ultimate convention rival, Pennsylvania Governor William Scranton, as a candidate who "too often casually prescribed nuclear war as a solution to a troubled world." George McGovern was attacked in the 1972 Nebraska primary as the "Triple A" candidate: "the candidate of acid, amnesty, and abortion."

In both cases, these nominees found themselves isolated from the mainstream of the electorate, if not of their parties. All their incumbent rivals had to do was occasionally to remind the electorate of what their own party members had said about them: a dictum taught by Napoleon, who once said, "Never interfere with the enemy when he is in the process of destroying himself." In fact, attacks from within a candidate's party are always more potent than attacks from the rival party. Americans are used to a two-party system in which Democrats and Republicans attack each other out of habit. When a Democrat attacks a Democrat, when a Republican attacks a Republican, it has the special authority of an argument in a child's baseball game, which is always settled when one side notes triumphantly, "Your own man says so!" And once the electorate concludes that one of two candidates is not trusted by substantial elements in the party that nominated him, the election is over.

In modern political campaigns, the job of discovering shortcomings in an opponent's position is called "negative research." There is no clear definition of what constitutes an attack within the bounds of political fairness, and what constitutes a smear campaign. It is easy enough to discover the clear cases: criticizing a rival's position on taxation or housing policy is obviously fair game; stealing an opponent's medical records from his physician to discover information about his physical or mental health is not. But suppose your opponent is Jewish, and has divorced his Jewish wife to marry a Gentile? There is nothing about that fact that reflects in any way on your opponent's capacity to do a job. It is also true that in certain Orthodox Jewish constituencies, this information would be devastating to your opponent. If you can deplore the kind of atmosphere in which this information could harm a politician, while simultaneously delighting in the fact that the proper constituency has learned of these facts, you are ready for a career in the world of politics.

"Murphy's Law" is alive and well in politics; if something can go wrong, it will—often disastrously.   When I was working with Jerry Bruno on *The Advance Man,* a book about Bruno's experiences in the political trenches, he kept returning again and again to one essential theme: in politics, you can never assume anything. If someone tells you not to worry about the cars being ready for the big motorcade, the cars will not be there. If you are told that the sound system for the rally has been installed by a great-grandnephew of Thomas Edison, the sound system will fail. If El Exigente himself says he will make the coffee for the reception, the coffee will not be ready.

What is true for simple political logistics is true at every other level. It is one of the examples of poetic justice that, in an endeavor in which the participants seek great power and believe themselves capable of heroic deeds, the smallest detail can upset not simply a political event, but an entire campaign.

A few examples should make the point abundantly clear. In 1916, Woodrow Wilson was running for reelection against Charles Evans Hughes. Hughes was making a swing into California, a state where the Republican Party was split into two bitter factions. The regular, highly conservative faction was led by William Crocker. The reform faction was led by Governor Hiram Johnson. The division was deep, and fused with mutual suspicions. One of the questions was who was to introduce Hughes at a big rally in San Francisco, a Crocker or a Johnson ally. This issue was supposed to be settled with a big peace meeting in Portland, but somebody forgot to make sure that both sides were showing up, and the Hughes campaign train pulled into San Francisco with the issue unsettled.

In addition, Hughes discovered that he was to speak at a private club in San Francisco which was the center of anti-union sentiment at a time when a strike of waiters was taking place just across the Bay. Hughes feared that canceling the speech would lack courage, and gave the address—losing thousands of votes in the San Francisco Bay Area. And, by the process of inertia, he was introduced at the meeting by Crocker, further alienating Hiram Johnson's allies.

The final blow, however, took place at a Long Beach hotel just outside of Los Angeles. Because the hotel was owned by a Crocker ally, Hughes's reception was filled with Crocker supporters. At the same time, Governor Johnson himself was resting from a campaign trip five floors above.

No one told Hughes that Johnson was there. The result was that the Governor became convinced that Hughes was out to snub him, and pointedly refused to help Hughes.

The result? Charles Evans Hughes, who went to bed in November 1916 convinced he had been elected President of the United States, woke up to find he had lost California by 1200 votes—and the loss of California's electoral votes cost him the Presidency.

Thirty-two years later, another Republican, Thomas E. Dewey, was in the midst of a presidential campaign he was certain to win. While campaigning by whistle-stop in the Midwest, Dewey's railroad engineer mistook a signal as the sign to pull out of the station; the train jerked ahead, and Dewey was jostled. He referred to the engineer as "a lunatic," saying, "He probably should be shot at sunrise, but we'll let him off this time."

Dewey was joking, of course. But there were two consequences. First, it is unpleasant to see a wealthy Wall Street lawyer figure, who looked, in Dorothy Parker's famous phrase, "like the groom on a wedding cake," treat a blue-collar worker as an indentured servant. Second, particularly in the Midwest, there are literally millions of people who are closely related to railroad workers. To them, the phrase "lunatic" did not sit well. The casual, unintended remark hurt Dewey badly in the Midwest, where Truman's surprising showing made the difference between victory and defeat.

No one who has ever worked in a campaign has escaped the sting of the little detail that no one bothered to think about. Richard Nixon's 1960 pledge to campaign in all fifty states put him on a bone-crushing schedule which left him physically weakened for his first debate with Kennedy, a debate which Kennedy won decisively on cosmetic grounds. McGovern's 1972 convention effort to overturn a Rules Committee decision taking away more than a hundred California delegates left his staff unprepared for a thorough examination of potential Vice Presidents—which led to the selection of Senator Thomas Eagleton of Missouri, his subsequent removal from the ticket in the wake of the discovery of emotional instability, and the final destruction of the entire McGovern campaign. In one memorable Senate campaign in which I worked, our client became very nervous before a televised debate, and took a tranquilizer to make sure he was calm and collected. He was so calm and collected during the debate that his answers sounded as if they'd been recorded at 78 rpms while being played at 33. In addition, the tranquilizer so thoroughly dried his throat and lips that he kept moistening his lips by slowly licking them with his tongue over and over, suggesting that his idea of servicing his constituents was of a highly illicit nature. He lost the election.

Adversity need not be disastrous. Under the right circumstances, with the right strategy, it can be an asset to the campaign (see chapter 13, on political jujitsu). The point to keep in mind is that it will happen as surely as night follows day. If you are the kind of personality who finds satisfaction in an orderly flow of problems and solutions, if sudden changes of schedule, strategy, and logistics make your stomach churn, then none of the pleasures of the political life will compensate for the torture you will endure. When H. R. Haldeman was testifying before the Senate Watergate Committee in 1973, he described his goal as White House Chief of Staff as creating a ''zero-defects system.'' This is as good an explanation as is possible for the behavior of the Nixon White House: since mistakes were intolerable, any means was considered acceptable to cure those mistakes. You must be prepared to live by Murphy's Law to have any chance of succeeding—or surviving—in politics.

CHAPTER III

GETTING INTO THE GAME

To anyone with a firm grasp of the eternal principles of politics, to anyone with a vague grasp of the pleasures of politics, the most important question is how does one enter the field? In offering some preliminary answers, I trust you will note that these routes into the corridors of campaigning may seem to violate the thesis set down earlier, that politics is a meritocracy. In the first place, I give you Walt Whitman, a great American, who said, "I contradict myself? Very well, I contradict myself." The fact is that the political world is no more immune to the unfair aspects of our society than any other part. It is still, in relative terms, a profession—or trade —or art—or hobby—where ability counts for a great deal. But the assets which weigh heavily in the balance of our national life count for a great deal in political life as well.

Thus, the easiest ways of making a successful entry into political life are these:

- Have a great deal of money
- Know people with a great deal of money
- Attend an elite university, preferably an elite law or graduate school
- Know someone well-placed in politics

I do not intend to suggest that these roads to political influence are the only ones. There are other ways to make your mark in politics, and I will not abandon those few readers without wealth, access to wealth, Harvard Law degrees, and friends in high places, to the world of computer programming and tractor-trailer-truck driving. But it is worthwhile to examine exactly how these more traditional sources of political access operate.

Having a great deal of money. In the wicked old days of politics, before the triumph of post-Watergate morality, politicians either were born to great wealth, made a great deal of money, or were forced to spend much of their time associating with people of great wealth.

This is *not,* contrary to those who regard television as the source of modern political evil, a recent development. California politician Jess Unruh's observation that "money is the mother's milk of politics," is a statement that has been true as long as we have had campaigns. In what many regard as the first real presidential campaign, the 1896 battle between Democrat William Jennings Bryan and Republican William McKinley that saw nationwide barnstorming and political merchandising, the Republicans used the specter of an easy-money, anticapital Bryan to raise and spend $4 million in that election—nearly eight times the $600,000 raised and spent by the Bryan forces. The endless need for money in political campaigns meant that every four years, candidates and finance chairmen would cultivate people of wealth, people like insurance executive W. Clement Stone, who gave hundreds of thousands of dollars to Richard Nixon in 1972, or people like Los Angeles's Max Palevsky, who helped keep the McGovern campaign alive in its early days.

After the Watergate scandal revealed—among other things—the widespread use of hidden money by corporations to help fuel political campaigns, as well as the use of implied threats by government agencies to coerce people into contributing, a raft of financing "reforms" was enacted by Congress. Among other things, these laws limited individual contributions to any one campaign to $1000. This, Congress was sure, would cut down "big-money" influence on our political system.

The original law also limited amounts that an individual could spend on his *own* campaign, but the Supreme Court said this was unconstitutional. Candidates had the right to spend whatever they wanted to in pursuit of their own candidacy; and outsiders could spend what they wanted, *provided* they spent the funds by themselves, with no coordination through a campaign.

The results were as wondrous as our political system could devise. It meant that a Eugene McCarthy, who had a group of loyal, affluent supporters, could not use their help in support of his own efforts, but that H. J. Heinz III, heir to the pickle-and-ketchup fortune, could spend more than $2 million of his own family's money to win a Pennsylvania Senate seat in 1978. It meant that a McCarthy supporter could spend millions of his own dollars, but only if the contributor promised on pain of criminal prosecution not to consult with McCarthy on how the money could best help his campaign. This is the legal equivalent of telling a wealthy army to buy all the bullets it can afford, while telling an impoverished army it can enlist wealthy allies only if it promises not to tell them in which direction to point the guns.

A 1979 study by the Harvard Institute of Politics Campaign Finance Study Group concluded, according to the *Washington Post,* that the law triggered a "dramatic increase in the use of a candidate's personal resources in campaigns, making it all the more difficult for average-income people to even contemplate running for federal office.'' What this means is that if you possess a healthy independent income, you are halfway down the highway to Washington, or whatever state capital you have in mind.

In some political circles, the preferred method of application of money is still traditional. It is understood, for example, that a lawyer wishing to be elected to a New York State judgeship can expect to spend a few tens of thousands of dollars "contributing" to his local Democratic organization in one of several counties in and around New York City. But there are far more creative methods of using your wealth to build a political following.

For example, if you live in a community with a large population of old people, you can fund the Sheldon Smithers Senior Citizen Care Center, where the elderly can go for recreation, counseling, and a good meal. Since the elderly vote in disproportionately large numbers—and since there will be more senior citizens each year from now until the year 2000—your funds will go not just toward making their lives better, but toward making your political recognition and popularity better. You can produce great numbers of Sheldon Smithers Citizens Aids—lists of emergency telephone numbers, schedules of football and baseball telecasts, plastic shopping bags, recycled paper shopping bags (if you are based in an ecology-minded community), all with your name and photograph prominently displayed. Whatever the device, it will establish you as someone who counts in your community.

You can, in effect, replace the discredited old-fashioned political organization, now buried in most of our towns and cities. They handed out buckets of coal and baskets of turkeys; you can feed and warm the needy—and unlike the bad political machines, you don't even have to make house calls. You can establish the Sheldon Smithers Foundation, and supply funds to local community groups, churches, and individuals whose gratitude on Election Day will return to you a thousandfold. You can organize a Sheldon Smithers Task

Force on any issue you choose, hiring pollsters, researchers, writers, and public-relations people to (a) make sure your views are popular, (b) make sure your facts are right, (c) make sure your language is eloquent, (d) make sure your views come to the attention of newspapers, radio and television stations, and those who count. Within a short time you will be invited to editorial board luncheons, and you will be appearing on local Sunday television public-service-so-we-don't-lose-our-broadcast-license programs with names like *Forum, Perspective, Viewpoint, Focus, Probe, Query, Insight, Searchlight, Background, Forefront, Meet the Press, Face the Nation, Issues and Answers, Let's Find Out, Live and Learn,* and *Who Cares?*

This process will, within a short time, give you the status sufficient to enable you to be thought of as a potential candidate for office. If the pace of the process does not suit you, you can hold small dinner parties in which you ask community leaders to discuss the crisis facing us—there is always a crisis facing us—and offer ideas for bringing new solutions to these problems. Do not worry; sooner or later, they will get the idea.

Know people with a great deal of money. In one sense, the post-Watergate reforms in federal campaign laws, and similar laws that have been enacted by most states, have lessened the value of contacts with people of wealth. Since even the most enthusiastic of supporters cannot contribute more than $1000 to a campaign, political veterans have found themselves freed of the necessity of spending hour upon hour meeting with thin-blooded heirs to great fortunes who exchange large amounts of money in return for (a) access to a candidate, and (b) serious consideration for their world-improvement schemes, such as building rooftop dance halls in every American city to give youths a chance to work off their energy without causing crime in the streets.

In another sense, however, it has increased the value of your wealthy connections. For one thing, money cannot be raised from two or three enthusiastic supporters. Instead, relatively large numbers of people with money have to be brought together, at dinners, cocktail parties, or other fund-raising benefits, in order to raise five-figure sums at one time. Since people who know others with money are the only ones who can bring such groups together, they are considered extremely valuable members of a campaign staff.

Since campaign staffs are very interested in keeping good relations with the wealthy, you will find that your chances of landing a job inside a political campaign increase in direct proportion to the net worth of your close friends and associates. A telephone call from the chairman of a board of a Fortune 500 corporation, or from a multimillionaire entrepreneur, will not go unanswered for long no matter what the status of the law is.

More specifically, the new campaign laws have put a special premium on a particular kind of wealthy associate: the entertainer. In one of the more ironic consequences of the post-Watergate reforms, the most powerful of all political personalities of the 1980s may well turn out to be the rock-and-roll promoter. The reason is that, as it now stands, the law does not count the real market value of a first-rank performer. If Linda Ronstadt, or Kiss, can fill an arena with 25,000 fans, each of whom has paid $20 for a ticket, the law counts 25,000 contributions of $20 each. In fact, the performer has contributed an appearance worth a gross of half a million dollars to a campaign, every bit as much as did a fat-cat industrialist of another time who wrote out a $500,000 check. This is no theoretical possibility. In 1975, a series of concerts put together by rock promoter Phil Waldren brought hundreds of thousands of dollars into Jimmy Carter's campaign—money without which that campaign would not have survived through the New Hampshire, Florida, and Pennsylvania primaries. And when Jerry Brown plunged into the race, his initial funding came in large measure from a series of rock concerts starring Linda Ronstadt and the Eagles. This is not to say that rock promoters such as Jeff Wald or Bill Graham will soon be taking their places inside a Presidential Cabinet (although if Jerry Brown makes it to the White House, all bets are off). It simply demonstrates that access to wealth is, as it has always been, an effective shortcut to the political life.

Attend an elite university, preferably an elite law or graduate school. In Great Britain, the old-boy network is a venerable tradition. People who first met up at Oxford or Cambridge go through their professional careers offering each other's names for responsible positions in government, finance, and academic life. For those who are not part of the network, entry is far more difficult.

Something very much like the old-boy network is very much at work in our own political process, although it has happily become more of a young-man-and-woman network. For reasons that have more to do with mythology than with merit, high-prestige schools such as Harvard and Yale carry with them an imprimatur of special ability. Why this is so is not entirely clear. A coterie of Harvard and Yale men have in our recent past been substantially responsible for such splendid triumphs of public policy as the Bay of Pigs invasion, the war in Vietnam, and our energy policy. Despite this record, you will have a far easier time moving into the world of politics with an impressive degree from an impressive law or graduate school than you will with a degree from a less distinguished institution.

I can offer personal testimony on this point. In 1967, during my last year at Yale Law School, Robert Kennedy's office was looking for a legislative aide to assist the two key assistants (one from Harvard Law, one from Yale). I happened to be in a class taught by a professor who was a good friend of Adam Walinsky, Robert Kennedy's speechwriter. Thanks to an unexpected, and unduplicated, performance in the professor's class one day, I found myself on the receiving end of an enthusiastic recommendation, and after graduation found myself working in Robert Kennedy's Senate office.

This path into public life is at least as old as the New Deal, when Franklin D. Roosevelt's "brain trust" made academic credentials not only respectable, but almost a prerequisite of an invitation to Washington. Felix Frankfurter, who went from a professorship at Harvard Law School to the Supreme Court, helped to recruit dozens of "little hot dogs" into the federal government and its rapidly expanding agencies. This path seems to be secure no matter who is elected President. Jimmy Carter's whole campaign for President in 1976 was keyed to the national resentment against the insiders, the elitists. Over and over again, we were told by Jimmy Carter that he was not a politician, not a lawyer, not a member of the Congress. Shortly before Carter's election, his top aide, Hamilton Jordan, promised an interviewer that "we're going to be bringing people in you've never heard of before." But if you look at the staff of the Domestic Policy Council, at the operational staffs of the Carter cabinet members, at the agency appointments made by this antielitist from a small town in Georgia, you find the Ivy League representation as strong as ever.

This is not to say that a Harvard or Yale diploma is a political advantage in every situation. When the South was fighting the last remnants of the Civil War—a period in political terms which lasted from 1865 to 1965—any hint of Yankee connections was a political liability. Sam Ervin, the former North Carolina Senator who gained fame during the Senate Watergate hearings, frequently described himself as "just a country lawyer." His Harvard Law School degree was not fully compatible with this "good-old-boy" image, and Ervin did his best to obscure the origins of his legal education. But for a young man or woman looking to enter the lists—as a member of a Congressional or gubernatorial staff, as a research aide in a political campaign—the possession of an impressive university degree is a powerful asset. In a world where harried, often desperate campaign organizers are searching for competence, the sheepskin often stands as a symbol—however distorted—that the possessor knows what he or she is doing. Should you hold one of these degrees, you may find it morally tempting to raise the performances in government of, let us say, Vietnam War strategists McGeorge Bundy or Walt Rostow. This is not advisable. Do not feel it necessary to shatter the illusions which will enhance your own stature.

Know someone well-placed in politics. When Lyndon Johnson came from Texas to Washington in the 1930s as a Congressional aide, he came to the attention of President Roosevelt. FDR chose LBJ as an official in the National Youth Administration, and later, when Johnson returned to Washington as a Congressman, Roosevelt made sure he received exceptionally careful treatment from the executive branch. Johnson, in turn, helped advance the political career of a young Texas lad named John Connally, whose protégés will no doubt soon be applying their considerable skills to the cause of the increased concentration of wealth and power.

Gail Sheehy refers in *Passages* to the crucial role of the "mentor" in helping along the careers of younger people, particularly women who lack traditional allies in the power structure. In politics, *the mentor is the single most certain way of moving into the field.* When an important personality becomes impressed with the capacity of a young man or woman, that is by itself a first-class ticket to power. Here all of the other factors—wealth, access to wealth, school ties—diminish in importance. For the figure at the center of politics, life is an exercise in uncertainty. Alliances can vanish overnight; a single neglected detail can cause a major crisis; for an overworked, underrested major figure, the days are a succession of meetings, speeches, conferences, votes, decisions, which come up from beyond the horizon at dizzying speed. There is no time to reflect, to think, to get a grasp of the issues. This is one reason why self-assured figures, who seem serenely confident of their judgment, are so appealing to Presidents—why men such as Connally and

James Schlesinger, Carter's former Secretary of Energy, gain access to the center of political power whatever the track record of their decisions may be.

At a lower level, the young man or woman who actually has a grasp of the facts at hand, and has any chance to demonstrate that grasp to a powerful political figure, is home free. One woman I know had been working in a campaign for months without ever having had a chance to exercise anything approaching real authority. During one meeting of the top staff, a specific question came up about the ethnic makeup of the Democratic Party in New York. Nobody knew the answer. One of the people in the meeting remembered that this woman knew a great deal about this area. She was summoned into the meeting, gave a quick, clear, accurate summary of the information—and from then on was part of the campaign "inner circle."

This opportunity, of course, presupposes that you have gained some foothold, however slight, into the political arena. What happens if you lack wealth, access to wealth, an Ivy League diploma, and acquaintances with powerful political muscle? However simplistic this advice will sound, it has the virtue of time-tested confirmation: get your foot in the door any way you can. *Once you are inside a political arena, anything can happen.*

This is true whether you are seeking political office or a career as a camp follower. No one can predict where a political crisis will strike, where a figure will have a chance to demonstrate skills. When a young Los Angeles College Board member named Jerry Brown was looking to move up the political ladder, he hit upon the office of California Secretary of State—a job that had been a comfortable burial ground for California politicians for decades. Among other things, the office was responsible for the solemn obligation of enforcing elections rules, and supervising commissions for notary publics. But Brown sensed something in the political air. Even before Watergate was anything more than a twinkle in Judge John Sirica's eye, Brown was using his office to attack legislative lobbyists and shady campaign contributions; and when the Watergate scandal broke, Brown's office was a highly visible participant. At one point during Nixon's tax troubles, Brown put himself into the story by threatening to revoke the notary commission of one of Nixon's tax preparers. Obviously, the fact that Brown was the son of a former Governor of California gave him access to political power and campaign funds. But by turning an all-but-abandoned office into a crusading center for political reform, he established himself as something more than daddy's little boy.

The analogy holds even at the lowest rung on the political ladder. Suppose you want to be a speechwriter. You have no credentials, since there *are* no credentials for speechwriting: even the editorship of a magazine and dozens of published articles guarantee nothing about your skills (see chapter 6 for surefire advice on speeches). Getting a job in this field is like breaking into the theater. You can't get an Actors' Equity card unless you have theatrical experience, and you can't get theatrical experience without an Equity card.

Here's a solution which will probably seem foolish to you. Walk into a campaign office and volunteer your time. Then make sure that you are working, however tenuously, in an area that has *something* to do with words. Perhaps you will be proofreading a brochure. Or clipping newspapers. Or answering the mail. *It doesn't matter.* All you are looking for is a reasonably plausible excuse to bring something to the attention of a speechwriter. (As with all writers, any speechwriter will welcome an interruption, as long as it is not twenty minutes before a deadline.) *As long as you know what you are talking about,* you will gain the attention you are looking for.

For example, if you are proofreading a brochure, spend enough time doing research in a library to find some useful additional information about the subject. Then tell the speechwriter, "I'm sorry to interrupt, but there's something you might want to know about this brochure on inflation. In this state, inflation's been running thirty-four percent *above* the national average." Even better, find a mistake in the brochure copy. "I'm sure this was just an oversight, but crime is up three point five percent, not seven point six percent." In politics, gratitude flows freely to anyone saving a participant from a potentially embarrassing mistake.

If you're clipping newspapers, find something in a small newspaper, and let a researcher or speechwriter see it as an example of a warm, personal anecdote. Political rhetoric is almost always better when it is personal, instead of a mere compilation of statistics. Consequently, speechwriters always look for the story with a moral. ("Last week, in the little town of Furburg, a seventy-eight-year-old woman was put on the street—because a computer down at City Hall said she'd died. She hadn't, of course. But the computer wouldn't listen. And that's what's wrong with government these days.") Even if you're looking through the mail, you may find a letter that sums up a prevailing point of view with earthy charm ("If these politicians would use all that hot air in winter, we wouldn't need that Arab oil."), or that raises a potentially valuable political issue: street repair incompetence, housing scandals, child neglect—all first-rate issues.

Once the speechwriting office sees you as the bearer of useful information, you should find little difficulty in moving out of the mail room or newspaper closet. Remember chapter 1—anyone at a reasonably important level in a political campaign is desperate for competent help. And once you are located anywhere around a speechwriter, you will sooner or later be asked to help out on one writing task or another. It is not likely to be a State of the Union speech, or the opening statement in a televised debate. More likely, it will be a telegram to the Friendly Sons and Daughters of Bosnia, sorrowfully explaining the candidate's absence at their annual Bowl-a-Line Dinner Dance ("For 27 years, you have courageously struggled to win for all Bosnians the dignity and respect to which they are entitled. Your Labor Day Car

Wash has inspired millions of Bosnians who once again know that they are not forgotten wherever the flag of freedom flies high. . . ."). But it is a beginning. At some point in the campaign, either because the chief speechwriter is out sick, or because there are simply too many papers to prepare, someone will throw you a real speech to draft. This is where the meritocracy of politics applies. If you are competent, you are home free. Not only will you have real work to do in that campaign, but when the next campaign season rolls around, and the telephone calls go out on the old-boy network ("Do you know any good speechwriters?"), your name will be on the official list until the time comes when you choose to take it off (I was still recommending one woman as a speechwriter months after she had become a successful theatrical producer).

There are similar examples which apply in the case of actual officeholders; the key is to fill a vacuum, even if nobody realized there was one. Richard Nixon entered politics in 1946 by answering a newspaper advertisement for a young man willing to run a hopeless Congressional race in California against the unbeatable Jerry Voorhis. George McGovern became a political figure in South Dakota by becoming head of the Democratic Party at a time when there *was* no Democratic Party in South Dakota; he spent years driving around the state, laboriously recording on file cards the names of scattered Democrats. By 1962, those file cards paid off with a United States Senate seat. Hubert Humphrey, Eugene McCarthy, and Orville Freeman were all struggling academics in Minnesota in the mid-1940s, often without the resources to feed themselves decently. Because of the Farmer-Labor Party's strength there, the Democratic Party was in shambles. Humphrey, McCarthy, and Freeman got into the effort to rebuild the party early, and among them wound up with two Senate seats and a governorship.

The central point you must never forget is that the ebb and flow of political tides are beyond anyone's capacity to predict. Harold Stassen in 1944 was the bright hope of the Republican Party: the youngest Governor (of Minnesota) in the land, one of the youngest in American history, a certain presidential nominee. In 1948, he was contesting Thomas Dewey for the nomination when an unexpected primary loss put him out of the race (see chapter 10 on debates). By 1952 he was a has-been, by 1956 a political joke, the symbol of a loser. By contrast, William Proxmire in 1956 was a three-time loser for Governor of Wisconsin, a perennial candidate who would begin running the day after the votes were counted. In 1957, he won an election to fill Joe McCarthy's unexpired Senate term. He has been in the Senate ever since, and is now considered as unbeatable a candidate as exists in a two-party state. Until 1978, Howard Jarvis was a political joke in California, a contentious old man somewhere toward the outer fringe of the conservative spectrum who cluttered up the balloting in California. But when tax-cut fever hit, with Jarvis leading the struggle for property tax relief with Proposition 13, he became a folk hero, and politicians crowded around him so they could be in camera range.

Just to take one other example from 1978: a young Massachusetts Congressman, Paul Tsongas, announced his candidacy for the United States Senate at a time when Republican Edward Brooke seemed absolutely impregnable. As a liberal Republican from a liberal state, as the only black member of the Senate since Reconstruction, Brooke was regularly supported by enough independents and Democrats to give him a landslide victory. So Tsongas appeared to be a Don Quixote figure. Then, in the spring of 1978, Brooke's divorce turned into front-page news, with his wife and children forcing revelations about Brooke's financial records— and forcing Brooke to admit that he had been less than candid in proceedings before courts and the Senate. Suddenly, Brooke seemed vulnerable. Yet that very vulnerability proved to be Tsongas's best asset against a flood of *other* Democrats. Any late entry by a more powerful Democratic politician would have looked like rank opportunism—kicking a man (and a black man at that) when he's down. Tsongas was immune to that charge, since he had entered the race when Brooke looked strong. He went on to win the primary, and to defeat Brooke.

Of course, not every campaign has even the slimmest possibility of victory. Running for Congress as a Republican on Manhattan's Upper West Side can safely be classified as unwinnable, even though in 1970 Bella Abzug's opponent came within a few thousand votes of beating her. There are districts in Kansas where Democrats have not been elected in decades, but Kansas *has* elected Democratic governors every tenth leap year or so. Yet even campaigns with no possibility of victory can serve a very useful purpose in getting your name and face before the voters, or in establishing your credibility as a candidate. Astronaut John Glenn first ran for the Senate in 1964, when an accidental injury forced him out of the race (he slipped in a bathtub). In 1970, he was beaten in the Democratic primary by industrialist Howard Metzenbaum, who went on to lose the general election. But in 1974, Glenn won a landslide victory—and two years later, Metzenbaum joined his fellow former loser in the Senate. When James Buckley ran on the Conservative Party ticket in New York State in 1968, he received a million votes, finishing third behind Jacob Javits and Paul O'Dwyer. Two years later, running again as a Conservative, Buckley won the seat as two liberals split the vote. His first race had, in effect, been a warm-up for his win. (In 1976, Buckley was handily defeated for a second term by Daniel Patrick Moynihan, proving that visibility isn't everything.)

The lesson, then, is clear: If there is no easy way to ease your entry into the political life, you must find it for yourself. And the only way that can be done is by putting yourself in a position where lightning can strike. There are no guarantees that this will work: perhaps the speechwriter you approach with your gem of an idea is a rigid, closed-minded person who fears competition; or perhaps the race you choose to enter is so unwinnable that you wind up looking like Alf Landon or Barry Goldwater or George McGovern.

A willingness to put your foot in the door is a necessary, but not a sufficient, condition for making a career in politics. In addition, it may turn out that you aren't any good at it. The Hollywood story line featuring the chorus girl who must replace the star at the last minute never shows us a case where the chorus girl never should have been taken out of the chorus in the first place.

It is, however, a better way to position yourself for a political career than any other way I know of, short of the possession of money, access to money, mystical credentials, or powerful friends. Most important, however, is that *when your chance comes, you must understand enough of the specific skills of politics to take advantage of your chance.* It is to that task that we now turn.

CHAPTER IV

CHOOSING YOUR CAMPAIGN
ISSUES

In his classic evocation of rural Mississippi childhood in his *North Toward Home,* Willie Morris recalls a political rally in Yazoo in the 1940s.

"Once Pearl Hanna . . . got up to announce her candidacy for sheriff of Yazoo County," he writes. "She said, 'my platform ain't got but one thing, and that's to clean up the jail. If you ain't never been in there, you should. It's a mess, the floors ain't been swept and the toilets ain't flushed. I intend to get it cleaned up or die tryin.' "

This is the best example I have seen of a perfect match between campaign and issue. Few of you who enter political life can hope to achieve this level of perfection. But given one of the central premises of this book—that issues decide elections—your first task in mapping out a campaign is to put aside all thought of alliances, marketing strategy, and

74

makeup artists, and figure out *what your campaign is all about. What is the premise on which you run for office?*

This is a very different question from drawing up every issue on which a question will arise during a campaign. This is one of those necessary, utterly irrelevant aspects of a campaign that can best be thought of as a religious ritual. In every campaign, you can (if you were so allowed) walk into a research office, pull down a fat loose-leaf book, and find an alphabetically arranged catalog of more positions than the *Kama Sutra,* all cleared with the relevant interest group, all with documented proof that a candidate has been on the correct side of this issue since high-school graduation. Under "Greece, Cyprus," you will almost certainly find a ringing affirmation of Greek rights and a denunciation of Turkish barbarities. Why? Because there are far more Greek-Americans than Turkish-Americans. In the book of any good liberal you will find support for making Martin Luther King, Jr.'s, birthday a national holiday, while the conservative's book will promise to begin paying off the national debt.

These kinds of issues are *not* what we are talking about here. We are talking about what the undergraduates at Princeton once labeled "megacepts," essential themes which knit the entire campaign, from speeches to advertising to slogan to press interviews, together. They can be encapsulated in a single, specific issue, provided that issue resonates with a broader political message. In 1961, Sam Yorty was running for Mayor of Los Angeles after a checkered public life—checkered mostly with defeat. Yorty discovered that among Los Angeles citizens, a major issue was triggering intense passion: garbage. The city administration required homeowners to separate their garbage into organic and nonorganic waste. Yorty made a specific promise to the people of Los Angeles: vote for me, and you will not have to separate your garbage. He won, he kept his promise, and this demonstration of Yorty's concern for the common folk of his city formed an important basis for his twelve years of occupancy at City Hall, in the face of a record that placed him well in the forefront of the worst of big-city mayors.

What made Yorty's issue a megacept is that it was an issue that went far beyond the specific issue of garbage. It was a way of interposing Yorty between the ordinary citizen and the ever-intrusive bureaucracy that always seems to demand one more form, one more concession to City Hall, one more step to make their life easier while yours became just that more difficult. *I will help you defeat these people,* Yorty's stand promised. *I will get them off your backs just this once.*

The choice of such a theme is extremely difficult, because it depends on a specific mix of the candidate and the political atmosphere. The same megacept which crashes on takeoff in one election year can take a candidate to victory in the next. Take, as an instructive example, the issue of trust as a fundamental campaign theme, and what happened to it over the course of four presidential elections.

In 1968, an exhausted electorate faced a choice among Hubert Humphrey, Richard Nixon, and George Wallace. Nixon's "Tricky Dick" reputation was still stalking him; Humphrey's reputation as a champion of liberalism had been badly tarnished by his service as the intellectual cheerleader of the Vietnam War, and George Wallace was too much the red-neck racist to translate the public's disaffection with mainstream politicians into votes for himself (particularly after he chose as his running mate retired General Curtis LeMay, who turned his initial press conference into a ringing endorsement of life under nuclear fallout). In the midst of this unappealing political season, the presence of Democratic vice-presidential nominee Ed Muskie was a breath of fresh air. His quiet rhetoric, his sense of old-fashioned New England solidity, his patience in inviting hecklers up to the podium to express their views, all seemed to promise relief from the bitter divisions of the past years. Muskie came out of the 1968 election the clear front-runner for 1972—a position enhanced when, in the 1970 Congressional elections, his calm election eve speech contrasted so effectively with a near-hysterical, poorly produced speech by President Nixon.

In preparing for the 1972 presidential campaign, then, Muskie's team believed, with good reason—that the character of Ed Muskie was his strongest asset. The theme, the megacept of 1972, would be "Trust Muskie," a plea to unite the divided Democratic Party by focusing on the appeal of the man instead of on the appeal of his stands. But as a theme, the "Trust Muskie" appeal ran directly into the bitter divisions within the Democratic Party that had not begun to heal. The antiwar activists, denied their triumph in Chicago in 1968, and encouraged by the new rules that opened party participation, had both organizational skills and a candidate of their choice, Senator George McGovern. They were in no mood to trust Muskie, who had supported the Administration position on the Vietnam War in 1968. At the same time, Muskie's attempts to reach out to the left wing of his party were anathema to its right wing. They had Henry Jackson, an unregenerate hawk, as their candidate, while the traditional labor–big-city Democrats had Hubert Humphrey as theirs. Muskie wound up in the middle of a polarized party with no constituency, and by the middle of the primary season Muskie's campaign was dead.

By 1976, the entire political picture had changed. The Watergate scandal had driven Nixon from office, and a payoff scandal had driven Vice-President Agnew from office. The corruption of the political process had been the single most dominant story in the national press. The win-at-all-costs philosophy had been temporarily discredited as a campaign philosophy, and in 1975, American troops had fled Saigon in the final chapter in the humiliation of the United States at the hands of a determined small nation. Now, in an atmosphere of disenchantment, the same campaign theme that was so wrong in 1972 was exactly right.

The campaign of Jimmy Carter was, in substance, nothing more than an echo of Ed Muskie's campaign. Had 1976 been a year when specific stands counted, Carter would have been

more vulnerable than Muskie had been four years earlier.
Carter had seconded the nomination of war-hawk Jackson in
'72; he had as Georgia's Governor staged a ceremony that
seemed very much an indication of support behind accused
My Lai massacre leader Lieutenant William Calley; and his
affection for such worthies as George Wallace and former
Georgia Governor Lester Maddox was at the least disturbing
to liberals.

But 1976 was not 1972. The Democratic Party, including
those idealists who had first entered politics in 1968, was
now impatient for victory, perhaps out of a lust to begin
making America better, perhaps out of a lust for those offices
and perquisites which have always beckoned less refined
figures. The war was over. As one former peace activist said,
half-jokingly at the time, "The statute of limitations on war
crimes has expired." Ideological purity was in remission.

Moreover, the endless analyses of Richard Nixon's character defects, the probing of his family life, his paranoid fear
of enemies, his lack of trust in friends or respect of foes, had
made us a nation of psychoanalysts. We wanted to see evidence of a candidate's personal strength. In such an atmosphere, Jimmy Carter was a perfect candidate. His very
vagueness on the issues made him a vessel into which disparate constituencies could pour their hopes. Each of us
heard what we wanted to hear, as Carter moved through the
primaries as the representative of cognitive dissonance. The
very lack of experience which would have made him a laugh-
ingstock in most election years made him attractive in 1976.
"I'm not a lawyer, I'm not a politician, I don't come from
the Congress," Carter boasted again and again, and America
thought of the lawyers and the politicians serving time in
federal prisons, or thought of the Congressmen in deep con-
sultation with secretaries who couldn't type or Koreans
bearing gifts. And when we looked at Carter's personal life,
his background, his roots, it almost looked too good to be
true.

He came from Plains, a town whose very name resonates
with a sense of trust: Plain, not fancy, the Great Plains (and

for Jewish voters, the two-cents Plains). The town looked
like a movie set, with appealing little storefronts up and
down Main Street. The family seemed out of general casting:
a sprightly old woman for the senior citizens and the femin-
ists, a cute eight-year-old for the motherly and fatherly in-
clined, a faith-healing sister to reinforce Carter's religiosity,
and a nephew in prison for the Willie Nelson–Waylon
Jennings outlaw fans. For those Southerners uncertain
of Carter's "good-old-boy" qualities, there was a beer-
guzzling, foulmouthed, overweight brother who ran a gas
station. For those of the counterculture, who feared that a
Southerner would be hostile to their way of life, there were
quotations from Bob Dylan songs scattered through his au-
tobiography and his speeches (although, when a Northern
reporter asked Carter which song, or which album, he especially liked, Carter proved especially vague on the work of
the singer he so admired). At the time, the whole campaign
seemed more like a carefully calculated situation comedy on
television, cast and set in appealing ways, rather than a presidential campaign. (This sense was fortified in a Fireside
Chat by President Carter, during which he wore a tie and a
sweater—an obvious steal from Ozzie Nelson.)

But it worked well enough to bring Jimmy Carter from
almost-total obscurity to the Democratic nomination. True,
the Carter general election campaign was a disaster, because
the questions that had been deferred during the primary campaign came up with a vengeance after the conventions: What
does Jimmy Carter intend to do as President? Does his distance from the mechanics of national government really
make him better qualified to run that government? The hunger to believe, however, along with Ford's pardon of Nixon
and the sluggish economy, proved strong enough to put him
into office.

By 1980, however, the idea of trust as a megacept had
become totally discredited. Whatever the final play of 1980's
cards, it is clear that electing an upright character as President is not good enough. The purchasing power of the dollar
is too low, gasoline and home-heating oil prices are too high,

to be charmed or inspired by a pleasant fellow. This explains how a figure such as John Connally could even aspire to the Presidency in 1980. Four years earlier, a candidate who had been indicted by a federal grand jury, who had been a Texas wheeler-dealer in the Lyndon Johnson mold, who was an unabashed champion of big business and the corporate elite, who had advised President Nixon to destroy the White House tapes, would have been a joke. In 1980, however, competence, not trust, is the key megacept.

To give you a broader sense of what will and will not work as a megacept, let's look at several important campaigns over the last decade or so, with special attention to the *slogans* that were used in these campaigns. For all their similarity to marketing and advertising techniques, slogans provide a splendid clue to the fundamental premises of a candidate. The Republicans dominated national politics throughout the last third of the nineteenth century by evoking memories of Civil War passions with the slogan: "Vote As You Shot." In 1946, the massive Republican gains in Congressional elections came about because of a widespread disaffection with scandal and incompetence in Washington, captured in the simple phrase, "Had Enough?" Slogans, then, can illuminate a megacept *because* of their very simplicity.

LINDSAY IN 1969. John Lindsay had been elected Mayor of New York in 1965 as a Republican-Liberal, in response to twenty years of traditional Democratic rule which had left the city in a crisis. Racial division, crime, and a pervasive sense of drift had seemed to call for a leader in the Kennedy image, free of the taint of the clubhouse and determined to reform city government from top to bottom. In the first years of Lindsay's term, it seemed to be working. His walks through dangerous city neighborhoods, his energy, his ability to keep the city from exploding, had won him strong support. By 1969, it was all unraveling. A bitter teachers' strike had split the city along racial lines. Police, fire fighters, sanitation workers, bridge handlers, had all at different times fought Lindsay bitterly, with job actions or strikes. In blue-collar neighborhoods, Lindsay was seen as a pro-black Mayor, and the police were saying that his administration had "handcuffed" them in cracking down on criminals.

In planning the campaign (I was working for Lindsay at the time), it was understood that the mistakes of the first term could not be ignored. They would have to be acknowledged and placed in context. At the same time, Lindsay's stature would have to be rebuilt, by measuring his performance against the size of the job—and in so doing, measure Lindsay against his rivals. Finally, since Lindsay had emerged as a leader for the urban centers of America, and since the need for more federal funds then going in such huge numbers to the Vietnam War was a key element in Lindsay's political approach, the national perspective had to be brought into the campaign for Mayor.

The slogan developed in this campaign was to the point: "Vote for Mayor Lindsay: It's the second toughest job in America." (At a benefit in that campaign, Woody Allen remarked that "the first toughest job is held by Mrs. Spiro Agnew.") It was a slogan that encompassed the megacept: that Lindsay's errors were due to the enormous burden of the job of Mayor, and that Lindsay's opponents lacked the ability to cope with this job. The campaign was greatly aided in this theme by the Democratic primary victory of Mario Procaccino, a florid, highly conservative politician who brought to mind The Great Gildersleeve. It was Procaccino who, when campaigning for Frank O'Connor, Democratic nominee for Governor in 1966, exclaimed to a crowd, "Frank O'Connor grows on you—like cancer!" and who explained his emotional, tearful announcement statement by saying, "Yes, I'm emotional; Jesus Christ was emotional." So in emphasizing the difficulty of the job, the Lindsay campaign was also saying, in effect, "Do you really think Procaccino is up to this job?" In addition, Lindsay's frequent references to the cost of the Vietnam War and the defense budget fit the megacept. Instead of appearing as a simplistic cop-out, it was a way of explaining why the job was so hard: because the city wasn't getting its fair share of funds. Not so incidentally, it was an issue that helped keep disaffected Jewish liberals in Lindsay's camp.

I don't want to exaggerate the impact of this slogan, nor the success of the campaign. As an incumbent Mayor, Lindsay won reelection on the Liberal Party line with 43 percent of the vote. Fifty-seven percent of the voters chose between Democrat Procaccino, and Republican John Marchi. But it is clear that without some basic premise to convince disillusioned supporters that Lindsay deserved a second term, even this victory would have been impossible.

JAMES BUCKLEY IN 1970.   Just as Lindsay had won as a liberal benefiting from two conservative opponents, James Buckley was elected Senator from New York as a conservative benefiting from two liberals as his opponents. But the key to Buckley's victory was his ability to draw traditional Democratic votes to himself, while running on the Conservative Party line. It was a time when the passions of the 1960s were still very much alive, when the scars of campus turmoil, violent street demonstrations, and the cultural divisions were very much with us. The Nixon Administration had launched a campaign to cash in on the "social issues": the anger on the part of the traditional majority with such behavior as drug use, sexual liberation—or libertinism—the "permissive" approaches to crime and school discipline. The whole premise of the Buckley campaign was that only he represented the true feelings of most New Yorkers, while both Democrat Richard Ottinger and Republican-Liberal Charles Goodell were more sympathetic to the dissidents.

The Buckley slogan in 1970 was: "Isn't it about time *we* had a Senator?" It was a perfect open-ended summation of the key campaign theme. Were you outraged at overprivileged students who burned down the campuses to which blue-collar workers were hoping to send their children? Then it was about time *we* had a Senator who understood that.

Were you in favor of the war in Vietnam, or at least against the opposition which seemed to denigrate our boys in the field? At last *we* could do something about it.

There was another constituency to which this slogan might well have appealed. New York's other Senator, Republican-Liberal Jacob Javits, is Jewish. Buckley's principal opponent in 1970, Richard Ottinger, is also Jewish. Whether it was intended or not—and there was not the least hint of any religious appeal in Buckley's campaign—the "we" in his slogan could have been read by some to mean that the Christian majority in New York was entitled to at least one of the two United States Senators. The advantage of such a slogan, and of a broad megacept of the kind Buckley was expressing, is that it does not have sharp limits. Unlike a particular issue or platform, it can reach into places even its creators did not fathom.

WALLACE IN 1972.   In 1968, George Wallace had won some ten million votes as a third-party candidate, moving from his Southern segregationist base to a national one. It was a process that had begun as far back as 1964, when Wallace had entered three Democratic primaries outside the South, and had won between 30 and 40 percent of the vote against stand-ins for President Johnson. Now, in 1972, Wallace was back in the Democratic Party, entering primaries, hoping to capitalize on the spreading unhappiness with such policies as school busing, smoothing out his segregationist line with a general attack on federal bureaucrats "who couldn't park a bicycle straight stickin' their noses into people's affairs," and attacking elitists such as the Ford Foundation for using tax-exempt funds for social engineering.

The key to the Wallace campaign was resentment—not just against blacks, but against the whole Establishment that seemed to be turning its back on traditions such as hard work, loyalty, and property rights. The slogan of the campaign was: "Send them a message." It was a slogan that, in the words of Nixon advertising director Peter Dailey, was "sheer genius. The slogan was open-ended. Whatever your beef was, if you voted for George, you got it off your mind." There was another dimension as well. A primary, unlike a general election, is something of a "free vote." It's a chance for disaffected voters of all varieties to express a sense of resentment without it "counting" for keeps. In a primary, voters tend to be more willing to vote for a candidate on the fringe, rather than in the mainstream of a party, because they are not *really* voting for the person whose finger will be on the button. It is exactly the right time to "send them a message," to let the people in power know how much they have failed us by shocking them with a vote. Because Wallace was shot and paralyzed just before the Maryland and Michigan primaries, the full appeal of the Wallace megacept is impossible to measure. But it was a theme which reached a wide constituency throughout the country.

TOM BRADLEY IN 1973.   When Tom Bradley ran for Mayor in 1969 in the Los Angeles municipal election, he ran far ahead of incumbent Mayor Sam Yorty in the first primary. But because he did not win 50 percent of the vote, he had to face Yorty in a runoff; and in a campaign as vicious and racist as any that had been seen outside the Deep South in the Dark Ages. Yorty had beaten back Bradley's effort to become the first black Mayor of Los Angeles.

In 1973, Bradley ran again. What the campaign was looking for was a theme that would go after a highly vulnerable Yorty, who was a constant seeker after higher office and who had set some kind of record for foreign travel by a visiting mayor. But we (Dave Garth was the media adviser) were also looking for a way to ease the obvious racial fears of the Los Angeles majority. It was not so much Bradley who frightened them—he had been a Los Angeles police officer for twenty years, a City Councilman for ten, and an "extreme moderate" on racial matters. The question, rather, was whether Bradley would somehow open the door to more radical elements, to more violent forces within the black community, and would somehow open the city treasury to welfare clients. (When you look at the political terrain before an election, it is easy to despair at the perceptions of the people you are trying to win over, but to ignore these feelings is like ignoring a navigation chart because you are philosophically opposed to reefs.)

The slogan that was developed was elaborate—much too long by traditional political standards. It read: "Isn't it about time we had a mayor who wanted to be mayor? Vote for Tom Bradley. He'll work as hard for his paycheck as you do for yours."

The first part of the slogan was designed to damage Yorty on two fronts. In 1966 and in 1970 he had sought the governorship of California. In 1972, he had run a brief race for the Presidency, largely with the help of *Manchester* (New Hampshire) *Union-Leader* publisher William Loeb. Both these efforts and his frequent travels—a source of great humor from Johnny Carson in his *Tonight* show monologues —suggested that he really didn't want the job, and that he was almost contemptuous of the Los Angeles electorate for asking them for this stepping-stone job again.

The second part of the slogan was more crucial to the campaign's central theme. By saying that Bradley would "work as hard for his paycheck as you do for yours," we were trying to say (a) Yorty wasn't working for his salary, (b) Bradley would earn the job of Mayor, (c) Bradley understood the premises of the work ethic and was no permissive open-the-treasury welfare enthusiast, (d) Bradley understands how hard you, the typical voter, work for your paycheck because *he is one of you.* The entire campaign was premised on the need to confront as directly as possible the specific racial uncertainties of white Los Angeles, and to answer them; to convince them that Bradley was the alternative to Yorty the city was looking for. He won a landslide victory.

HUGH CAREY IN 1974. When Hugh Carey entered the Democratic primary for New York Governor in 1974, he was known to less than 10 percent of the electorate. His key opponent, Off-Track Betting chief Howard Samuels, had been running for Governor since 1962, had run a respectable primary effort in 1970, and held a highly visible job running the city's legalized horse-betting system. As a seven-term Congressman from Brooklyn, Carey had compiled a good legislative record. But nobody knew who he was.

Nineteen seventy-four was also the year of Watergate, when the whole political world was in disrepute. No campaign could succeed in this year by proudly embracing the great traditions of the American system of government. But Carey was clearly a politician: a Brooklyn, Irish politician who was a Congressional insider as a member of the tax-writing Ways and Means Committee. The key for the Carey campaign was to recognize the cynicism, and to make Carey's record the answer to that cynicism.

Thus the slogan: "This year, before they tell you what they want to do—make them show you what they've done." In strictly rhetorical terms, the slogan was designed to echo the clear distance between the governed and the governors in this particular year. You may have trusted political people before, the slogan said, but this year you're "you," they're "they," and you'd better not forget it if you don't want to get fooled again. But beyond this point, we were trying to turn a potential disadvantage—the fact that Hugh Carey was a practicing politician—into an advantage (see chapter 13, on political jujitsu). By defining the central issue of the Democratic primary as one of achievement, we were looking to make a virtue out of necessity. Further, the fact was that Howard Samuels, while a visible presence in the New York political scene, did not have a record other than his service as Off-Track Betting chief.

Here, Carey's theme was greatly strengthened by two errors in strategy on the part of the Samuels campaign. They assumed that Samuels's recognition could be translated into votes. People knew him, yes; but they knew him as New York's chief gambler, as "Howie the Horse." The fact that a public figure is a recognized celebrity does not mean that voters will automatically, or even probably, turn to him as the person to be placed in high political office. This is one more refutation of the idea that a candidate is a product. When you market soap, recognition is always a positive, unless your soap is in the news because it gives people plague. But in politics, you can judge very little by recognition—except that if you don't have it, you'd better get it. But you'd better get it on *your* terms. Carey's whole theme, expressed with a very heavy advertising campaign, was that it did not *matter* that you had vaguely heard of Samuels, or that you knew he was running for Governor: for your own sake, you had better look past the promises to the actual record. Given Samuels's background, he could not offer that kind of record.

Second, Samuels was by nature a manager. He had been a highly successful entrepreneur, Under Secretary of Commerce, a man used to being at the head of operations. Had he stressed the achievements of the institutions he'd headed, he might well have competed with Carey. Instead, he made his theme one of management—"New York needs a manager." It was consistent with Samuels's background. But it was inconsistent with the political mood of 1974. In the first place, New York had, until 1973, been governed for fifteen years by Nelson Rockefeller, not a man known for his timidity in running the affairs of state with a vigorous hand. Second, most citizens are not enamored of "managers." Managers are the people who tell them they cannot have an extra day off; managers are the bank officials who call in loans; managers are the people who disconnect your telephones, or tell you why you are not eligible for extra Social Security. Arguing, especially in the climate of Watergate, that you were going to be a manager was almost like proclaiming that "what New York needs is a bureaucrat, and I've been a bureaucrat all my life."

There were a lot of reasons why Carey defeated Samuels in a landslide in the primary, not the least of which was the fact that Hugh Carey's brother owned an oil company, which enabled him to underwrite a massive advertising campaign. The money, however, would have been irrelevant without the proper theme.

These examples offer some clue to the contours of successful campaign themes. There are, in addition, some basic principles a politician must keep in mind if his or her campaign themes, and the issues supporting them, are to be successful.

Never make your central theme specific unless you are absolutely confident of its wholesale appeal.   Contrary to the popular notion about politics, specifics are a valuable part of a campaign. But, with rare exceptions—Yorty's garbage issue comes to mind—it is suicidal to make so specific an issue the centerpiece of your campaign. Why? Because voters will forgive you a wrongheaded notion about a particular decision if they believe that you are fundamentally on their side; if, however, you persist in telling them that this particular issue is how you choose to define yourself, you cannot be shocked or disappointed if they turn on you. In a sense, it is like having as a friend a man who believes that UFOs have landed in his driveway. If he is otherwise agreeable, considerate, and caring, you may forgive him his eccentricity. If, however, he devotes hours at each social gathering to discussing his latest conversation with the people from Neptune, you will probably not choose to keep him as a friend for long.

Take these two examples. In 1972, busing became an inflammatory issue in Florida. George Wallace won that state's presidential primary with 40 percent of the vote in a crowded field by clearly standing as *the* most intense antibusing candidate. The state's Governor, Reubin Askew, was foursquare in favor of busing—a position that was opposed by nearly 80 percent of the state. But it was just one position, and Askew was not running that year. He was a politician of unquestioned integrity, who was an effective and compassionate Governor. Floridians forgave him his trespass on their sensibilities, and in 1974 Askew won an overwhelming reelection victory.

In contrast, the leaders of the Republican Party in Ohio in 1958 decided to make the right-to-work issue—a state law forbidding union shops—the central issue of their campaign. They believed that they needed to make absolutely clear their conviction that the open shop was an integral part of a free society. They also managed to bestir the Ohio trade-union movement into ceaseless activity until Election Day, and, in the highest nonpresidential turnout in Ohio history, the Republicans went down to a defeat of historic proportions.

There will be time enough to arouse the passions of those interests concerned with specific ideas once you have won office; as a rule, those affected by your ideas are always more passionate than the general populace, which would be marginally affected by your idea to stop limiting beef imports, or to deregulate artificially high trucking rates. When you become specific about what you intend to do, you run the danger of stumbling into what the late Ohio Congressman Mike Kirwan called "The Overriding Issue." As longtime chairman of the House Democratic Campaign Committee he had said, The Overriding Issue is "possibly the one factor over which the candidate has no control. . . . Good candidates, good campaigns, gimmicks, superior financial resources, all pale to insignificance when a compelling issue appears. The problem is to recognize such issues. The further problem is to make sure you're on the right side of it."

And by far the easiest way to avoid this trap is to subordinate your issues within a general campaign theme which is acceptable, and to make your issues reflections of your theme. This has the advantage to the public of offering them a coherent, integrated view of the kind of policies you intend to produce. It has the advantage to you of creating watertight compartments. When an enemy or the press scores a direct hit on one of your pet ideas, there is less chance of your entire ship sinking.

Never put a price tag on your ideas, and never phrase your ideas so that a price tag is necessary. Nothing unsettles an uncertain electorate more surely than the idea that you intend to spend a great deal of their tax money. Peculiarly, nothing delights an electorate more than the idea that you intend to inaugurate a program that will provide them with an additional service. The distance between these two notions, so small in reality, has always been immense in our political life. It is similar to the inability of some primitive societies to fathom the link between sexual intercourse and pregnancy, since the two seem so discrete in time. The key, then, to advancing your ideas is to avoid, at all costs, "pricing them out"—that is, telling the people how much they will cost. As soon as the citizenry, or the press, hears a monetary figure named, the suspicions are inflamed, and you are in trouble.

This problem can afflict liberals and conservatives alike. When George McGovern proposed a welfare reform that, for the sake of calculations, presumed a $1000 "demogrant" for every member of every family, to be taken into account during tax and/or income-guarantee purposes, it gave people the impression that McGovern was going to sit in Washington mailing out $1000 bills to every man, woman, and child in America. Everything people believed in their heart of hearts about wild, free-spending liberals seemed to be coming true. And this impression was reinforced during a nationally televised debate with Hubert Humphrey shortly before the California primary, when columnist Robert Novak— a commentator bitterly hostile to McGovern—asked him the perfectly fair question of what his welfare reform programs would cost. When McGovern answered, in effect, "I don't know"—in part because such calculations would depend on the economy, in part because he had been inadequately prepared for the question—you could almost feel the ground shifting out from under him.

Four years later, during the New Hampshire primary, Ronald Reagan promulgated the notion of a transfer of programs away from the federal government, back to the states, so that they might decide the levels of spending they wished to pursue. It was not an idea designed to stir the heart of a low-income family in a state such as Utah or New Hampshire. It was, nonetheless, an idea consistent with the conservative notion of moving power and resources out of Washington, back to the states. The dilemma for Reagan was that a dollar figure was put on the plan—a $90 billion figure —as a way of estimating the level of the shift that was being talked about. Suddenly, the plan became "Reagan's $90 billion scheme." Did it mean that the states were going to have to come up with $90 billion more in state taxes? Did it mean that every state would have to adopt an income tax, or jack up their sales tax rates? Whatever it truly meant, it also meant that Reagan was forced to explain a complicated tax proposal over and over again, in the midst of a presidential campaign, where complexity is always the first casualty.

The solution is never to mention a dollar figure, *unless* you are talking about *cuts* in spending or taxation. This is always easy to defend, because it depends only on your ability to tap the deepest, least disputable belief of the American electorate: the conviction that a huge chunk of government spending is wasted.

For instance, suppose you intend to propose a 10 percent cut in federal or state spending. Or suppose you want to claim that all of your new proposals can be paid for by cutting 10 percent from existing programs. How? you are asked.

"By cutting some of the fat out of the government," you reply. "Don't you believe that this government wastes ten cents out of every dollar it spends?" Of course they believe it; everybody believes it. It may even be true. The problem is, of course, that nobody knows which ten cents is wasted —or how to get it out of the budget without (a) destroying important programs or (b) petrifying the interests who depend on government spending. This problem, however, can wait until later—after you are sworn into office.

If you want to duck an issue, find a creative way to do it. The image of the politician running away from an issue, or surrounding it with great gobs of hot air, has gone with the wind. We are simply too much aware of the image of the evasive candidate to accept it. When we begin to believe that a candidate is, in fact, evading an issue, that candidate is in trouble. Richard Nixon's steady decline in the polls in 1968 came in part from his refusal to explain in any concrete sense at all what he would do with respect to Vietnam, except to imply that he had a secret plan to end the war. Similarly, the feeling in the fall of 1976 that Carter was, in the cliché, "fuzzy" on the issues made him a less appealing alternative to Gerald Ford.

There are other ways to put an issue to one side:

SAY, "I DON'T KNOW." Although parodied effectively by Joseph Heller in *Good as Gold,* this answer is still a very effective way of dealing with a complicated or divisive issue, provided it is not used as the answer to more than one, or at most two, questions. Amid all the certainties candidates bring to so many issues, an occasional confession of ignorance is bound to impress an audience as engaging and candid. A neat variation on this theme was often struck by President Kennedy in his press conferences: He would first recite a series of figures on the question ("As you know, these incidents rose 53.7 percent over the last decade, with a total cost adjustment of 7.3 billion dollars just in the last fiscal year.") and then promise to do something about it ("So this is a matter which seriously affects the United States, and I would hope to make a judgment on it at an appropriate time in the future."). Kennedy sounded as if he knew more about the issue than the questioner, without making himself vulnerable.

TAKE THE OFFENSIVE; DENY THAT YOU SHOULD KNOW ANYTHING ABOUT IT. I first saw this remarkable tactic

employed by S. I. Hayakawa when he was running against
—and beating—Senator John Tunney of California, in
whose campaign I was involved. As always in California,
there were a series of propositions on the state ballot, one of
which would have legalized dog racing in the state.

When he was asked for his position, Hayakawa replied,
"I don't give a good goddamn about dog racing. I'm running
for United States Senator." Not only did he not have to take
a position on the issue—which, in fairness, might well have
had some effect on the economy of California—but he put
himself in the position of being above it.

BLOW THE WHISTLE ON IT.   By far the most creative device
for avoiding a stand in the history of American politics was
employed by the first Adlai E. Stevenson, who was elected
Vice President of the United States in 1892 on Grover Cleveland's ticket. While campaigning in the Northwest, Stevenson found that one of the most controversial issues in the
region was what to name the highest mountain in the region.
Some favored Mount Rainier as the name; others favored
Mount Tacoma. It was not only a heated issue, it was one on
which compromise was impossible. At every campaign appearance on his whistle-stop tour of the region, Adlai would
end his speech by saying, "I pledge myself, here and now,
that if elected I will not rest until this glorious mountain is
properly named. And . . ."

At this point Adlai would pull a hidden cord to signal the
engineer, who would blow his whistle, start up the engine,
and pull the train out of the station, as Adlai Stevenson's
courageous words were "drowned out."

CHAPTER V

HOW TO READ—AND USE—A POLL

Here is a dilemma which confronted a recent campaign: specifically, the reelection campaign of New York's Governor Hugh Carey in 1978:

He was, by every poll, very unpopular, indeed, the most unpopular major politician in the state. He was running almost twenty points behind the Republican nominee with barely two months until election. These same polls showed, among other things, that crime was a major issue on the minds of the electorate, that capital punishment was favored by nearly three-fourths of the electorate, and that nearly half of those favoring capital punishment would vote for Governor on that issue alone. Hugh Carey had twice vetoed capital punishment bills, and had stated flatly that he would commute the death sentence of any prisoner sentenced to the electric chair. And just a year before, Carey's own running mate, then candidate for Mayor Mario Cuomo, had lost the Democratic primary to a pro-capital punishment rival.

That was what the polls said. Now, if you believe the conventional critique of contemporary politics, you know exactly what was supposed to happen. After all, politicians read the polls, and then shape their issues according to what the polls say the people want. And this is precisely what many second-rate politicians do. But leaving aside the heretical notion that there are people in political life who act upon principle, taking the most cynical view possible of Carey's intentions, ask yourself, What could Governor Carey do? Could he drop his persistent opposition to the death penalty in an election year? Of course not. In the first place, so blatant a change of position in an election year would have lacked all credibility. The press may be reluctant to judge the merits of a proposal, but one thing it does know how to emphasize—and ridicule—is an obvious change of heart (see chapter 7, on the press).

In the second place, it would have undermined his own support among those opponents of the death penalty, who include two of the three major newspapers in the city of New York, who were vigorously supporting his bid for reelection (their reappearance after a lengthy strike just before Election Day and their editorial support of Carey on election eve were contributing factors to his late surge).

And in the third place, Carey had made his position so much a matter of personal conscience that to alter his position in the middle of an election would have earned him the contempt of the electorate no matter what their position. It would have been an act similar in effect to George McGovern's dumping of Tom Eagleton as his running mate in 1972. Those who thought he never should have picked Eagleton were more convinced than ever that he had made a bad mistake, while those who wanted him to keep Eagleton felt he had stabbed an innocent man in the back.

If Carey had acted the way politicians are supposed to act when reading a poll, he would have scrambled to get on the right side of this decisive issue. Instead, he concluded otherwise. He knew he had to do two things: first, he had to convince the legitimately concerned citizens of New York that he was prepared to take vigorous action against violent criminals, since the death penalty sentiment was, in large measure, a reaction not to the relatively few murders that would be punished by death under any possible law, but to the continuing epidemic of violent crime in the streets. Second, he had to convince those who favored the death penalty that Carey deserved, if not their support, then their respect for a principled position.

The first goal was met with a package of anticrime proposals, including a lowering of the age at which juvenile offenders could be tried as adults, and a proposal for life sentence without parole for a variety of heinous crimes. This proposal *was* a change in the Governor's position. But because this specific issue was not a major element in Carey's political makeup, he was able to get away with this (relatively) minor shift without incurring the suspicion of the press or the wrath of the electorate. The second goal was met by Carey's own behavior during the campaign, arguing that he was bound by conscience to oppose the death penalty regardless of the political consequences. These positions were not responsible for his reelection, but they did serve to ease the pressure that might otherwise have brought Carey down.

This lesson must become an instinctive part of your thinking. Nothing is easier than to misread a poll; nothing is more dangerous than the temptation to take a set of numbers on a computer printout and to turn them into certainties of the most mistaken and dangerous kind. Properly interpreted, and placed in perspective, a poll is a valuable piece of information. Used without restraint, a poll is like a pistol that is pointed at your own head.

To understand how to use a poll, it is first necessary to dispel some of the foolishness that surrounds discussion of polls. Pick up a newspaper, or turn on a television set, and you are likely to read or see a ringing denunciation of this malevolent mechanism out of *1984*. These same newspapers will spend tens of thousands of dollars on readership surveys which tell them the public wants less "complicated" hard news and more features on how to grow status plants. These same television stations commit millions of dollars worth of programming based on Nielsen ratings, and hire news reporters based on the reactions of people who are wired to determine which reporter evokes more glandular responses. These are the guardians of the principle that there is something evil in trying to determine what the people whose votes you seek are thinking about. It is this hostility to polls that has forced anyone seeking political office into a ritual response when asked about polls during a campaign. There is only one correct answer to the question, "What do you think of the poll that just came out?"

Answer: "The only poll that counts is the one on Election Day." You know you do not believe this, the press knows you do not believe this, and the press does not believe this, either. But it proves that you are not a slave to the mysterious technology of the modern age, and it soothes the feelings of reporters, who dislike any mechanism that interferes with their role as the interpreter of great events.

A poll, when stripped of the demonology that surrounds it, is nothing more than a way of measuring the attitudes of a random sample of a given population, *at a particular point in time, in response to a particular set of questions.* It is a tool that is usually accurate within these limits. It is a poor predictor, because it is not supposed to be a predictor. It cannot assure you that your candidate who is twenty points ahead in September will win in November, any more than a radar speed check can tell a police officer how fast you will be going five miles farther down the road. It cannot tell you that the American people who oppose the Panama Canal Treaty in 1977 will oppose it in 1978, because a poll has no way of measuring the power of the arguments that will be advanced for or against that treaty. It cannot tell you what side of a political issue is always the "popular" side, because a poll only reflects the contradictions about our political beliefs—it cannot settle them. If the American people oppose higher taxes, but favor more government programs, if they claim they want budget cuts but oppose cuts in defense, education, Social Security, and everything else except welfare payments to Cadillac owners, the poll will show that. But it will not tell you what to do about it.

If the polls are limited, however, they are not wrong; not usually. George Gallup, Jr., has remarked that "in every election year, open season on polltakers is declared. . . . People across the nation write or telephone us to remind us of 1948, to ask why they haven't been interviewed. . . ." For the political Luddite, "1948" is not a year, it is a battle cry, the year when the people proved the experts wrong by electing Harry Truman when all the polls and experts were certain that Thomas Dewey would win. The pollsters stopped polling ten days before that election, and they have not made that mistake, or been that wrong since, but it does not stop people from citing 1948 as the triumph of the individual over Big Brother.

Why this hostility to the poll? If a candidate for office could talk to 800 or 1200 people, randomly selected by a system that provided a mix of education, ethnicity, and income so as to provide a rough equivalent of the population, would we condemn it? If he had the time to read a thousand letters a week, would we think this a cynical attempt to manipulate public opinion? Even the most loyal disciple of Edmund Burke's political philosophy would not suggest that a representative ignore public opinion, even if he chose not to reflect that opinion. At base, that is what a poll is for. It gives a candidate a sense of what people are thinking. If a candidate is a coward, he will do nothing more than try to create an echo of that sentiment. If he is a leader, he will try to move that sentiment closer to his own deepest beliefs. But the idea that a candidate is demeaned by trying to tap into the public opinion of the moment is a curious one in a nation which prides itself on a democratic form of government.

Having said this, it must also be said that politicians them-

selves have on several occasions been guilty of flagrant mis-
use of the polls. The most memorable such occasion was in
1968, when the late-starting campaign of Nelson Rockefeller
spent $4.5 million in barely eight weeks in a blitz of news-
paper, magazine, and radio and television ads, not so much
to win primaries, but to move the public-opinion polls so that
the delegates to the Republican National Convention would
become convinced that only Rockefeller could be elected in
November. The idea was that as the polls changed, the delegates would change their minds. The reality, as the Rockefeller forces found out, was that the delegates had either
been chosen in primaries, or else had convictions of their
own which would not be swayed by the movement of the
polls.

That same year, when the Humphrey campaign was far
behind Nixon's, a vicious cycle was crippling that campaign.
Because Humphrey was behind in the polls, money was
scarce, since contributors do not like to put their money on
a probable loser. And since money was scarce, there was no
way to battle back from the underdog position. According to
Melvyn Bloom's *Public Relations and Presidential Campaigns,* Humphrey campaign manager William Connell prepared a memorandum based on highly questionable poll data
favorable to Humphrey, which made its way into some press
reports. The strategy was that if the press wrote that Humphrey was gaining in the polls, money would flow into the
campaign, the television advertising and other campaign devices could go forward, and ultimately Humphrey *would* rise
in the polls. This relationship between image and reality recalls the scene in *Catch-22,* when Yossarian and his fellow
airmen must fly a dangerous bombing mission over Piamosa
because the troop line shows that city still is in enemy hands.
In the middle of the night, someone moves the line across
Piamosa; the next morning, the bombing run is scrubbed.

Let us assume, however, that you are not in the business
of trying to persuade the press or convention delegates to
turn poll results into a major story or a change of vote. Let

us assume, rather, that you are beginning your own campaign for office, as candidate or key campaign aide, and you are trying to make sense out of the poll for which you have paid somewhere between $10,000 and $30,000. Your first instinct will be to thumb to the "horse-race" results, the "who's winning? who's losing?" question, much in the manner that *Playboy* readers whip past the Teilhard de Chardin essay to examine the centerfold. This is understandable; but once your curiosity is satisfied, once you have discovered that you are thirty points ahead, or thirty points behind, put that question out of your mind and attend to the following critical points:

What are the numbers saying?   You have just discovered that, if the election were being held today, you would receive 39 percent of the vote, while your opponent would receive 11 percent of the vote. If you believe that you are almost certainly going to win the election, or even if you believe that you are substantially ahead of your opponent, you are very likely to be mistaken.

Why? Because the numbers may not be telling you what you think they are telling you. If you are known reasonably well by 85 percent of likely voters, and 39 percent say they are for you, you may well have a serious problem. In spite of your high "recognition factor," or maybe because of it, a lot of voters who know you are not favorably disposed toward you. If your opponent is known by, say, 16 percent of the likely electorate, his 11 percent represents a strong correlation between recognition and support (it may also mean that those 11 percent of the voters would choose anyone on the ballot, including Attila the Hun, over you). This spells serious trouble; if your opponent has the resources to get well known as a reasonable alternative to you, he has a good chance of winning.

The numbers also may be telling you that you are far ahead among all eligible voters, but not among *likely* voters. In many states, primaries for major offices are decided by a fourth of the eligible voters, or less. If you are very popular among the young, the poor, and the black, and much less popular among the older, more educated, Jewish and Catholic voters, you are in trouble—because young people, poor people, and black people tend not to vote in heavy numbers, especially in primaries.

In addition, once you move beyond the horse-race numbers, you may find that your potential for victory or defeat is very different from the picture painted by the "who's ahead?" question. You may find that a lot of the opposition to your candidacy stems from disagreement on the issues. This is (believe it or not) hopeful, because it is possible to change people's minds on issues through rhetoric, advertising, endorsements, the errors of your opponent, or, as a last resort, logic. But if the voters sense that you are not trustworthy, you have a much more difficult role. As columnist Murray Kempton once said of Lyndon Johnson, "A politician can survive voters who disagree with him; the voters who destroy him are the voters who don't trust him even though they agree with him."

What are the numbers unable to tell you?   In the three elections in which New York Governor Nelson Rockefeller ran for reelection, he always entered the election year well behind any potential Democratic opposition. He never won reelection by less than 400,000 votes. Were the polls wrong each election spring? No. But they were useless as a predictor. They not only could not measure the impact of the millions of dollars Rockefeller had to spend on his campaigns, or the power of his family to call on financial and political obligations, they could not measure the performance of his opponents once the campaign had begun. There is no way a poll in March could predict that the Liberal Party would run an independent candidate in 1966, who would draw enough votes off the Democratic line to provide Republican Rockefeller with his margin of victory. There is no way that a poll could predict that Arthur Goldberg, an honorable, prestigious man who had occupied such noble offices as Secretary of Labor, Justice of the United States Supreme

Court, and Ambassador to the United Nations, would turn out to be a thundering incompetent as a political campaigner.

What issues can your candidate reasonably exploit?   Suppose your poll tells you that inflation is the most important issue in this election. Suppose your opponent is an incumbent Senator who has been serving in Washington for twelve years. One of the classic temptations for a challenger is to add up the spending bills passed by Congress and attempt to link the incumbent to massive federal deficits, and therefore to inflation. But the evidence of recent elections shows that this strategy will not work; the connection is simply too difficult to make, and the defense too easy: "Yes, I voted for the Furburg dam, which brought ten thousand jobs to our state. I voted for defense to keep our nation strong. I voted for Social Security to enable our senior citizens to live in dignity. And I voted against fifty billion dollars in needless spending" (needless spending is a dam to be built in another state).

Conversely, you may find a single specific case of federal spending which appears so ridiculous that it makes your identification with tax saving strong. Senator William Proxmire has made a career with his "Golden Fleece" awards to some government expenditures, many of which were far more reasonable than Proxmire made them out to be. (For example, he ridiculed a study of airline stewardesses' figures. There was every good reason to study the configuration of airline personnel, because it was part of a study to design safer airplanes. But stated baldly, it sounded as if the government was paying somebody money to measure the hips of stewardesses.) The danger to avoid is to assume that, because a poll shows that voters are bothered by something, you can run for office using that issue.

What attitudes about you cannot be changed?   When Richard Nixon was running for reelection in 1972, his pollsters found that people did not find him a warm, likable man. Had the Nixon campaign attempted to "position" the President as a hail-fellow-well-met figure, they would have run into the stone wall of credibility. Instead, they positioned him as a *competent* man, one who was engaged in the serious business of running the country.

If you read a poll which shows that you do not excite the electorate, you cannot meet that problem by trying to be what you are not. Instead, it makes much more sense to look at the attitudes you are admired for, or that can reasonably be attributed to you (see chapter 13, on political jujitsu). When Ed Koch ran for Mayor of New York, he was a virtual unknown whose looks were compared to Frank Perdue's. Instead of trying to invest Koch with sex appeal, his campaign chose a slogan designed to contrast him with former Mayor John Lindsay and incumbent Mayor Abe Beame: "After eight years of charisma, and four years of the clubhouse, why not try competence?" When New Jersey Governor Brendan Byrne ran for reelection in 1977, after having pushed through a state income tax he had promised to avoid, he did not try to convince the people that he had not angered them. Instead, he acknowledged his error in not seeing the need for a tax. And the campaign argued that, however angry you were with Byrne, "On the record, you've *got* to respect what he's done."

If you read a poll, decide what the voters want, and attempt to make yourself into that image by wrenching yourself away from reality, you are likely to forget who you are and what qualities you may have to bring to public office in the first place. (If, on a careful reading of a poll, it turns out that you have *no* qualities likely to appeal to voters, you are most likely in the wrong profession.) A campaign, contrary to the notions of many prominent political experts, is not an exercise in marketing, and a candidate is not a product. A cigarette is whatever the packaging and advertising says it is. It can, with enough money, be changed completely, as Marlboro cigarettes were changed in the 1950s from an elegant "woman's" cigarette into the embodiment of the John Wayne West. A beer can be "positioned" in the marketplace as a product for swinging singles, young marrieds, blue-collar workers, or junior executives.

Products have not made speeches, they have not cast votes, they have not advocated or opposed programs and policies. A poll tells you how voters have perceived, or misunderstood, the attitudes you have embodied in your public life—or in your private life which has become public. Whether you are capable of reshaping those attitudes into a successful campaign is what a campaign is all about.

Where are your likely voters?   When you are commissioning a poll, one of the things you are looking at is where to spend your campaign efforts, in organization, time spent by a candidate, and money. But in any given year, your candidate may appeal to voters in one section of a state—or the nation—out of all proportion to the population. Since you are not out to win a unanimous verdict, you must find out where your likely voters are concentrated. In 1970, when James Buckley won his New York Senate seat, his pollster calculated a county-by-county "reasonable vote total" for Buckley, and the campaign spent its funds not where the population was, but based on a percentage of Buckley's "reasonable vote totals." His victory was made possible by impressive pluralities in Westchester, Nassau, and Suffolk counties, where traditional Republicans and disaffected blue-collar Democrats joined to give their votes to a millionaire oilman running as a conservative.

Where do the voters get their information from?   One of the most crucial pieces of data a poll can give you is how the voters will learn about you and your campaign. In days gone by, the opinions of most voters were in place before a campaign began; party loyalty, and the network of information provided by friends, family, and occasional contacts, provided the shaping influences behind a vote. In older cities, you can still stumble fatally by ignoring such traditional sources of neighborhood information as the parish church or the butcher shop. What you are looking for, however, is not "retail" but "wholesale" sources of information: what do they read, what television programs do they watch, what are the patterns by which voters inform themselves?

Ratings and newspaper circulation statistics are not what you are looking for in your poll, because they will not tell you what you want to know. It is frequently true that "likely voters" learn about campaigns in ways television ratings cannot begin to measure. Suppose, for example, you are trying to reach older voters with information about your stands. In television's universe, older citizens are "nonpersons"; after the magic age of forty-nine, they are banished from the heavenly city of desirable demographics, on the theory that they have bought their major purchases, or else because their buying preferences are too rigidly held to be changed by advertising. In political terms, however, this "some viewers are more equal than other viewers" does not apply the same way. If anything, older viewers are more desirable than younger viewers, since voting turnout rises on a curve more or less parallel with age. If your poll shows that these older viewers watch the news far more heavily than younger viewers, it will save you a lot of money wasted buying television time on programs seen by stay-at-homes. For these voters, Walter Cronkite will probably be worth a lot more to you than Mork and the Fonz put together.

These numbers can do more. They can confirm the idea, or rebut it, that your older voters watch the independent station's ten o'clock news in significant numbers, since they go to sleep earlier. They can take a common notion—that sports events are watched by the less-educated—and knock it into a cocked hat. If you ask the right questions, a poll can tell you not only what newspapers are relied on by what groups of voters, but what features they care most about—so that you can put your print ad on the page where it will be most helpful to you.

How should your record and platform be presented?   If the politics-is-just-a-marketing-campaign approach is misleading, this does not mean that a campaign has no choice about how it presents the reality of a candidate's credentials and proposals. By using a poll as a fever chart of the public's mood, you will be able to get a much better fix on the manner in which your arguments should be made.

For example, assume that your opponent is a wealthy man, who is fully prepared to spend as much of his money as he can to get himself elected. If you are like every other candidate of modest means facing great sums of money, you will be tempted to attack your opponent for "buying" the election. This tactic is an excellent method of ensuring your rapid return to private life. As an issue, it has never worked. Hubert Humphrey complained long and loud in 1960, in Wisconsin and West Virginia, that Kennedy was buying his primary victories, that he felt like "the corner grocery store running against the supermarket chain." Nelson Rockefeller's rivals in New York inveighed against his millions, particularly evident in 1966 when he was able to put forty television commercials on the air for every one of the Democrats'. Democrat William J. Green of Pennsylvania protested again and again at the massive sums spent by Republican H. J. Heinz III in 1978 in their battle for the Pennsylvania Senate seat. In none of these cases did the issue cut at all. If anything, people seem to believe that wealthy candidates will be free of the temptation to help themselves to samples from the tax coffers. When it comes to the issue of wealth, the populace seems to embrace the view of Rose Kennedy, who said of son Robert's 1968 presidential campaign, "It's our money, and we have a right to spend it."

Suppose, however, your poll shows the public to be agitated by the issue of taxes. As we have seen, when people learn that an affluent public figure has paid a lower share of taxes than middle-income citizens, the reaction is likely to be harsh. For now we have an issue: not the possession of wealth, not even the use of that wealth to advance one's personal political well-being, but the use of special rules to exempt oneself from the obligations ordinary people have to bear. This is what undid Tennessee Senator William Brock in 1976; it is what undid President Nixon as much as the Watergate tapes. When people discovered that Nixon paid less tax on a $250,000 income than did people with one-twentieth of that amount, an essential core of his support broke away.

So: if a poll shows this kind of resentment about unfair tax regulations—and it is hard to imagine such resentment not showing up assuming you are not running for First Select-man of Grosse Pointe—you have a way of going at your opponent's wealth without sounding like a whiner. Here is what you do: When you announce your candidacy, release your income tax records for the last five years, along with a notarized statement of your net worth. Explain that, given the corruption that has recently pervaded politics, it is important that people trust their elected officials. But trust has to be earned. You call on your opponents to follow your lead.

What you now have is a no-lose proposition. If your wealthy rival refuses to disclose tax returns and net worth, you have a cover-up going. Why? you will ask again and again. What is he hiding? Why won't Dithers do what Smith-ers has done: tell us what he owns and what he owes? If your rival does disclose, he will almost certainly reveal something discomfiting to his campaign. For it is a truth universally acknowledged that a mature American in possession of a sizable fortune must have all but carnal knowledge of tax loopholes. Unless your rival's tax attorneys are candidates for sainthood, he will have paid a far smaller percentage of his income in taxes than did the average man on the street. And there is your opening: "Dithers committed no crime," you will say (a generous refutation of what no one has alleged). "He was technically within the limits of the

law. But if a millionaire like Dithers can pay less in taxes
than the gas-station operator or the cabdriver, then something is wrong with our tax system; and as your Senator, I
intend to fight to change that system."

A good political poll, then, is nothing more elaborate than
a different way of delivering information about the people
whose votes you are trying to win. The fact that the information is printed on computerized forms, rather than being
gleaned from late-night meetings with canvassers, does not
make it less authentic, or more malevolent, than more
"human" forms of communication.

The key to its use is not to be mesmerized by a poll. If you
let its findings frighten you away from your deepest convictions, if you let it push you into trying to mold yourself into
a walking reflection of current moods, you will do yourself a
great disservice. But don't blame polls for timidity. Politicians were trimming their sails in the face of prevailing political winds long before the first pollster knocked on the first
door of the first interviewee; for decades in the South, people
of essential decency felt unable to stand against the racial
attitudes of their constituents, and defended segregation and
disenfranchisement with their every breath—knowing all the
while they were speaking dangerous nonsense. (One Southern Senator, who had compiled a consistent segregationist
record, once listened to South Carolina segregationist Strom
Thurmond bellowing in defense of white womanhood and
against integration, and muttered disgustedly to a colleague,
"listen to ole Strom—he really *believes* that stuff.") Now, a
poll at least gives you a deeper sense of what the populace
believes, and a chance of cutting through that prejudice. Do
politicians use polls this way? Not usually; they are subject
to the same weaknesses as a private citizen filling out an
Internal Revenue Service form outside the presence of a
federal law-enforcement official. But the fault is in politicians, and not in the polls.

CHAPTER VI

HOW TO GIVE A SPEECH

The speech is the centerpiece of political life. You can hire a media consultant, you can buy a poll, you can engage a direct-mail expert who will help you raise millions of dollars, you can rent a fashion designer to advise you on the cut of your suits and the shape of your collars. But if you do not know how to talk to an audience, you are placing yourself at a crippling disadvantage.

Indeed, it is a political proposition that has remained true for more than a century that the surest way to catapult yourself into national prominence is to deliver a notable public address. In our past, only the command of the armed forces of the United States has more definitely established a figure as a worthy leader. And with the results of the Vietnam War still alive in our national memory, this is likely to be an uncertain route to political power. The great speech, by contrast, is as powerful a weapon now as it has ever been. Consider some political history in light of the contribution of rhetoric:

• Abraham Lincoln was a much-defeated candidate for political office when he came to New York City early in 1860 to deliver a speech at Cooper Union college. The impact of that speech, and its national distribution over a period of months, was a direct cause of his nomination for President that same year.

• William Jennings Bryan was a free-silver youth from Kansas when he came to the Democratic convention in 1896 to oppose the gold-standard views of Grover Cleveland, the incumbent President of his own party. His famous "Cross of Gold" speech at the convention was the emotional spark that won him the first of three presidential nominations.

• Franklin D. Roosevelt's entire career was shaped by the quality of his speeches. His 1924 nominating speech for Alfred E. Smith not only demonstrated his recovery from polio, but marked him for the first time as a charismatic figure in his own right, rather than as a distant relative of Theodore. His 1933 Inaugural Address, carried by radio to a nation desperately short of self-confidence, asserting his "firm belief that the only thing we have to fear is—fear itself," set the tone for FDR's entire first term, establishing a level of trust between a President and the citizenry that has not been seen since. And his infrequent but powerful Fireside Chats gave Roosevelt a forum for a continuing reinforcement of his political appeal.

• John Kennedy made the substance and style of his speeches an implicit rebuttal to the charge in 1960 that he was too young, too callow, for the burdens of the Presidency. His speeches reached back into American history, recalling the words and lives of Adams, Jefferson, the Founding Fathers; his style was consciously imperial, with a deliberately formal style ("From those to whom much is given, much is expected . . . Let the word go forth from this time and place . . ."). It was almost as if, by investing his words with weight and moment, Kennedy could better demonstrate his right to hold such an office. Further, at least one

speech—his address to the Houston ministers' meeting in
the 1960 campaign, with its direct confrontation of the religious issue—may well have made the difference in persuad-
ing reluctant Democrats to vote for a Catholic candidate, at
least enough of them to decide so close a contest as the 1960
election.

• Three speeches in 1964 had a notable effect on presidential politics. Barry Goldwater's acceptance speech, which
seemed an almost purposeful attempt to exaggerate fears of
his radicalism ("extremism in the defense of liberty is no
vice; moderation in the pursuit of justice is no virtue"),
helped millions of Republicans decide to abandon the GOP
ticket that year. Hubert Humphrey's Vice-Presidential acceptance speech nailed down the Democratic effort to ex-
clude Goldwater from the mainstream of politics, with its
recitation of the things most Democrats and most Republicans believed in—"but not Senator Goldwater, not the tem-
porary leader of the Republican Party." And Ronald
Reagan's election eve speech for Goldwater, a nationally
televised address filled with brilliant conservative rhetoric,
made Reagan an instant national hero among the Republican
Right. It was that speech that kicked off Reagan's 1966 campaign for Governor of California, and it was that speech
which established Reagan's national base which has survived almost intact since.

These are small fragments of evidence. Add to it Adlai
Stevenson's welcoming speech at the 1952 Democratic convention, which made his draft candidacy possible; Nixon's
"silent majority" speech of 1969 and Spiro Agnew's attack
on the press that same month in October which put liberalism on the defensive until Watergate; Reagan's 1976 half-
hour foreign policy speech which won him the North Carolina primary and gave him the strength nearly to take the
nomination away from the incumbent President; and you
begin to see why the neglect of speechmaking is a political
blunder of the first magnitude. It does not matter if your
speech is nationally televised or not; one good address to the

National Press Club in Washington is worth twenty appearances on a TV panel show, because the columnists and reporters who will hear you at the National Press Club will delight in discovering a "comer" who has not been overexposed on the tube. ("In the dreary lineup of perennial political power-seekers," a typical postspeech column will begin, "the name of John Smithers will not be found. Yet this quietly eloquent presence"—I don't know how it is possible to be quietly eloquent, either, but that's what they'll write—"seems to many observers"—that's two other people at the bar—"to be more formidable than a dozen others." A few write-ups like that, and Gallup and Harris are all but required to place you on the list of presidential possibilities.) Conversely, a few bad speeches can fatally impair an otherwise promising campaign. In 1976, Senator Henry Jackson had strong support from labor, Jewish groups, defense-minded Democrats, and big-city organizations. He also had a speechmaking ability bordering on the nonexistent. When a national press corps begins to report the kind of joke Washington humorist Mark Russell once made ("Jackson gave a fireside chat last night and the fire went out") that candidacy is on the road to oblivion.

Can a good speech be defined by rules? Probably not. Recognizing the power of words to move people, to arouse them, to inspire them, is as complicated in the political arena as it is in the literary arena. Perhaps it will help to show you two different excerpts from speeches dealing with the same point: the futility of measuring national achievement by material possessions.

The first excerpt is from a speech by Senator Robert Kennedy, which he gave frequently in 1966 and 1967, and which was drafted in substantial measure by his chief speechwriter, Adam Walinsky:

> Let us be clear at the outset that we will find neither national purpose or personal satisfaction in a mere continuation of economic progress, in an endless amassing of

worldly goods. We cannot measure national spirit by the Dow Jones Average, or national achievement by the Gross National Product.

For the Gross National Product includes air pollution and advertising for cigarettes, and ambulances to clear our highways of carnage. It counts special locks for our doors, and jails for the people who break them. The Gross National Product includes the destruction of the redwoods, and the death of Lake Superior. It grows with the production of napalm, and missiles, and nuclear warheads, and it even includes research on the improved dissemination of bubonic plague.

The Gross National Product swells with equipment for the police to put down riots in our cities. And though it is not diminished by the damage these riots do, still it goes up as slums are rebuilt on their ashes. It includes Whitman's rifle and Speck's knife, and the broadcasting of television programs which glorify violence to sell goods to our children.

Here is Jimmy Carter, speaking on the same theme at Emory University in Atlanta in the summer of 1979:

What is true for an individual is also true for a nation. We can measure gross national product, imports and exports, the growth of industry and manufacturing. We can see how many tanks we have, how many nuclear warheads. We can be thankful for strength and grateful for material blessings. But we know that these things are not the most important characteristics of our national life. They do not hold us together as a unique people. They are not the essence of what makes us Americans.

The real meaning of America is not encompassed in the material wealth and military power of our country, for wealth and power can have potential for both evil and for good. We measure the real meaning of America in our intangible values—values which do not change: our care

for each other, our commitment to freedom, our search
for justice, our devotion to human rights and to world
peace, and the patriotism and basic goodness of our people.

These qualities cannot be measured: they are invisible.
Yet these are the true strengths of America which can
channel our wealth and strength—not for evil, but for
good.

The Kennedy speech has a sense of rhythm; read it aloud
and you will understand why the words have been put together in this way. The Carter speech has all of the rhetorical
organization of an inventory, which is why the last paragraph
repeats the idea of the first paragraph. The Kennedy speech
is specific; it evokes concrete images over and over again
(Lake Superior, mass murderers' weapons, violent television). The Carter speech is, in a sense, an abstraction of
Robert Kennedy's speech, a summary of the idea with no
specific reference for a listener to grasp. The point is not
whether the substance of this argument is correct: many
free-market economists, neoconservatives, and stockholders
in advertising agencies would argue that our material abun-
dance is very closely linked to America's pride in itself and
our sense of accomplishment. The point, rather, is that you
can at least understand the nature of Robert Kennedy's
point. All you can do with Carter's is slowly nod off.

Rhetoric, then, cannot be judged by the content of the idea
it is embellishing; nor is ideology any guide to speechmaking
effectiveness. Ronald Reagan, whatever your opinion of his
politics, is the most gifted political rhetorician of our time,
and not because he was an actor or hosted the *General Electric Theatre* on television in the 1950s. He has a sense of how
words can ignite the attention and the enthusiasm of his audience. When he opposed the Panama Canal treaties in his
1976 campaign, he cut right to the core of his case: a case
resting as much on America's resentment at the loss of world
power to smaller nations as on the canal issue itself. Over

and over, Reagan would say: "We bought it, we paid for it, it's ours, and we're going to keep it." Look at these words carefully, and they begin to sound like the whine of a child whose toy is being borrowed by a playmate. But heard in an arena, they bring an audience out of their seats to cheer this affirmation of our strength. When he was attacking Ford's foreign policy in that same year, he referred over and over again to "Dr. Kissinger and Mr. Ford"—not only taking away President Ford's honorific, but evoking a vaguely sinister sense of Ford's foreign policy with echoes of "Dr. Jekyll and Mr. Hyde." In arguing against the Democratic Party's 1976 platform, Reagan listed all of the platform's promises—full employment, national health insurance, a balanced budget, and lower inflation—and said, "Now if you believe this, I've got a bridge in Brooklyn I'd like to talk to you about."

Nor is there any particular style that defines good speechmaking. The technique used by John Kennedy in 1960 was shaped to a particular candidate in a particular time: it was an imperial rhetoric, evoking America's past and summoning us to challenges, in part because Kennedy could embody that sense of power, in part because we had been through eight years of beneficent passivity, and in part because Vietnam and other disasters had not yet taught us the cost of hubris. For the next ten years, we had to endure dozens of politicians attempting to ape John Kennedy's style. Richard Nixon's 1969 Inaugural Address was the most egregious example of this most sincere form of flattery. Apparently suffering from a permanent inferiority complex at the hands of the royal family, Nixon sounded like a man with one drink too many trying to recite the 1960 Inaugural Address:

"In throwing wide the horizons of space, we have discovered new horizons on earth . . . we find ourselves rich in goods but ragged in spirit . . . we cannot make everyone our friend, but we can try to make no one our enemy . . . our destiny offers not the cup of despair, but the chalice of opportunity."

So enamored did Mr. Nixon become of this device that, in his finest example of parallelism, he told the Air Force Academy in June 1969: "The American defense establishment should never be a sacred *cow*, but, on the other hand, the American military should never be anybody's scapegoat."

Hot *dog*.

President Nixon's lust to be seen as a bold, far-reaching leader was blatantly apparent in his rhetorical lunge for the "historic first." Visiting Indonesia in 1969, he exclaimed, ". . . for the first time in history a President of the United States is visiting Indonesia." A day later, he observed, "This is the first time that I have ever said good-bye to the people of this country." He also noted that "because I am the first American President ever to pay a state visit to Indonesia, the next American President who comes here will not be in the position I presently find myself in." He told a Boys' Club Dinner once that "this is the first evening dinner that has been held in this room since I have been President. . . ." And when something genuinely historic occurred —the moon landing—Nixon called it "the greatest day since the Creation." Ironically, Nixon did manage to achieve a historic first beyond all peradventure on August 9, 1974; the manner of his departure will almost surely remain an event of singular historical importance.

Despite the fact that borrowed rhetoric almost always shows its point of origin, there has evolved in American political life a kind of standard speech. If you are to move beyond the convention, you must first understand it. Accordingly, I want to lead you through the bowels—metaphorically speaking—of a typical important meaningful speech. It is designed to impress your audience, to impress the press, to provide you with a meaningful-looking document on an important national issue that you can have reprinted at low cost and mailed out to anyone writing you a letter on a remotely related subject. Writing this kind of speech is easy, once you have mastered the tricks of the trade; like pizza making, it depends on a sense of touch. To help you through this maze, I will interrupt to show you the purpose of what is being said.

Smithers Speaks Out on Health Care

Thank you. [*This shows you are polite.*]

I am delighted to be here in Cincinnati. [*This shows you have taken the trouble to find out exactly where you are.*] Your town bears the name of a dedicated citizen of Rome who left his plow for the work of saving his country [*you are a scholar and just may know more about their town than they do*]. And that is what we must do today—in our homes, our cities, our state, our nation [*you have a broad perspective, suitable for a place on the national ticket*]— particularly in the critical, too often neglected [*you see what others do not*] field of health.

Heraclitus once said, "He who is sick is not well—nor is his nation." [*Heraclitus almost certainly said nothing of the sort, but no one is going to spend time looking it up, and you have demonstrated some learning. If you are worried about being found out, change "Heraclitus" to "The Poet."*] So it is with us today; for the grim fact is [*facts are never just "facts"—they are "grim," "brutal," "disquieting," anything to convey a sense of crisis which the present speaker has the wisdom and fore-sight to identify*] that America faces a crisis in health care greater than any since the plagues of Europe half a millennium ago [*always count time in formidable categories— decades, centuries, millennia—to suggest mastery of scope*].

The federal government tells us that in 1934, twenty-six percent of low-income urban Americans suffered pulmonary dysfunction. Today, that figure has doubled. In 1946, one in four middle-aged men feared cardiovascular illness —today, that anxiety has tripled. More than five in nine children miss school at least three times because of illness. [*Note: you can cite facts to suggest any reality. If percentages look skimpy, switch to absolute numbers: seventy-four million Americans sounds like much more than a third of the population.*]

The numbers are brutal enough [*like facts*]. But numbers alone do not tell the whole story [*you can see through to the human dilemma*]. They do not tell us of the elderly widow in Altoona burdened by psoriasis. They do not tell us of the youth in Chicago, crippled by migraines, deprived of his birthright, of a fair chance. They do not speak of the steelworker in Pittsburgh, the waitress in El Monte, the truck driver in Nashville [*you have made the speech broad enough for national attention, and have brought the audience a glimpse of individual human suffering, suggesting you are in direct contact with The People*].

We must hear beyond the marble halls and closed doors of Washington [*a bit of polite populism*]. We must hear the real voices of our people—and of their need for genuinely effective health care [*you are foursquare against phony, ineffective health care*].

I therefore propose today [*you are making news*] a five point program [*there is your news lead—"Smithers Urges Five-Point Health Plan"*] to provide a comprehensive [*crucially important moderate-liberal buzz word*] program of health care.

First [*making lists shows organizational ability*]: I urge full funding of the Regional Health-Care Act, which I have cosponsored for five years [*you signed your name to a bill somebody else wrote*].

Second, I urge immediate, total review of the duplicative, wasteful federal health policy [*you are for efficient government, you can now claim that eliminating waste will fund your other points, and perhaps you can appoint a friend to a government commission*].

Third, I call for a federal coordinator to help local and state officials provide uniform, fair, comprehensive health care to get a dollar's worth of service for a dollar's worth of government [*this means just about nothing, but it gives you a chance to recite a nifty slogan*].

Fourth, I urge business, labor, foundations, and universities to begin examination of new, innovative [*another officially okay word*] approaches to health;

Fifth, I urge the President to convene an emergency White House conference on health this year [*you brook no delay*] to get the most knowledgeable advice from a broad cross section of the people [*you believe in listening to everybody; in addition, the professionals will have another paid vacation to thank you for*].

The task before us is immense [*if it were trivial, it would be silly to talk about it. Immensity suggests the need for somebody important—like yourself—to get involved*]. But it is not beyond America [*love it or leave it*]. The nation that conquered the Plains, spanned the continent, vanquished aggressive aliens and domestic discord [*alliteration still is okay*] can meet the challenge. We have the resources. What is needed is leadership of courage [*here you are*], will [*here you are*], and dedication [*here you are*] to lead this nation into the future.

If we find this leadership [*here you are*], we will build together a healthier, stronger land. And we will say, with Lincoln, Jefferson, Roosevelt, and John F. Kennedy [*note the occupation you identify with*], "the nation is healed; the nation is one." Thank you.

Speeches like this one are perfectly serviceable. They will properly establish your record on the issues. But a good speech has to do more. Although this model attempts to fulfill some of the requirements for a good speech, it is too contrived to be successful—especially since effective rhetoric has to be defined by its distance from convention. (The Kennedy-style exhortation was stirring in 1960; by 1970, it was leaden, because it had been imitated so often. By 1980, after the homilies of Jimmy Carter, it may be effective once again.) What, then, are the essentials of a good speech?

IT MUST FIT THE SPEAKER. Talking in a style alien to your own nature is like a fifty-year-old man who is forty pounds overweight walking around in an open-throat shirt and tight-fitting jeans. Rather than making him look younger, it emphasizes his distance from youth. It may be that in one

year, voters will seek glamour; in another, they will seek
competence; in another, personal honesty. What they will
almost never seek is a public figure trying to put on rhetorical
clothing that clearly does not fit. Both Lyndon Johnson and
Jimmy Carter paid a heavy political price for their refusal to
speak in a tongue comfortable to them. Lyndon Johnson,
who in informal speech was as persuasive a figure as ever
occupied the White House, persisted in trying to deliver
mealymouthed, high-sounding homilies that lacked credibility. Jimmy Carter, whose whole campaign evolved from the
personal, found himself paralyzed when required to explain
difficult, controversial policy choices because he had won
political success by filtering policy through his personality
—something a President cannot do.

IT MUST BE CONCRETE, NOT ABSTRACT.   In his classic
essay "Politics and the English Language"—which should
be your speechwriting bible—George Orwell notes that a
characteristic of dishonest speech is that "as soon as certain
topics are raised, the concrete melts into the abstract and no
one seems able to think of turns of speech that are not hack-
neyed; prose consists less and less of *words* chosen for the
sake of their meaning, and more of *phrases* tacked together
like the sections of a prefabricated hen house."
    This is your watchword when thinking about what you
want to say. "Fiscal irresponsibility" means nothing. In contrast, "The dollar today would buy what a quarter bought
twenty-five years ago" is a statement about inflation everyone can understand. "Poor people suffer from inadequate
housing" is what former presidential speechwriter William
Safire likes to call a "MEGO" (My Eyes Glaze Over), and
what my former employer David Garth calls "a-ga-bu"
(meaning it is incomprehensible). "Last year four hundred
children under the age of ten were paralyzed by lead poison-
ing" provides a specific image of what it is you are angry
about.
    The use of the concrete, however, goes well beyond lines

in a speech. It goes to the kind of evidence you marshal as well. One of the qualities that makes Ronald Reagan so powerful a speaker is that he takes items from the current news —from papers and from television reports—and weaves these items into the fabric of his addresses. Reagan does not denounce welfare chiselers; he cites the woman in Chicago who gave the welfare department dozens of aliases and collected checks for each different name. He does not denounce some abstract bureaucracy; he recalls the story in the papers of the retiree who was "lost" by the Social Security system, and who was advised to declare himself dead so that he could collect death benefits. The framework of his philosophy gains credence because his evidence is drawn from the sources which we use to inform ourselves. *Of course*, the listener says, *I remember seeing that story of the welfare mother collecting tens of thousands of dollars.* And since the pieces of evidence are known to be true by the listener, Reagan has gained an important step toward acceptance of his more general philosophy.

There are limits, however. One candidate for high office never tired of telling the story of an elderly woman who came to a reception to hear the candidate speak, ate half a sandwich, and carefully wrapped the other half up to take home for her dinner. The story was supposed to express the candidate's indignation at the plight of the elderly. Unfortunately, the candidate kept changing the time and place of this moving event, and the press began to express a certain sense of jocularity when the candidate launched into his story. In *Nixon Agonistes*, Garry Wills describes a 1968 Nixon appearance at Gallaudet College for the Deaf in Washington, D.C., when the students "serenaded" him in sign language and Nixon was emotionally overcome—which happened to be a replay of precisely the same incident, evoking precisely the same reaction, in 1960.

IT OUGHT TO UNSETTLE THE EXPECTATIONS OF THE AUDIENCE. When politicians address an audience, both parties to the transaction know what to expect. The speakers will tell the group they are speaking to that they occupy a special position in the ranks of the honored; that were it not for their tireless work, the Republic would have fallen to the Hordes long ago. They will then recite a list of those concerns they can comfortably endorse which meet the needs of the group to which they are speaking. The speakers are rewarded by having the toastmaster praise them for their "truly eloquent and unforgettable remarks."

A good speech takes as its premise the notion that the typical audience, being composed of more-or-less intelligent people, is as weary of this bad faith transaction as most speakers are. (There are exceptions, of course, the most obvious one being the dinner of a political organization. President Eisenhower was exactly right when, while running for reelection, he told speechwriter Emmet John Hughes to put "a few more 'cheer lines' in this speech. 'Cause a mob like this doesn't want to think—they just want to yowl.") The easiest way to show respect for your audience is to challenge them. I fully acknowledge a "romantic" political attachment to Senator Robert Kennedy, but it is clear to anyone who covered his 1968 presidential campaign that he almost relished the chance to shake up an audience by disagreeing with its most cherished assumptions.

He would step before a college audience and ask how many favored continuation or escalation of the Vietnam War, and even in 1968, about half the audience would usually raise their hands. How many of you favor the draft exemption for college students? he would ask. Almost everyone in the arena would raise a hand. So in other words, he would go on, you favor "escalation without participation." *What you want,* Kennedy would say, *is for the war to go on but not for you to fight it. This is a generation that talks about injustice; but don't you understand that the places in the army you don't fill will be filled by the blacks and the browns and the whites who are too poor to get into college?* He would batter them with stories he had heard from mothers who had lost a son in Vietnam, whose two younger sons were in combat, and whose fourth son had just received his draft notice. By the end of that talk, what had begun as a conventional political talk had turned into something much more like an opening of minds.

This is the same tactic that was used by John Kennedy in 1960 when he went before that group of Protestant ministers in Houston, spoke bluntly about the religious issue in the campaign, and then answered questions about every conceivable fear that could arise about the prospect of a Catholic in the White House. It is the same tactic that was used by Jimmy Carter when he went before the American Legion and said flatly that he would indeed pardon those who had fled the country to avoid serving in Vietnam. It has a way of jolting an audience into realizing that they are in the presence of an unusual politician.

On a smaller scale, I saw Ed Koch, then an underdog candidate for Mayor of New York, tell a small group of homeowners who passionately favored a multibillion-dollar highway project that he was opposed to it. The discussion went back and forth, and then Koch said: "Look. I am not going to change my mind about it. If it means the difference between getting your vote and losing your vote, then I am not going to get your vote." More than one member of the audience—who disagreed with Koch's stand—said they were seriously thinking of voting for him *because* he had challenged their beliefs. "He didn't tell us what we wanted to hear; I like that," one said. (After the election, Koch abandoned his position and embraced the project, but that is a story about political consistency, not rhetoric.)

Clearly, this tactic has limits. It is unwise to stand before an audience and tell them that they embody every character trait you have found repellent through the years. It is also poor strategy to believe that *any* disagreement can be turned into exciting rhetoric, or that this is necessarily good. You could, I am sure, trigger great excitement at a convention of the American Jewish Committee by revealing your support for the aims and methods of the Palestine Liberation Organization, but it will not be of assistance to your political career. (On the other hand, should you have a fundamental disagreement with an interest group, you have nothing to lose by appearing before it to explain your position. You have nothing to lose, and you might earn points for courage.)

There is, of course, another reason why opposing the thinking of an audience has clear political benefit. Every speech by a reasonably prominent figure has two audiences: the one he is speaking to, and the audience that hears about the speech. The very fact that you have shown yourself willing to confront an angry audience will almost surely benefit you in the wider community, which does not share your immediate audience's passion for the specific issue involved. In fact, a reporter who can be persuaded to begin his story, "Confronting an angry audience last night, Smithers . . ." has already done your campaign an enormous favor.) The people in the hall may be incensed with you, but the greater populace may well say to itself, "I like that fellow Smithers; he's got the guts to stand his ground." This view of you will ripen into genuine political affection, until you stand in front of his group and take them on. You must be careful to limit this tactic; if you confront enough different groups, you may find you have alienated more than half of the electorate. This is not advisable.

A Special Word About Humor

Humor is the nitroglycerin of political speech. It is a substance of great power when handled properly; mishandled, it can explode with fatal consequences.

At least two presidential campaigns have been directly, perhaps irretrievably, altered by humor. In 1944, Franklin D. Roosevelt was under attack for having sent a navy destroyer back to an installation in Alaska to pick up FDR's dog Fala. It was a charge of potential power, especially because FDR's family was constantly being accused of using its power to obtain special privileges. One of his sons, James, had "bumped" returning American combat veterans from a transport plane to make room for his pets which were being shipped to his new California home. In a speech, Roosevelt mockingly deplored the foul play of his rivals; not content to attack my family, he said, "they now attack my little dog Fala. . . . Fala is Scottish, you know," said Roosevelt, and since hearing the charges of wasted tax money, "he hasn't been the same since."

In 1976, a reporter overheard Secretary of Agriculture Earl Butz repeat a joke in answering a question about why Republicans could not attract black voters. The only thing coloreds were interested in, the joke went, was "tight pussy, loose shoes, and a warm place to shit." Since the eavesdropper was John Dean, on assignment for a magazine, the story made its way into print, and President Ford fired Butz in the wake of the fully justifiable outrage.

Beyond these extreme examples, humor can often make a point more sharply, and more memorably, than a dozen position papers. The only effective answer to the politically popular attack on bureaucrats in American history was given by Harry Truman in his 1948 campaign. "You know what a 'bureaucrat' is?" he asked. "A 'bureaucrat' is a Democrat who's got a job a Republican wants."

When he first ran for the Senate in 1962, Ted Kennedy told this story to rebut the charge—not entirely outrageous —that he was running as the child of privilege and wealth. He was, Teddy said, attacked at a factory speech by a listener who said that Teddy hadn't worked a day in his life. After the speech, another worker came up to him, and said, "You ain't worked a day in your life, eh? Let me tell you something, son, you ain't missed a thing."

What Ted Kennedy was attempting to do with this story, what most politicians attempt to do, is to use humor to relax their audiences, to get the audience to treat them as "real people." We have a tradition in America of deep-seated, but good-natured skepticism about our politicians. What we suspect is that, beneath their noble words, they are all four-flushers, putting on airs and thinking themselves better than the rest of us. Humor is a way a politician uses to say to his audience, "See? I can laugh. I can make you laugh. I'm one of you, not one of those martini-swilling, secretary-pinching high livers in Washington."

The problem is that most politicians do not know how to make humor a part of their speeches. They, or their ghostwriters, will thumb through the *Compleat Guide to After-Dinner Humor* and staple three or four prepackaged jokes to the top of their speech texts. Thus, the speaker is "reminded of what the judge said to the inebriated defendant" (or, in the days when all-male audiences were common, he would be "reminded of what the eunuch said to the sultan's twenty-fifth wife"). After three or four of these thigh slappers, the politician's face would suddenly pull itself together, and the audience would receive a signal that the light moments are over, and that the serious part of the speech has begun.

This is not the way to use humor. Instead, remember these two rules:

- If humor is appropriate, use it throughout your speech, and in answer to questions as well.
- If humor is not appropriate, do not use it at all—and make your opponents uncomfortable for having used it.

The appearance of wit somewhere beyond the first three minutes of a speech produces an effect much like finding that a beautiful, unapproachably erotic stranger across the room harbors an unquenchable lust for you. The sense of shock is quickly replaced by a sense of overwhelming gratitude. No matter what the (wrong) lessons drawn from Adlai Stevenson's sense of humor in 1952—running against Eisenhower was impossible no matter what Stevenson's demeanor—wit delights an audience. It immediately sets you apart from the other politicians whom they have been listening to, and it proves that you respect an audience enough, and are confident enough in your ability, to relax in their presence to free yourself from the tyranny of prerecorded words.

When S. I. Hayakawa was running for the Senate in 1976, and was asked about turning the Panama Canal over to Panama, his answer was: "We should keep it. We stole it fair and square."

Consider the benefits of that answer. It was unexpectedly funny (at least, the first few times; later audiences almost demanded it, as fans of *Mork and Mindy* insist Robin Williams say "na-no, na-no" in each episode). To liberals, it suggested that Hayakawa understood the injustice of the foreign possession. To conservatives, it suggested enthusiasm for the John Wayne style of international diplomacy. Not bad for a single sentence.

George Wallace, in 1968 and 1972, was especially skilled at flaying the hides of liberals by venting the darkest fantasies of citizens about their government. After scorning all those Washington bureaucrats who couldn't park a bicycle straight telling you how to run your lives, he'd scornfully wonder what was inside all those briefcases they carried around. Open one up, he'd say, and you'd probably find a peanut butter sandwich and a newspaper.

Alternatively, the Kennedys constantly resorted to humor as a self-deprecating device. They understood that there was a fine line between the movie-star celebrification of the family, and a potential resentment against their money and political power. Thus, when John Kennedy was asked how he got to be a war hero, he would reply, "It was involuntary— they sank my boat." A more complicated version of this was Robert Kennedy's remarks while whistle-stopping through Nebraska in 1968. The train would stop at a small town, one which had probably not seen a presidential candidate since William Jennings Bryan, and Kennedy would begin something like this: "Perhaps you're wondering why I decided to run for President. I was talking it over with my wife, and she said, 'You should run for President.' I said, 'Why?' She said, 'Because then you'd run in the Nebraska primary.' I said, 'And?' She said, 'Well, then you could visit Furburg.' And here I am."

It was more complicated, because Kennedy was not only mocking himself and his fellow politicians, he was mocking the whole ritual by which political figures found it necessary to extol the virtues of every community they happened to find themselves passing through. At times, Robert Kennedy could almost become whimsical. When asked at one stop how he felt about the North Koreans seizing the ship *Pueblo*, he replied: "Badly."

The use of humor is a splendid political device assuming you have a sense of humor. The mistake many political figures make is to demonstrate a sense of humor they do not possess. When Richard Nixon would stand up and say, as he did to college audiences in 1968, "I sympathize with your effort to graduate from college. I'm trying to graduate from a college, too—the Electoral College," the result was excruciating. And watching Nixon's smile instantly disappearing from his face, to be replaced by the grim visage of concern, contributed in no small part to his reputation for insincerity.

The answer to a lack of a sense of humor is *not to go near a joke*. Rhetoric works best when it fits your own character, your own personality, when the public face of your words is as close as possible to the private face. (Obviously, there are limits to this advice. If your private vocabulary runs to the grossly obscene, this is not something to display at the Commonwealth Club speech. But, as Harry Truman demonstrated, a certain earthiness of speech can be politically effective.) A serious demeanor, then, will prove much more acceptable to your audience than a strained attempt to tell a humorous story.

It can even be a distinct advantage. Suppose you are at a candidates' meeting, with several of your competitors. Each of them has stood up and attempted to make some ingratiating, pleasant, humorous remark. Now it is your turn. You approach the rostrum. You nod pleasantly, if a little coolly, to your fellow candidates. You wait a beat or two. And you begin:

"You know, I find it interesting that my opponents believe that you need a little joke in order to pay attention to this critical election. I like a good laugh as much as the next guy. But I wonder, when you look at what we face in the coming years, whether there's much to laugh about. I don't happen to think it's funny that it costs a dollar to buy what a quarter bought thirty years ago. I don't happen to think it's funny that our older Americans subsist on an income that condemns them to poverty. I admit to you that my opponents are a lot better at making you laugh than I am. But I think the ideas I have—the record I have—proves that I take seriously the business of protecting you and your money."

What you have done, in a few short words, is to redefine the mood; you have gone *with* your weakness, instead of trying to fight against it. And in so doing, you have managed to make your opponents look like a handful of insensitive, callow fools.

There is one other point to keep in mind about humor: it is the easiest, most efficient tool available to vent potentially damaging ideas about you and your candidacy. Even though voters are skeptical of candidates, they are usually too polite to ask what is really bothering them about you. If, for example, you are a black candidate for office, you are not likely to be asked whether you think too many special privileges have been given to blacks. You are not likely to be asked, if you are divorced, whether you believe in the sanctity of the family (although Theodore White does report that at the 1964 Republican convention, when Nelson Rockefeller's speech was booed by angry Goldwater supporters, a delegate incensed by his remarriage stood up screaming again and again, "You lousy lover! You lousy lover!"). A humorous jest about what you know is on everyone's mind can break the tension quickly.

Ronald Reagan will sometimes raise the issue of age, saying he has frequently been asked the question in Japan, where age is venerated. "They thought I was too young." Congresswoman Pat Schroeder, when asked how she could combine a political career and motherhood, usually says, "I have a brain and a uterus—and they both work." And a black candidate for office could do a lot worse than raise the issue of "this fundamental difference we face—the fact that I do not like professional football." This is not to say, I hasten to add, that Ted Kennedy will be spending much time joking about bad drivers. But John Connally has said for two years, when asked about his indictment—and acquittal—on bribery charges, "I am the only certified not guilty candidate of either party." The general rule here is to follow the example of defense attorneys in murder cases. If they can keep the mood light, the jury is less likely to believe the heinous charges against their clients. Your ability to make light of a liability can help convince an audience that you do not really fear that liability, or you would not be joking about it.

CHAPTER VII

HOW TO USE THE PRESS

You will frequently hear, in discussions on political life, about the "adversary" relationship between politicians and the press. You will hear it at seminars in journalism school. You will hear it on television commentary when a President gets annoyed with the press, as has happened with every President since Jefferson. You will hear it repeatedly at editors' or publishers' conventions. It is true, if what is meant is that reporters can become famous exposing politicians, and that politicians bitterly resent anything unpleasant printed about them. It is also a wildly simplistic description of a relationship which is as symbiotic as it is adversarial. What you must keep in mind at the outset is that politicians need the press, and the press needs politicians.

It is obvious that the candidate for office needs the press. In an age of "wholesale" as opposed to "retail" politics, a candidate's name must get in the papers and on the news or that candidate does not exist. As a perceptive political analyst (me) once said, "If a tree falls in the forest and it isn't on the six o'clock news, did it in fact fall? Maybe, but who cares?" Any candidate running for high office understands that a major part of his job is to get himself in the columns and on the news shows (see chapter 8 for a specific discussion of television).

When Jimmy Carter was Governor of Georgia, he went out of his way to accommodate visiting journalists, and we can mark his first plunge into national attention with his appearance on the cover of *Time* magazine as the symbol of the New South. (A puzzling choice given his frequently expressed admiration while running for Governor for Lester Maddox, and given the presence in Florida of Reubin Askew. It was made more puzzling by the remarkable likeness between the final cover portrait and the image of John Kennedy.) And during the 1976 Iowa Democratic caucus voting, Carter went to New York, so he could more easily appear on the late-night and next-morning network shows.

But the press needs politicians (maybe "welcomes" would be a better word), for a host of reasons. First, campaigns make exciting stories. Unlike subtle news which takes years or decades to develop—the shifts in population, the decline of the dollar, the worsening environment, the shift in economically powerful regions and nations—politics has all the drama up front. Bands, crowds, airplanes taking off and landing, movement, charges, countercharges, all take place in a contained, easily coverable setting. Unlike a war, where reporters risk their lives, campaign coverage is a piece of cake. Your luggage is picked up and delivered by campaign aides, and your rooms are booked as well. You pay for nothing; the paper or magazine or broadcast outlet gets—and pays—the bills.

Second, politics is a way for a reporter to make it big. Forty years ago, foreign correspondents came back from faraway climes with tales of European monarchs and foreign ministers, and speculations about war and peace. They wrote books which featured pictures of themselves wearing trench coats, perhaps smoking pipes. They lectured to women's clubs, and got the best tables at restaurants in New York.

Today, the political correspondent is the first among journalistic unequals. Today, it is the well-informed seer of presidential politics who lectures at clubs and colleges for $1500 a throw, who appears on *Washington Week in Review,* who is jetted to London to explain American politics to the British, and whose books find publishers. Without the inherent drama of politics, journalists might well find themselves stripped of the rewards of their craft—summer homes, European vacations, good clothes—and find themselves returned to the impecunious, rumpled image of *The Front Page.*

But most important of all, the press needs politicians to help tell the public what is going on. Whatever the cynicism with which a reporter jokes about politicians, most journalists know full well that the average candidate or officeholder is a treasure trove of information. Politicians must have a sense of the public mood, not because they are more dedicated to the public well-being, but because they need this instinct to survive, the way a fragile forest animal must have an acute sense of the smell of danger. So a journalist looking for an accurate reading of the public mood knows to seek out a politician. The politician's tale of a disaffected constituent, an embittered onetime loyalist of the President, is a nearly infallible guide to a good story. This is true in matters of substance as well. For all the delight we take in the portrait of a dunderheaded legislator—and there are enough to make that portrait plausible—most members of the legislature are immersed in the details of bills, at least those bills that directly affect the people who elect them to office. Scratch a Senator from Iowa and you will find an expert on agricultural subsidy programs; talk to any California Congressman and you will learn more about the politics of water than you would ever care to know. In the relentless torrent of information that pours out of public and private sources, the politician is a highly useful guide to interpretation.

If you understand the press, its values, its needs, you are

a long way to achieving political success. If you distrust the press, fear it, assume it is an adversary, you are, in effect, running a race with a fifty-pound weight on your shoulders. Reporters and journalists, no more than any human being, cannot pretend to omniscience and, with the exception of such as Joseph Alsop and Joe Kraft, they do not make such pretensions. But they do have a clear set of judgmental tools, and you must understand what these tools are if your campaign is to use properly the press as an ally. For that is what your task is: to *use* the press, to take advantage of their assumptions, in order to aid your own prospects. Here are some basic guideposts. If you ignore them, the more subtle points about relations with the press are not worth discussing.

Never lie.   A journalist may not feel competent to pass judgment on your program for tax reform, or housing, or welfare reform, but a lie is something always remembered, never forgiven. If a reporter asks you something you do not want to talk about, say so. One of the early signs of Lyndon Johnson's crumbling political fortunes came when the press discovered his tendency to dissemble. A reporter asking LBJ about Richard Goodwin's speechwriting role in the White House was told that he was not writing speeches at all, even though that reporter had just come from talking with Goodwin about speeches he was working on. When a 1966 campaign stop was canceled, the White House announced that Johnson had never intended to make such a stop, even though the reporters had talked to advance men and other technicians working on Johnson's appearance.

These little lies helped solidify the press's sense of Johnson as a dissembler, and made the media far more willing to listen to the argument that the whole truth was not being told about the Vietnam War, either. There is nothing wrong at all with saying, "No comment," or even, "I can't answer that question," when the subject matter is too sensitive for a straightforward reply.

Do not change your position on an issue unless that change can be made to seem an act of political courage. In an analysis of the 1976 press coverage, political scientist Donald Matthews, in *The Media and the Nominating Process,* concluded that "a candidate's statement on public issues is most likely to be reported if it represents a *change* in the candidate's position, or if the statement is *inconsistent* with other positions the candidate holds at the same time. . . . Reporters place a premium on internal consistency. 'A politician can get away with a great deal,' one of the best reporters in the business said a few years ago, 'so long as he is consistent.' "

Again, a journalist may find it uncomfortable to write flatly that "Smithers' position on financing Social Security through nationally televised bingo games is ridiculous." That calls for a policy conclusion, and reporters do not like to be put in the position of making such conclusions. But a *change* in position is a far more easily detectable fact. Reporters love to seize on such an inconsistency, because it is the closest thing to a value judgment they get to make. Thus: "Smithers' position on financing Social Security through nationally televised bingo games represents a sharp departure from his previous position in favor of financing Social Security through a compulsory baby-sitting service for senior citizens."

The only way that change will help you is if you outflank the press by reveling in it. The press likes to believe it is uncovering something by trapping a politician into admitting he has changed. Thus, the only way to accomplish such a change in public policy is to take the offensive, to hold hearings, listen to experts, and then stand up and declare that "The facts are beyond dispute, and it is our duty to respect the facts. We can no longer cling to outmoded ideas of the 1960s to solve the problems of the 1980s. This is a matter beyond partisan dispute or petty bickering. It is a matter of conscience."

In this kind of case, it would be trivial for a reporter to "expose" what you have already conceded. Otherwise, "a foolish consistency is not only the hobgoblin of little minds," it is your hobgoblin as well.

The press is bewitched by character and by detail. Ever since Theodore White's *The Making of the President: 1960,* the press has found itself in the grip of what has been called "the Teddy White syndrome"—a fascination with the mechanics of a political campaign, with its backstage detail, its organization, its staff, its strategy, its polling, with everything except a detached examination of what a candidate intends to do with the office he is seeking. This is part of the reason why George McGovern's demogrant scheme, announced in late 1971, did not become an issue until it was raised in the late primary season of 1972 by Hubert Humphrey and Henry Jackson; and why Ronald Reagan's $90 billion transfer idea did not get picked up by the press for several months. It is simply not as exciting to sit down and read through position papers as it is to probe the backgrounds of a candidate's family and aides.

Essentially, political journalists have become novelists in training. A detailed examination of a position is all right for a *New York Times* "The Week in Review" column; but to get the cover of a magazine or a shot at a big book, a reporter needs detail, character insights, literary probes. One of the reasons why Jimmy Carter so captivated the press after his initial primary victories was that his hometown of Plains was so rich in the fabric of good literature: once a writer got finished describing Main Street in Plains, the red clay dirt, the temperature, the quaint folk sayings of Miz Lillian and Brother Billy, the first thousand words of the profile were already written. Similarly, America was dazzled in the first days of the Ford Administration by the revelation that the new President toasted his own English muffins: a clear sign that the days of the Imperial Presidency were over.

The surest way to play off this lust for the detail is to *plan* for it. You cannot approach the press without a careful package of the following:

THE REVELATORY BIOGRAPHICAL ANECDOTE. Jimmy Carter told us over and over of the signposts of his life, of watching the black workers hovering outside his father's home, listening to Joe Louis knock out Max Schmeling, then quietly going home to their neighborhood and then celebrating; of meeting Admiral Hyman Rickover who sternly demanded of him if he had done his best in school; of being challenged by a pastor to demonstrate his Christianity.

You need this kind of material. You need, for example, a schoolyard confrontation with a bully. Or a life-changing talk with a kindly teacher (preferably, a teacher long since deceased to prevent embarrassing conflicts of detail). Or a scarring loss of a good friend. What you need is something to give the press the raw meat of character development they are all seeking.

In addition, you need to give to your staff one good story that you never tell. This is the story the staff will tell late at night in a barroom conversation with a reporter, and should be preceded by the comment that "The old man will kill me if he finds out I told this story." It should be the kind of story that reveals a "weakness" which is in fact admirable; for example, the time the candidate blew his temper and became almost violent when faced with a man abusing an animal. "The old man's never forgiven himself for almost blowing up like that," the aide will say.

THE VALUABLE MISTAKE. In Jimmy Carter's case, he referred often in 1976 to the fact that he had been guilty of the sin of pride, caring too much about worldly success before finding his born-again Christian faith. In this age of anything goes, when reporters no longer cover up any of a candidate's shortcomings, whether venal or mortal, you cannot hope to impress the press with an image of perfection. Some flaw in your character must be revealed.

My own preference in these times is a past undervaluing of your spouse (assuming you are a male). More specifically, I would suggest that you tell a reporter that when you were first married, you took your wife for granted and expected her to serve you in a traditional way. Then (you say) your wife grew. You did not understand. There were strains in your marriage. She left—for a few weeks, maybe months. Now you have a stronger relationship, and you do not feel threatened by her job. In fact, you're learning to understand the pleasures of nurturing a child.

THE FAMILY IN CRISIS. At one time, the political family was a carefully controlled image: beloved wife, well-scrubbed children, attractive pet. Few people remember this, but one of the features of Richard Nixon's famous 1952 "Checkers" speech was that, in the middle of his live telecast, he left the desk and sat down beside Pat, whose smile appeared to have been sprayed on with Renuzit. And John Kennedy's political fortunes were greatly aided by a glamorous wife and two adorable children, who filled the pages of magazines such as *Look* and *Life* scampering about the White House and Hyannis Port in high spirits. (Their father, it is now clear, was scampering about on other, less photographed pursuits.)

Now, troubled families are all but compulsory. Betty Ford gave her book a powerful lift by publicly confessing alcohol and drug dependence, and solidified her position as the most admired woman in America. Howard Baker, a powerful Senator and a presidential contender, acknowledged his wife's past alcoholism. Ted Kennedy's wife Joan has waged the same struggle. And divorce, as has been mentioned earlier, carries the same weight as a case of the flu.

Offering up a troubled family member to the press is a first-rate form of political inoculation. By acknowledging that a spouse, or child, is going through a difficult period, you ensure (a) that the press will treat that family member sympathetically, and (b) that the problem of your family member will help insulate you from frontal attack. Even if it is your fault that your wife has turned to drink or your child to controlled substances, there is something potent about a politician publicly grappling with a private crisis. I do not go so far as to suggest that you rent a dipsomaniac to pose as a close family member. I only suggest that a family crisis can help, and it cannot possibly hurt, in the effort to let the press unconsciously serve you.

The press loves a politician with vision. Nothing tires out a political writer faster than covering the internecine wars among candidates and their coat holders; no matter how clean a campaign, there is always mileage to be gained by offering a ringing denunciation of the grubby lack of issues that have turned a campaign into a personality contest. And nothing excites a political writer—especially an important columnist—more than the prospect of listening to Real Ideas. One of the reasons why Daniel Patrick Moynihan was so beloved by the normally skeptical national press was that, from the time he entered the Kennedy Administration as a junior Cabinet member, he threw out an endless stream of visionary ideas and arcane knowledge. In a world of politicians living for the next poll and the next campaign, Moynihan would offer them obscure studies of rural elections in India, or insist that it was impossible to understand the Third World without reading a Ph.D. study about the malevolent influence of the London School of Economics on African heads of government. Since Moynihan is an authentic intellectual, at home in the world of scholarship, it gave him a cachet which placed him far above the level of ordinary political folk; so much so that when he and Henry Kissinger published a dialogue in which both decried ''elitism''—a feat similar to critic John Simon attacking snobbism—not one political reporter cocked a journalistic eyebrow.

This should be a lesson you take to heart. You must make it a point, especially with columnists whose opinions influence other writers and leading citizens (these are people who make more than $150,000 a year), to express your impatience and discontent with the run-of-the-mill issues clogging the circulatory system of our politics.

"You know, Scotty (or Joe, or Dave, or Haynes, or Elizabeth)," you say to your inquisitor, "here we are struggling to talk about energy and inflation. But have you heard a single word about farming the seabed? Or the future of weather control? Do you realize in five years we may be able to send newspapers around the world by satellite? Where will we be then? Do you realize that not a single Presidential commission is studying any of these problems?" This approach need not be limited, by the way, to presidential office seeking. If you are running for local or state office, you can always prove your vision by (a) calling for regionalization if everything in your region is run locally, or (b) calling for decentralization if everything in your region is run regionally. Any talk about reorganization carries with it the imprimatur of vision, without requiring you to say what it is this new form of organization will do.

The more general method of proving yourself a figure of vision is to talk about what the future might hold for us fifty or a hundred years down the road. This not only ensures that you will not be proven wrong—at least, not until you and the members of the current press corps are beyond caring— it also takes the pressure off you, since none of the journalists listening to you are going to feel threatened by your vision. You can paint all the pictures you want of mining on the moon, or transcontinental bus service for the poor, and you will be listened to respectfully. This will not happen, in contrast, if you suggest a plan to relocate low-income blacks in public housing in and around Georgetown.

The press has become spoiled. Because the logistics of campaigning have become so complicated, the press has grown accustomed to a kind of service that would have made an old newshound like Hildy Johnson from *The Front Page* gasp with astonishment. On a national campaign, it is impossible to follow the movements of a major candidate for major office without adhering to the campaign's structure. You move when the candidate moves; you stay (more or less) where the candidate stays. You get yourself listed on the airplane manifest, or you do not follow the campaign, since you cannot keep up with a chartered aircraft by resorting to scheduled airlines. You file your stories when the campaign gives you the time and the facilities to do so. You rest when the candidate decides that the campaign day is over. You find companionship among the people traveling with the campaign party.

This means that the old-fashioned view of the politician-press relationship is out the window. Out of necessity, campaigns must supply the press with much of what they used to gather by themselves. A member of the press cannot cover a major campaign with a notebook and a pencil. Cameras, microphones, and lights must be in place; speech text releases must be prepared and distributed enough in advance so that reporters can digest the substance of a speech (if there is any) and write an accurate story reflecting its major points. And they must be fed and housed properly; for nothing more absolutely demonstrates to a reporter a candidate's unfitness to govern the nation than that candidate's inability to deliver the reporter's luggage to the right hotel room.

Part of your campaign's obligation, then, is to meet the press's expectations. Pierre Salinger, reflecting on his experience as John Kennedy's press secretary in the 1960 campaign, writes that "from the beginning, we attempted to create a climate in the campaign entourage that would make the reporter's work agreeable . . . more than one reporter, switching back to the Kennedy camp after traveling for a while with the Vice-President's party, told me that they felt like they were 'coming home' when they rejoined us." After twenty years of this kind of treatment, the press has grown to believe that the right to drinks on the plane is something close to a footnote to the First Amendment.

But the very isolation that demands you serve as concierge

to the press also enables you to exercise a considerable degree of control over what the press can cover. One of the clearest lessons of recent campaigns—at least, presidential campaigns—is that the Heisenberg Effect is very much in evidence. (As any county committeeman can tell you, the Heisenberg Effect occurs when the act of observation alters the character of that which is observed; as when the light emanating from the eye of a scientist looking through an electron microscope changes the movement of tiny particles of matter being watched.) McGovern campaign manager— now U.S. Senator—Gary Hart, found himself "intrigued" during the fall campaign by "the degree to which logistics conditioned the way McGovern campaigned. The size of the press corps traveling with us conditioned the kind of campaign we waged; we had to plan around what airports we could land at (because the size of the press corps determined the size of the aircraft). . . . We tried those factory appearances and going into hospitals. But you . . . know what it's like to go into a hospital with a hundred and fifty reporters behind you—with all the pads and the overcoats and everything and knocking people out of bed?"

Given this unwieldy body, you as a candidate have every good reason to shape it to whatever purpose you choose. This does not mean that you should bar the press from meetings with fund-raisers, as President Nixon did in 1972; in the suspicious post-Watergate era, this is likely to trigger a certain degree of suspicion. What it does mean is that your schedule is what the press will cover; they go where you take them. Specifically: if you have a major endorsement lined up in your next day's schedule, make that the centerpiece of your entire day. Do not succumb to the temptation to feed the press more than you want them to digest. You arrive in a city in the morning. You make your endorsement press conference for 10:00 A.M., thus guaranteeing that it will make the evening news. You follow this endorsement with a closed meeting, but one about which the press cannot complain—for instance, a meeting with the editorial board at a local newspaper (no abuse of freedom of the press there). You then get out of town with a long trip to another media market. Why? Because the only thing the press will have to write about will be your endorsement.

None of this should be done with anything other than a spirit of full cooperation. The text of the endorsement should be distributed well in advance; a brief biography of the endorser should accompany the text. The point is that you have it within your power, through the very logistics that have spoiled the press, to ensure that the story you want makes the news. As the candidate, you can help by curbing your boundless enthusiasm for answering the probing questions of reporters *on that day*. That way, there is no chance of supplying a journalist with a quotation that, in his judgment, is more important than your endorsement. You can make sure that your campaign staff is not releasing your position paper on energy which a major news organization might deem more important than your support from this key political figure. In other words, don't trump your own ace. In yet another set of words, one of the most effective, least objectionable ways to control the way the press covers you is to limit the flow of news to the press corps which, whatever its protestations, is fundamentally dependent upon you.

The press is most easily manipulated by those who are not intimidated by its language. The conventional exchange between politicians and reporters follows a ritual as elaborate, as implicitly understood, as the Balinese dance or the Noh play is understood by those immersed in those cultures. This ritual is observable on any Sunday when the networks and local stations present their public-service, please-do-not-take-our-licenses-away interview shows, or at any press conference in any hotel suite on any given weekday. The reporter asks a sharp, but neutral question: *On Monday, you said X, Mr. Smithers. But last June, you said Y. Why this change in your position?* You reply: *I don't think this represents any change at all, Bill. You see, X is a part of the* *greater effort we must all make to accomplish Y.* Another thrust and parry: *A recent report says your proposal would cause plague and pestilence among thirty percent of American youth, Mr. Smithers.* You caution that *this is completely at variance with the facts. I am hopeful that flowers will bloom in fetid swamps.*

It is understandable, of course, that politicians would tend to talk this way, since they have grown up listening to other politicians. It recalls the hoodlum Joey Gallo, who developed his "gangster" talk from watching old George Raft films. But it is not the way to talk to the press. What most politicians do not understand is that the press is required to talk this way. You are not. If you have the confidence to do it, you can break the rules of this ritual and there is nothing the press can do about it.

For all of the railing about the manipulations of the media, the fact is that the press is all but imprisoned by its sense of responsibility. Senator Joseph McCarthy realized this when he would make his charges about Communist penetration of the military, the State Department, the churches, and other institutions of American life. He knew, that is, that the press would write that McCarthy charged (fact), Jones denied (fact), but *not* that McCarthy charged and he is either a dolt or a liar for believing this (conclusion). Without suggesting that you emulate the tactics of the unlamented late Senator, you must take to heart the fact that the press cannot step outside of its role. It cannot, that is, simultaneously play its part in the ritual while interrupting to tell the audience how the ritual is progressing.

The politician can. This is what Senator *Eugene* McCarthy did throughout his 1968 primary campaign, when he answered virtually every reporter's question by saying, "Well, I don't really think that's the most important question," and proceeded to talk about whatever he was interested in talking about. It is what George Wallace did throughout his political career when he would insert, more or less at will, the comment that "the national press, *The New York Times,* the

Washington Post, Time, Newsweek, CBS, they all ignorin'
the ordinary people of this country.'' It is what Spiro Agnew
did in his famous Des Moines speech in 1969, when he reminded his audience that the decision on whether America
would hear his comments was ''not my decision; it is not
your decision; it is *their* decision''—whereupon the networks carried, live, the remarks of a Vice President of the
United States.

It is what California Governor Jerry Brown does as well
as any politician in recent memory. He has a way of altering
the thrust of a question by putting a reverse English on the
words used by a reporter, and winds up sounding better
informed, and more thoughtful, than he would by answering
the question honestly.

During a scandal in California's hospital administration, in
which, because of inadequate funding, mental patients were
abandoned to terrible conditions in state facilities, reporters
would ask Brown about the state of public health institutions.

''What do we mean by health?'' Brown would say, and
soar off into philosophical discourse about holistic medicine,
proper exercise and nutrition, and environmental concerns.
But no reporter could possibly fulfill his or her role while
writing in the story, ''One thing health probably means is the
absence of a condition where a ward of the state spends the
day sitting in a hospital corridor in his own filth.''

An even more impressive example of the way Brown
bends the language of politics to his own devices occurred in
the summer of 1979, when he appointed a former Vietnam
prisoner of war to an unexpired term as a county supervisor.
The POW, a political ally of Tom Hayden and Jane Fonda,
had been accused of collaborating with the North Vietnam-
ese, in return for special favors, such as extra provisions at
mealtime. To a conventional politician, this would have been
an embarrassment of major proportions. Instead, Brown answered charges by saying (a) that the Vietnam War critics
were more right than those who prosecuted the war, (b) that

it was time to put the divisions of the 1960s behind us, (c) that it was not very important to find out what people ate for breakfast.

An ordinary citizen might have felt compelled to express a sense of shock, or perhaps a desire to laugh in the Governor's face, at this response. POWs who collaborate with a military foe are not precisely comparable to Senator William Fulbright or war resisters, and the issue wasn't what was eaten for breakfast, but whether such conduct—if the charge was true—should be rewarded with appointment to a public job. But reporters cannot rebut such an approach *at the time it is being made*. They can write a column two days later, but by then the force of the objection is largely depleted. As long as the press is obligated to play it straight in covering the political world, you as a candidate possess an advantage which you would be foolish to ignore. It enables you, just as an example, to characterize any past failure, no matter how embarrassing, in a positive light. The business you ran into the ground was "not only a learning experience, but a lesson I've taken with me for the rest of my life. I saw what excessive government regulations can do to destroy a hardworking businessman, and I vowed to spend the rest of my life making sure that what happened to me would never happen to another American enterprise." The bill you sponsored to provide federal tax loopholes for your home state's big industry is "one of the ways I think I've demonstrated an understanding of this tax system. A Senator who can't fight for his constituents doesn't deserve to be in the Senate. Who do *you* think should get the tax breaks? The corporations who can hire two-hundred-and-fifty-dollar-an-hour lawyers? The multinational corporations? It's about time we used the laws we have to protect American companies and American jobs."

The key to using the press in this manner is that a reporter, in general, will be too honest, too responsible, and too restrained to get in a debate with you. If someone from *Rolling Stone* wants to attack your manipulative approach, fine—it will appear weeks after your statement and the *Rolling Stone* readership doesn't vote anyway. But the method will not work if you are intimidated by the game the press is playing. Most politicians hire media consultants to teach them how to play this game. What you want is someone to teach you how to sweep away the rules, and play the game you want to play.

With the press, everything counts. Twenty-five years ago, the press was very much a part of the political inside. On campaign trips, poker games between political aides and reporters might feature an exchange of views, and language, which would have shocked the nation. But these exchanges were kept strictly confidential. So were the after-hours recreational tastes of candidates for office. So were the marital strains such tastes might have imposed on a marriage. When I was on my first campaign flight West in 1968, a veteran of many campaigns intoned the basic rule of press coverage, designed to protect politicians and journalists alike: "Nothing that happens west of the Potomac is mentioned east of the Potomac"; this clearly applied to working definitions of sobriety and fidelity.

Now the rules have been changed. The "Teddy White" syndrome has made revelations about character and mood valuable commodities. The Watergate melodrama, and the increased emphasis on political personality as a clue to performance, has made fair game out of every careless statement, every misstep. The antics of Wilbur Mills and Wayne Hays, Fanne Foxe and Elizabeth Ray, have given new meaning to the term "Acts of Congress," while the public confessions of past alcoholism on the part of everyone from Betty Ford to Billy Carter to New Jersey's Senator Harrison Williams to former Iowa Senator Harold Hughes to Georgia Senator Herman Talmadge have obliterated the distinction between private and public conduct.

From the public-interest view, this is probably a good thing. From politicians' point of view—and never confuse their point of view with the public interest—it is a potential disaster. There is no such thing as a private moment in the presence of a public figure. Even the change in journalistic tastes has stripped away this barrier. Magazine features are so heavily geared to personality profiles, which in turn depend on the recording of furniture and other artifacts, that a candidate is on view from the moment he opens the door of your hotel room to a visiting journalist.

(" 'Just a moment,' Smithers mumbled, and opened the door to his room. His unshaven face bore a hesitant smile, and his breath suggested a dash of Close-Up toothpaste in an effort to erase the smell of last night's Don Diego cigar. The red terry-cloth robe concealed a middle-aged body beginning to hint of flab, while the copy of *Penthouse* half-hidden under the sofa cushion bespoke a man both pursuing, and uncomfortable with, an adolescent sexual fantasy life. . . .")

In other words, *everything counts*. If you say something to a reporter off the record, it may not be printed in the next-day's reports. But sooner or later, you will see or hear stories that say, "While Smithers is publicly pleased with his fund-raisers' advice, he is known to believe privately that they are as big a collective group of fools as he has ever been forced to suffer, and wishes they would just give him the money and get lost." If you yell at your aides in front of reporters, your temper will become a political issue. The way you order food, the way you hold your knife, the way you embrace your children—or do not—will all go into the public conveyer belt no matter what ground rules you set down; perhaps it will be a less *public* public conveyer belt —the one that circulates through newsrooms and cocktail parties—but sooner or later it will see the light of day.

Here, too, adversity creates opportunity. As long as you know that everything counts, and as long as the press does not realize that you realize everything counts, you have a magnificent chance to make points, as long as you prepare properly for the task. Suppose a reporter is going to spend the day with you to develop an important magazine profile.

Here are some examples of artifacts and anecdotal incidents that will help turn the profile into a free advertisement:

PICK ONE ARTICLE OF CLOTHING FOR WHICH THERE IS AN AMUSING OR MOVING STORY. You may, for example, wear a conventional three-piece suit, along with a rumpled raincoat. You will hold the raincoat up to view, and say ruefully, "My wife calls this my 'Columbo' coat. She keeps trying to throw it out, but I won't let her. I wore it in my first campaign, and it's always been kind of a good-luck charm."

Alternatively, you might look at the raincoat somberly and explain, "It belonged to a buddy of mine in the service. Just before he left camp, he gave me this coat and told me to hold onto it until he came back. I . . . I guess it has a special symbol for me . . . maybe, maybe of hope." (You do not have to tell the reporter that your buddy never came back because he went AWOL.)

PLAN FOR AN UNEXPECTED INTERRUPTION IN YOUR DAY THAT GIVES YOU A CHANCE TO DEMONSTRATE GOOD CHARACTER. You are traveling to your next stop; suddenly, you see somebody in trouble along the way, perhaps a lost child, perhaps a victim of a minor accident. Stop the motorcade. Get out of the car. Exchange a few words with the victim. Call for help, or insist that one of your aides be left behind. Then move on. With good advance work, you can all but ensure that an event casting favorable light on you will appear in the profile—perhaps in the first paragraph.

Warning! Do not attempt to insinuate yourself into uncontrollable situations unless you have a very strong sense of self-confidence. During one of Richard Nixon's motorcades, a motorcycle officer was knocked off his bike. Mr. Nixon sped to the side of the groggy officer, leaned down, and asked, "Do you like your job?" Even "setup" situations have danger lurking at every turn. In 1969, Congressman John Murphy, one of the least impressive members of the House of Representatives, launched a campaign for Mayor of New York. Taking a rare break from his preferred pastime of consorting with dictatorial heads of state, Murphy decided to paint himself as the symbol of rectitude by staging raids on pornographic bookstores. Accompanied by the press, he threw himself into a Times Square emporium, only to have a wily bookstore owner gaze at him coolly and say, "Hey— you look like one of my best customers." The press event collapsed and, shortly thereafter, so did John Murphy's mayoral campaign.

GIVE THE REPORTER MORE TIME THAN YOU ARE "SUPPOSED" TO.   Flattery is a powerful weapon with anyone, and reporters, no less than ordinary folk, are susceptible to its charm. Let us say you have given a journalist the promise of a forty-five-minute interview. What you do is to cancel the rest of your schedule a good twenty-four hours in advance. After the reporter has been talking to you for forty-five minutes, have an aide come in to inform you that it is time for your next appointment. Brush him aside. Fifteen minutes later, have the aide return apologetically to inform you that it is getting late. Dismiss him angrily. When the aide returns a third time, tell him, "It's been a long time since I've been able to have an intelligent conversation—cancel the rest of my schedule."

Should the reporter run out of questions, or should he be sufficiently bored by you to wrap up the interview in another twenty minutes, you can get in some tennis or a movie, more or less secure in the knowledge that the reporter's estimate of you has increased in direct proportion to your opinion of his journalistic ability.

AT LEAST ONCE—BUT NO MORE—CONFESS TO THE SKILL OF A REPORTER'S QUESTIONING.   You do not want to be constantly knocked back by a question from a reporter, because that implies incompetence on your part. But at some point in the interview, you ought to pause, smile sheepishly, and "confess" that "that's the question I was afraid you'd

ask. I frankly don't know—and neither does anybody else''
(this gets you off the hook). It is a rare journalistic bird who
will use a knife on a subject who has acknowledged the wisdom of the journalist.

IF YOU ARE FACED WITH THE PROSPECT OF AN INTERVIEW
BY A KILLER JOURNALIST, DO NOT GRANT THE INTER-
VIEW. Washington is littered with the bones of people who
believed they could survive a profile by Sally Quinn, the
Washington Post's premier feature writer. Time after time,
Ms. Quinn has examined the lives of the powerful people of
that city, and time after time has painted merciless portraits.
Yet there are always those who believe they can charm, or
stonewall Ms. Quinn into painting a sympathetic picture.

Do not make this mistake. If a journalist has made his
reputation by carving his initials into the hides of subjects,
do not grant an interview. And do not be intimidated by the
threat that "we won't be able to get your side of the story."
A personality profile without the personality is very hard to
get into print, since editors are likely to believe the animus
stems from sour grapes.

The press, then, must be treated as a dangerous, but potentially valuable animal. You must house it, feed it, pet it
once in a while. You must never show it fear, or it will turn
on you. You must gently, but firmly, guide it in the direction
you want it to go. You must respect its power, but realize
that its power is limited to primeval instincts about the pro-
priety of its own behavior. Once you master it, it will serve
you well in your political life—as long as you remember
never to turn your back to it.

CHAPTER VIII

HOW TO USE TELEVISION WITHOUT FEAR

In no area of political life has mythology more thoroughly displaced reality than in the discussion of what television has done to political life. Of course it has changed it dramatically; so did every other invention of communication; so, for that matter, did every other major shift in the way we work, play, travel, learn, and live. What you must do, to succeed in politics, is to face television without fear. You must respect its power, but you must never lose sight of one fundamental fact: *television has changed our political life far less radically than you have been told.* You cannot appreciate the way to use television in a political career unless you first sweep away the myths and recognize the difference between the *real* impact of television and the ways in which our political life have remained remarkably constant.

152

Has television produced a politics of symbolism? The famous "log cabin" in which American Presidents are supposed to be born was an image created in the 1840 campaign of William Henry Harrison, actually the product of an affluent family. The whole tradition of military heroes as especially fit for the job of President—a tradition extending from George Washington through Andrew Jackson through Zachary Taylor through Ulysses S. Grant through Theodore Roosevelt through Dwight Eisenhower—is itself an expression of a symbolic link between battlefield command and political prowess. And if you think that television commercials uniquely exploit personal traits for political gain, consider this extract from a piece by Artemus Ward in 1860, poking fun at Abraham Lincoln's rail-splitter image by "reporting" on what happened when a delegation from the Republican National Convention went to inform Lincoln that he'd been nominated for President:

> The Official Committee arrived in Springfield at dewy eve, and went to Honest Old Abe's house. Honest Old Abe was not in. Mrs. Honest Old Abe said Honest Old Abe was out in the woods splitting rails. So the Official Committee went out into the woods, where sure enough they found Honest Old Abe splitting rails with his two boys. It was a grand, a magnificent spectacle. There stood Honest Old Abe in his shirt-sleeves, a pair of leather home-made suspenders holding up a pair of home-made pantaloons, the seat of which was neatly patched with substantial cloth of a different color.
>
> "Mr. Lincoln, Sir, you've been nominated, Sir, for the highest office, Sir—"
>
> "Oh, don't bother me," said Honest Old Abe. "I took a *stent* this mornin' to split three million rails afore night, I don't want to be pestered with no stuff about no Conventions till I get my *stent* done. . . ." And the great man went right on splitting rails, paying no attention to the Committee whatever. . . .

Obviously, the Lincoln presidential campaign did not neglect the symbolic value of Lincoln's hardworking, log-cabin background. And neither has any major political campaign. We have had plumed knights, and happy warriors, and giantkillers as long as we have had campaigns.

Has television placed a premium on good looks? We hear often that in the television age, candidates must appear smooth, telegenic, or, in the words of one observer, "look like a heroic marble bust." When Arizona Republican Congressman John Rhodes praised Gerald Ford in 1976, he declared that Ford "looks like a President." And it is a staple of political satire, good for one free column every four years, that a candidate who looked like Abraham Lincoln, with his gaunt features, mole, deep-set eyes, and beard, would never make it in today's media age.

To begin with, a handsome face has always been a political advantage. The same praise heaped on Gerald Ford was also heaped on Warren Harding in 1920. With his white hair and firm jaw, he, too, "looked like a President." Teddy Roosevelt's muscularity was an important aspect of his political appeal, as was William Jennings Bryan's youthful vitality. (One wonders, by the way, whether Lincoln's massive height advantage over the minute Stephen Douglas was not, in part, a triumph of physical presence.)

But more important, the Age of Television has by no means brought about the Age of Charm School Candidates. Granted, Senators Birch Bayh, Ted Kennedy, Mark Hatfield and Charles Percy, are immaculately groomed, good-looking candidates. But then how explain the victory of S. I. Hayakawa over John Tunney in California, of all places, the ultimate media state? How explain the triumph of Ed Koch as Mayor of New York, or the political durability of Senators Ed Muskie and Jacob Javits, neither of whom are likely to be drafted by Bloomingdale's store in New York for a Fall Fashion Preview. It is certainly true that television has made it more possible to campaign on the basis of character—or what you want people to think of as your character—but that is a very different proposition than arguing that cosmetics is now the dominant factor in making presidential choices.

Has television altered the basis on which political campaigns are built? Without question, television—specifically, television advertising—has made it easier than it ever was for a political unknown with a lot of money to enter the political world without spending years building a political base in the sense in which we used to use that term. A look at the kinds of people successfully running for the United States Senate in this decade shows a break with the tradition of going from school board to state legislature to Congress to the Senate. Candidates such as New Hampshire's Gordon Humphreys (airline pilot), John Glenn and Harrison Schmidt (astronauts), Bill Bradley (basketball player), S. I. Hayakawa (academician and college president), all could be used to prove that television has short-circuited the road to political achievement.

But look again: Schmidt and Glenn were contemporary versions of military commanders, proving their ability to lead by having the courage to fly into space. Moreover, both men had spent long years building political bases in their respective states; Glenn had run for the Senate in 1964 and again in 1970 before finally winning his seat in 1974. Hayakawa, too, had been a kind of military commander, beating back the dreaded student radicals as president of San Francisco State in 1969, and had been speaking at political gatherings ever since before ousting Tunney in 1976. Bradley had put in years as well on the rubber-chicken circuit in New Jersey, surely enough to qualify him for a gastronomic medal of honor.

These politicians were made famous by television. But that tells us no more than does the fact that General Grant was made famous by telegraphic dispatches back to newspapers during the Civil War. Whatever TV did for these figures, it did not relieve them of the responsibility of slowly building up their political bases with very traditional activity —in part to prove to the voters of their states that they were more than media personalities.

The vitality of traditional politics is even clearer if we look at who has been nominated for President in the Age of Television and how. If we begin in 1964—the year after network news had expanded to a half hour, and the year after the Kennedy assassination had demonstrated television's full news potential—the facts add up to something less than a demonstration of TV's dominant influence.

1964. Lyndon Johnson was renominated automatically by virtue of his incumbency. He had initially risen to political prominence as Senate Majority Leader, and was defeated for the Democratic presidential nomination in 1960 less because of television than because he did not understand the growing importance of presidential primaries. The ultimate 1964 Republican nominee, Barry Goldwater, had been a national spokesman for the conservative ideology since his entrance into the Senate years before. In fact, his name had been placed in nomination at the 1960 convention by the Louisiana delegation, and in his speech withdrawing his name, he exhorted conservatives to take the Republican Party back by getting to work. They did. Goldwater's candidacy was, in effect, begun by his supporters the moment Richard Nixon lost the 1960 election. In 1964, even though Goldwater did not by any means dominate the primaries, his devoted followers outworked every other campaign in winning huge blocs of delegates in the party caucuses. One primary—California's—gave Goldwater the delegates and the momentum that made his nomination inevitable.

1968. Richard Nixon won the Republican nomination by cashing in on twenty years' worth of political prominence or notoriety. Far from being a "media creation," Richard

Nixon had by 1968 already been involved in three national campaigns. In 1966, he had crisscrossed America, campaigning for Republican candidates at every level; a large measure of his broad-based support that year came from the network of political alliances he had built up, ranging from Senator Strom Thurmond of South Carolina to Governor John Volpe of Massachusetts and the then-liberal Governor Spiro Agnew of Maryland. This was, by any measurement, a traditional, "nonmedia" method of gaining political support.

In the Democratic Party, Eugene McCarthy's insurgency in New Hampshire was written off by almost every national political journalist and reporter. It was only after four months of work by an army of volunteers going door to door, canvassing cities and small towns alike, that McCarthy "won" the primary with 42 percent of the vote to Johnson's "loss" with 49 percent. Robert Kennedy, who then entered the presidential campaign, was a national political figure by virtue of a family legacy, and by a deliberate decision on his part to turn his Senate work into a kind of campaign for the dispossessed. And the ultimate nominee, Hubert Humphrey, had for twenty years been one of the most familiar, outspoken figures in the Democratic Party, a figure who evoked in 1968 support from big-city Democrats, big labor, and a faction of traditional liberals—now called neoconservatives —who saw in the McCarthy and Kennedy campaigns a threat to their values. In no sense could Hubert Humphrey's support be traced to anything other than a long history of political combat in Washington and around the country.

1972. Richard Nixon was renominated without serious difficulty. Senator George McGovern won the Democratic nomination by virtually duplicating Goldwater's victory (and ultimate defeat). He had been a last-minute candidate four years earlier, inheriting much of the late Robert Kennedy's support at the Chicago convention. He was the choice of a committed faction within the Democratic Party which was in dissent against the Vietnam War, and which had become convinced in 1968 that they had been denied their victory at Chicago. From this faction, McGovern built a cadre of tens of thousands of dedicated workers. As late as January 1972, McGovern was the choice of barely 3 percent of registered Democrats, and most commentators had all but conceded the nomination to Senator Ed Muskie. Only with Mc-Govern's second-place "victory" and Muskie's first-place "defeat" in New Hampshire did the networks begin to regard McGovern as a serious contender for the nomination. He had announced his candidacy some twenty months before the 1972 election.

1976. Both nominations were seriously contested. Ronald Reagan, who almost took the Republican designation from President Gerald Ford, has been described as the ultimate media candidate, and certainly the onetime sportscaster-actor-television host is fully comfortable in front of the cameras. But by 1976, Reagan was also a former two-term Governor of the most populous state in the union. It is probable that as many votes were cast for Reagan in his two campaigns in California as had been cast for Ford in all of his Congressional races in Michigan. He had, as had Goldwater and McGovern, surfaced as a last-minute presidential contender in an earlier convention—1968—and had followers who believed his strong conservative policies to be the salvation of the Republican Party.

And Democrat Jimmy Carter was the consummate outsider: former Governor of a Southern state whose chances for the nomination were ridiculed by his home-state newspapers ("Jimmy *Who* Is Running for *What?*" was the *Atlanta Constitution* headline when he announced). Carter, too, declared for the nomination very early—two years before the 1976 election—and spent all of 1975 talking to people in shopping centers, supermarkets, and small-town Democratic dinners, far from the reach of a television camera. Only when *New York Times* reporter R. W. Apple, Jr., reported that Carter had won a straw ballot at an Iowa Democratic dinner in late 1975 (a dinner Carter supporters had packed) did the media begin to treat Carter with minimal seriousness.

Of course, had television ignored these candidates throughout the campaign, they would almost certainly have been defeated. But that would have required a conscious, malicious effort to distort the political process; and it is a far cry from arguing that these candidates were *made* by television. To say that TV "created" these candidacies is to say that when cameras record a flood that has been cresting for days, it is somehow responsible for that flood.

How, then, should one think about television in planning a journey into politics? You must understand that it is the latest in a continually changing mode of communicating with each other. And you must understand that politics has always moved into these new modes of communication, for the most obvious of reasons: that is where they are going to find the people.

A hundred years ago, our form of communication was to gather together, because the methods of reaching people separately had not yet been invented. If we wanted to be entertained, or diverted, we had to leave our homes and travel a good distance in order to hear preachers, or debates, or find some release from the cares of the world. And politics used this mode for its own purposes.

As historian Jules Abel describes it in his book *The Degradation of the American Presidency:* "In days gone by, particularly in the 19th century, the Presidential election was an all-consuming interest for the public. It was not a spectator interest. . . . It was an event for mass participation in parades, torchlight processions, meetings and barbecues, not only for adults, but for teenage boys and girls. There was endless speech-making and discussion. Contemporary observers noted that the carnival proceedings provided an emotional outlet and even communal recreation for the masses, at a time when there was little else available that would give the same emotional release or stimulus."

Historian David Hackett Fischer tells us that the Fourth

of July itself was converted into a huge cause for celebration by opportunistic political parties: "During the 1790's," he writes, "Independence Day had been observed intermittently, at best. After 1800, however, the two parties, even in the most insignificant hamlets, sponsored separate celebrations which became ever more elaborate. They became all-day affairs with speeches, odes, dinners, toasts, parades, fireworks. . . ." As early as 1840, politics featured huge encampments, which were attended by thousands of people who had traveled by wagons for days to attend these affairs. According to an 1884 tome, *American Commonwealth,* Americans took to political campaigning as Europeans did to boat or horse races.

The point is that politicians have, throughout American history, adopted the techniques of entertainment to reach an audience, because that's where the audience was. Today, the audience is at home, in front of the television set. And that is where the politician wants to be. Candidates advertise on television for the same reason candidates used to—and still do—speak at barbecues, church picnics, political dinners, and school graduations: because that is where the people are (see chapter 9 for a discussion of advertising).

The same kinds of criticism that are now aimed at "media" candidacies used to be aimed at politicians who followed crowds in earlier days. During Stephen Douglas's 1860 campaign for President, an Illinois newspaper complained that "Douglas is going about peddling his opinions as a tin man peddles his wares . . . small business it is for a candidate for the Presidency to be strolling around the country begging for votes like a town constable." When Theodore Roosevelt, running for Vice President in 1896 on William McKinley's ticket, saw that Republican boss Mark Hanna was buying billboards, he complained that "Hanna was selling McKinley like a patent medicine." Jules Abel, an eye-opening chronicler of presidential history, judged in 1968 that support for primaries "has steadily evaporated . . . it is certainly undignified for a man who will be the Pres-

ident of the United States to be darting in and out of drug-
stores, supermarkets, and beauty shops clasping hands. . . ."

Critics, in other words, seem offended whenever politicians pursue the people whose votes they seek by whatever
method, apart from publishing position papers and holding
forth in auditoria where music is not played and food is not
served. So they will criticize you for attempting to reach
your voters through television. If it pleases you, you can
from time to time bemoan the "image makers" and the "me-
diacrats" and wistfully long for a return to a (mythical) past
where candidates could really discuss issues. As Joe Mc-
Ginniss noted in *The Selling of the President, 1968,* Richard
Nixon liked to assail the "damn image experts," and concluded that a candidate "should express distaste for television, suspicion that there is something 'phony' about it. This
guarantees him a good press, because newspaper reporters,
bitter over their loss of prestige to the television men, are
certain to stress anti-television remarks. Thus, the sophisticated candidate, while analyzing his own on-the-air technique as carefully as a golf pro studies his swing, will state
frequently that there is no place for 'public relations gimmicks' or 'those show-business guys' in the campaign."

My own preference, however, is to be completely unapol-
ogetic. We have now had television in our homes for over
thirty years; while those over fifty may still regard it as an
unfamiliar intrusion, most Americans regard it as something
like a member of the family—often with a lot more fondness
than the flesh-and-blood members. You are on television to
let the people know where you stand, because a candidate
who won't face the people and let them know his concerns
is a candidate who doesn't trust the people. If *Commentary*
or *The Nation* doesn't like it, that is too bad, and you will
have to take the consequences of alienating the 113 people
who devotedly follow the judgments of those magazines.

What, then, do you do to use television effectively? You
do not turn over your campaign to a television expert. Unless you are dealing with a rare breed who is fundamentally

a political animal who happens to be in television, you are likely to sign on with someone whose résumé boasts of spectacular success in gaining television exposure for the *Marina '77 Extravaganza,* or for the NowChow Organic Puppy Meal campaign. These people really do believe that politics is all marketing. They do not understand the difference between a toothpaste that politely sits in its box on the supermarket shelf, and a candidate who can by turns act courageously, cowardly, brilliantly, stupidly, and who is facing an opponent and an outside world, both of which can completely alter the nature of a campaign. These people are terrific at reading numbers and drawing the obvious conclusions, but they have no notion at all of how essentially political skills can alter those numbers by the force of logic or emotion. You can, with a clear conscience, follow their advice on the size of your lapels, the pattern of your tie, the timbre of your voice. Unless they are politicians first, and media experts incidentally, do not listen to them at all when they advise you of the content of your ideas.

There *are* specific devices that are important to remember when appearing on television, either in a news or interview setting. They are elementary, but as with many elementary principles, they are often forgotten:

Do Not Orate. Talk.   When radio was still young, President Franklin D. Roosevelt made a few radio talks that people still remember or study. These Fireside Chats were so-called because FDR understood that people do not listen to political talk on radio the way they do in huge halls. They are usually alone, or with two or three other people at most. They are at home, in their living rooms. They are in a state of repose. They are not like a crowd at a rally, which wants to be fed red meat. You are, in the great cliché of old-fashioned broadcasting, "coming into their homes," at their invitation. So he "chatted." Oddly, a lot of politicians never learned this lesson. They still speak into a microphone the way older people talk on the telephone when the call is long distance, by assuming that if the people you're talking to are far away, you have to talk loudly. Some politicians get away with this stentorian approach, most notably New York Senator Jacob Javits, arguably the most pompous figure in modern politics, who cannot say hello without bellowing about his firm hope and deep determination that the sun will keep shining. But if you are starting out, you should learn to respect the medium's intimacy. Television stations and networks spend a lot of money on sophisticated equipment. It will pick up your voice.

NEVER TURN DOWN AN INVITATION TO APPEAR ON TELEVISION, NO MATTER HOW UNIMPRESSIVE THE HOUR. Most television stations slot a few hours of interview shows on Sunday morning. If you so much as appear on the program of a political dinner, you will sooner or later be invited to appear on one of these programs. Do it. Do not be insulted by the fact that the program is on at nine thirty in the morning when most civilized people are either asleep or reading the Sunday papers. Just do it.

Why? Three reasons. The first is that it is good practice. You do not have to be at your best, and you can learn from your mistakes. Second, remember that television is a *mass* medium. If you live in Los Angeles, the station you are on has a potential reach of seven million television households. If one-half of 1 percent of those households are tuned into your program, you will be seen in 35,000 households. Ask yourself if you would turn down an invitation to speak to a local audience of 35,000 people. Third, local television stations usually have weekend news programs which will run pictures of almost anything that has moved in their community that weekend. An appearance on a local public-affairs show is almost certain to buy you a place on the local news, which will be seen by a few hundred thousand households. ("Appearing on Channel One's NewsDepth, civic leader Smithers declared today . . .")

Do Not Look at the Camera.   Political candidates are told to do the opposite by everyone from the high-priced media consultant to the cabdriver. It sounds logical; after all, a politician should be far more concerned with the home audience than with the interviewer in the studio. It is, however, very bad advice. In the first place, the camera operators know full well what shots the producers want. They will find you. If you talk straight ahead at the camera, averting your glance from the interviewer, you are asking for trouble. It is, for example, a lot easier to remember the question you have been asked if you are paying visual attention to the questioner. In addition, if you are asked a particularly compelling question—highly unlikely given the political acumen of the average local TV reporter, but one never knows—you will look like a fool if you suddenly swivel your head away from the camera to look at the interviewer for the first time. Third, you may find yourself in the hands of a malicious director, who will call up a wide shot of you and the interviewer. Nothing looks quite so ridiculous on television as the sudden shattering of the illusion of intimacy—as when the camera angle reveals an earnest politician staring straight ahead at a mechanical device, while ignoring the human beings ten feet away from him.

Television Treasures Brevity—but Make Sure the Answers You Give Can Only Be Used on Your Terms.   Network news broadcasts are thirty minutes, some twenty-two minutes of news once you discount the commercials and other announcements. Every one of those minutes is golden. Even when a network show carves out five minutes for a special report, there is no room for the leisurely examination of an idea. Local news programs, which run as long as two and a half hours, also treasure brevity, because they have in general paid a great deal of money to consultants who have carefully determined that what keeps an audience tuned in is a sense of urgency—rapidly edited news footage, preferably of fires, shots, or moving objects, with nothing lasting more than a minute and a half or so.

What this means is that your deeply-thought-out, carefully-substantiated arguments about policy issues will not find a place on television unless you pay for it yourself. Even then (see chapter 9), you are likely to be refused the opportunity to spend your own money on a lengthy expression of your views. If you understand this, you will be able to treat television for what it is: a shorthand method of getting your ideas across to the people. This *does not mean that you should abandon ideas as the centerpiece of your campaign,* any more than newspapers should abandon details because the stories they print will have headlines on top of them. What it means is that you must express your ideas in a form that will be usable on television. What it also means, given that broadcasters in effect control how ideas are heard on their government-licensed outlets, is that you must have no compunctions about manipulating this process to get every second you can out of it.

Jimmy Carter showed either a superb instinctive sense of this process or a shrewdly designed tactical approach to it. When Carter was asked a question, he would pause for a deep breath. This immediately made viewers at home, so used to the complete absence of quiet on television, prick up their ears. It also gave Carter the impression of being immersed in deep thought. When he finally offered his answer, it was delivered in a cadence that suggested Carter was running for the Presidency of Bob and Ray's "Slow Talkers of America." Most important, Carter would often pause in the middle of a sentence . . . and pause . . . and pause . . . But because there was no way to edit the sentence without losing the train of thought completely, the same answer that would have taken another politician fifteen seconds to deliver could take Carter forty-five seconds to a minute. This also ensured that there would be no time for follow-up questions; a single generalization, delivered in that meandering style of negative upon negative, was all that television had room for ("I would not favor a constitutional amendment on abortion unless I was unconvinced that no other method . . .")

I do not suggest that Carter's desperate attempt to avoid stating a flat substantive position should become your model of how to use television. (For one thing, as soon as Carter became President and actually had to make decisions, he found whole categories of voters who, having read their own hopes into his ambiguous remarks, felt themselves betrayed. Do not rely on cognitive dissonance to provide a loyal base of support.) What I do suggest you take to heart is how Carter structured his replies to gain maximum time on the air.

For example: You are asked why you believe you're better qualified for the job than your rivals. You reply: "Three reasons. First, I'm closer to the mood of the people than my rivals. . . ." An editor cannot take just that reply, because you already have told the interviewer that there are three reasons. Similarly, you are asked what the most important issue in the campaign is. You answer, "I don't disagree with those who believe that crime, or energy, or the outrageous levels of taxation are important issues. They are, but they are not the most critical dilemmas we face. . . ." You are again *requiring* the packagers of the news to take you on your own terms.

In case you are concerned about the prospect of a television news program not using any of your answers at all, do not be. Every news director in the history of broadcast journalism has been petrified by the prospect of being accused of inefficiency. When a news crew and a reporter are sent out, that footage has to be used in order to amortize costs and pay for the sportscaster's blazers. Once you find yourself in the presence of a local news crew, you are all but assured of getting on the air.

Television cannot resist a visual angle.   Some years ago, politicians began to realize a curious fact about television news. Coverage of a statement was always better if a politician *went* somewhere, if an issue could be directly tied to something at which a camera could be pointed. If you had a position paper on housing, you held your press conference outside an abandoned building. If you wanted to attack crime, you visited a dangerous neighborhood (in the daytime, of course) and appeared in the role of Kojak on his day off. For years I waited for this ludicrous trend to abate. Instead, it has intensified.

Today, politicians find themselves in the role of investigative reporters on television. Local news programs have a taste for "exposés," but they mean by this something quite alien to the honorable tradition of exposing wrongdoing by poring over records and documents, unearthing complex conspiracies. The average TV investigative reporter prefers to find a case of horrible wrongdoing on a news wire or police report. The reporter, with a crew, then rushes to the scene of this horrible event, and is photographed by the news crew racing into some building. (No one asks, by the way, how the reporter, so anxious to find the blackguard responsible for this outrage, managed to run slowly enough to get photographed by the camera crew.) The reporter then pounds on doors and thrusts into offices, confronting some civil servant or private underling who, finding himself blinded by lights, demands that the reporter leave the premises, or else flees with the avenging reporter and camera crew in full pursuit. (This footage always makes the news broadcast, because it is visually exciting and is the closest thing to a car chase that can get on the evening news. It also makes the reporter look good, since flight implies guilt.)

This taste for the hunt offers you a tempting if repellent opportunity to put yourself into the local limelight. All you need do is wait for an official or semiofficial report on some kind of official or semiofficial wrongdoing. (This is as easy to find in our time as a disaffected taxpayer.) It may be a controller's report alleging waste in the schools, or a citizen's group alleging inadequate garbage collection, or a legislative staff investigation on water pollution. Armed with this report, you advise the press of a press conference, to be held at the site of the wrong. This gives your indignation a visible focal point.

"Behind those walls, the bureaucrats shuffle their paper while people suffer," you say, assuming you hold your press conference outside City Hall. If you actually want to visit the site of the injustice—an uncomfortable prospect, since this is usually far from midtown in a neighborhood with many poor people and abandoned automobiles—you say, "Behind these walls, people suffer while the bureaucrats downtown shuffle their paper." If one of these bureaucrats or administrators happens to show up, you can engage him in a heated debate as the cameras roll. There is no way for this adversary to win, no matter how reasonable, because (a) he will have no idea what is happening until it is too late, (b) you are armed with official—or semiofficial—proof, (c) the reporters will be thrusting microphones into your adversary's face, demanding an answer. If you are really lucky, your adversary will demand the cameras be shut off, or threaten to call the police, whereupon you talk about the public's right to know. This approach will work as long as ratings-obsessed news directors and producers sacrifice any sense of responsible journalism in a cynical attempt to put hopped-up, manufactured news events on the air.

In other words, you can't miss.

The link between the television hunger for the visual and your own specific political goals is not, in any sense, confined to the early stages of a political campaign. In fact, the higher you stand on the political ladder, the more you can use television to serve your interests. When a presidential primary campaign reaches its climax, an army of reporters, cameramen, sound technicians, columnists, and engineers jams into press planes and buses to follow a candidate's movements. They are there to take pictures of that candidate —to record what he does—to match the story of the campaign against pictures. No matter how devotedly the broadcast news determines to cover issues this year, that candidate's movements will help shape the story.

Jimmy Carter's primary campaign scored its last, perhaps its most important triumph, by understanding this rule. By June 8, 1976, the upstart candidacy of California Governor Jerry Brown had begun to sting Carter's drive toward the nomination. Along with Senator Frank Church, Brown— both because of his own appeal and because he represented the hopes of Hubert Humphrey supporters for a brokered convention—had stopped Carter in Maryland, Rhode Island, Nevada, and Oregon. Now it was Super Tuesday, when three big state primaries would be held on the same day: New Jersey, Ohio, and California, representing a total of more than 23 percent of Democratic convention votes, 540 delegates. With Governor Jerry Brown a clear favorite in California, Carter originally placed substantial hopes for a good showing in New Jersey, until it became clear that an uncommitted slate, divided between supporters of Brown and Hubert Humphrey, was going to defeat Carter soundly.

In effect, Carter conceded these states, and spent almost all of his time campaigning in Ohio, against the fading candidacy of Congressman Morris Udall. Objectively speaking, Carter was acknowledging that in two critical states, New Jersey and California, he had so little support that campaigning would be futile. But by campaigning all over Ohio, Carter was, in effect, forcing the television cameras to make Ohio the major state of the three. They could not show a picture of Carter collapsing in California, because he wasn't there. They couldn't show Carter being greeted by massive indifference in New Jersey, because he wasn't there. Instead, Ohio became the important primary because Carter threw down the gauntlet there, and because Chicago Mayor Richard Daley decreed that *he* would make Ohio the test.

What happened? Carter was resoundingly defeated in New Jersey and California, but won Ohio with 52 percent of the vote. As Jerry Brown prepared to go on television to claim victory, he was told by correspondent Richard Wagner that

Eric Sevareid was already saying that Carter could not be stopped.

"Jesus, he lost two out of three tonight!" Brown exclaimed. But Daley, Wallace, Church, and Udall were all conceding to Carter, and the demonstration of Carter's electoral weakness—a weakness demonstrated by his November losses in both New Jersey and Calfornia—went all but ignored. The only way that television could have accurately reported the primary story would have been by technique; by showing the absence of Carter activity in New Jersey and California, and by *instructing* the audience as to the implications of Carter's absence. That is simply too much like "editorializing" for television news. Most correspondents know full well that when former NBC reporter Catherine Mackin went on the network news in 1972 to contrast McGovern's positions with the description of those positions by the Nixon campaign, she was severely criticized for "biased" reporting. No TV reporter will stand in a hall and say, "Jimmy Carter was not here in New Jersey because he knows he's going to lose." That is the great advantage you have in bending the visual hunger of television to your own ends.

There is, of course, another way to use this hunger. You could use the magnetism of a campaign to drag television to those parts of our national life which generally do not make the evening newscasts. You need not share my affection for Robert Kennedy to recognize the impact of his travels during his Senate years on our political landscape. Indeed, you are entitled to believe that his journeys into Appalachia, into the ghettos of New York and Chicago, into the migrant work camps of Delano, California, were nothing more than efforts to win political support for himself. The point is that as a national figure, as a political celebrity, Robert Kennedy's travels made news. Since he was treated as a potential President from the moment his brother was elected in 1960, television followed him wherever he went. And in addition to attending Democratic Party dinners, Kennedy went everywhere from Indian reservations to Bedford-Stuyvesant in Brooklyn, knowing that television would follow him.

If you really want to make your campaign one of substance, you can force television to help you by your choice of where you go. Once you have achieved sufficient political stature, you no longer have to stand outside empty public buildings on a weekend haranguing absent civil servants. TV is your hostage. If your campaign really means to talk about those Americans left behind, you can intensify your travels through poor neighborhoods and communities. The cameras will be there. You can visit working-class areas where chemical plant employees have been made ill by conditions in the workplace. The TV cameras will be there. And if you choose not to wage such a campaign, you can, of course, blame the media for "not concentrating on the issues." No one will realize that their agenda is your agenda, and that their failure is really yours. Speeches on the malevolent influence of TV on politics make first-rate reading, and will win you a small but devoted following. It is a lot easier to attack television than it is to use the power you have to force television to cover what you claim is at the center of your campaign.

CHAPTER IX

HOW TO ADVERTISE

If political television has come under a cloud, then political advertising on television has been in the midst of a thunderstorm ever since 1952, when the Madison Avenue agency of Batten Barton Durstine & Osborn (BBDO) designed the first nationally televised short political commercials for the Eisenhower-Nixon campaign. In sixty-second segments, these advertisements featured a Westbrook Van Voorhis the-world-is-ending voice presenting *"The Man from Abilene!"* and exclaiming, "Eisenhower Answers the Nation!" as an "ordinary" citizen posed "questions" about taxes and defense, while Ike offered one- and two-sentence answers. Other ads presented animated cartoon figures singing jingles, all while Adlai Stevenson was on television giving long speeches in huge halls.

Critics were horrified by this technique. Writer Marya Mannes summed up the prevailing attitude when she wrote:

172

Hail to B.B.D. & O.
It told the nation how to go;
It managed by advertisement
To sell us a new President.

. . . .

Philip Morris, Lucky Strike,
Alka-Seltzer, I Like Ike.

Today, the television advertisement has come to be a dominant part of any major political campaign, and it is still scorned as the central symbol of a political climate in which candidates are sold like soap. In the 1976 campaign, the first conducted under the public financing law which allocated roughly $25 million to the two major-party nominees, the huge amounts spent by Jimmy Carter and Gerald Ford on paid television were held largely responsible for the absence of grass-roots activity, for the sense in the "real world" that there was no presidential campaign happening at all. TV advertising is, we are told, a tool for demagogues, and for empty-headed candidates who are selling their smooth personalities.

Nothing anyone says will deter the use of advertising in major political campaigns; yield to this view of politics and nobly abandon television advertising and you will be able to afford a lot of money to hire the world's most prestigious writer to draft your concession speech. And there is no defense at all to the charge that advertising puts a special premium on money, that those who can afford to buy huge chunks of television and radio time have a huge advantage over less affluent candidates. (If you do not understand this in the deepest recesses of your soul, you are almost surely not ready for a political career.) What you should realize, if only to set your mind at ease, is that much of the objection to political advertising is wildly off base, that, in many senses, advertising is a more democratic, more reasonable—and can even be a more substantive—method of informing the public than traditional methods such as speeches, position papers, and direct contact with the people.

Look at some of the principal objections to political advertising, and see how legitimate these objections are, especially when matched against the political tools of earlier years.

Advertising is all packaged—we get no chance to find out how the candidate really feels. It is true that many politicians feel intimidated by the media experts they hire. They are well paid to know how television works, so why not listen to the professionals? I've already suggested that trusting any outside technician on a question of substance is a serious mistake, and this applies to advertising experts as much, not more, as to anyone. But the fact is that politicians have been packaged since the dawn of politics. The only difference is that the techniques of packaging have grown more sophisticated. From Alexander Hamilton's ghostwriting of Washington's Farewell Address to Carter adman Gerald Rafshoon's appointment to a $56,000-a-year White House staff job, the behind-the-scenes manipulator has played an important, often honorable role in our political life. Andrew Jackson had newspaper editor Amos Kendall stashed away as fourth auditor of the Treasury, from which position he served as Jackson's ghostwriter-confidant. Charles Michaelson was an important, mostly anonymous wordsmith for the Democratic Party in the late 1920s and early 1930s, and Robert Humphreys served in the same role for the Republicans. And no adman's advice could be more manipulative than that given to Warren Harding by Boies Penrose, who ran Pennsylvania's Republican Party for more than a quarter of a century. Insisting that Harding do no real campaigning, Penrose warned: "If he goes across the country, someone might ask him a question and he might try to answer it."

Moreover, the idea that advertising must be a packaged view of a candidate's campaign tells us a lot more about the passivity of a candidate than it does about the technique of advertising. *Advertising is nothing more than the purchase of time for the presentation of a message.* Its truth or falsehood, its content, is a matter of choice. Gerald Ford chose, toward the end of his 1976 campaign, to be introduced by broadcaster Joe Garagiola, because Garagiola had the "regular guy" quality that would keep an audience's attention on a paid political commercial. Jimmy Carter chose in his campaign to trade in his jeans for a business suit because the voters were indicating skepticism about his capacity to govern. Ronald Reagan, the much-attacked "media candidate," chose in 1976 to give a thirty-minute address on foreign policy, because he had come to the conclusion that Republican conservatives could be wooed on that basis, and because he had confidence in his rhetorical ability to reach these voters with a detailed speech on his view of foreign policy (it is interesting that none of the "nonmedia" candidates, not Udall, not Carter, not Ford, not Bayh, none of them had enough confidence in the voter to adopt this form of address).

You can't say anything of substance in thirty or sixty seconds. Certainly a speech or a position paper offers you far more range to explain your view on a complicated subject than does a short political ad. Indeed, in the early days of television, it was traditional to buy fifteen- and thirty-minute chunks of time, and to substitute political speeches for whole programs. More than that: it was the deliberate strategy of BBDO—when they were not employing short spot ads—to substitute lengthy political broadcasts for the most popular television fare of 1952. They bought out the time slots for Arthur Godfrey, Sid Caesar, and other highly rated shows on the "theory that it was necessary to reduce competition to a minimum by pre-empting the most popular shows, and at the same time attempt to capture at least part of the audience."

But preemption proved to be a disastrous strategy. When Adlai Stevenson bought time in 1952 to replace the last few

minutes of a *Name That Tune* show, on which two contes-
tants were being married, the campaign was flooded by angry
complaints, and Stevenson felt compelled to issue a statement apologizing for the preemption. In 1970, when Senator
Charles Goodell's campaign against James Buckley and
Richard Ottinger was in desperate trouble, he bought a half
hour on Sunday night before the election to explain why he
was not withdrawing to aid fellow liberal Richard Ottinger
—and began by forcefully apologizing to the television audience for replacing *Lassie*.

More than anger, the longer political broadcasts induced
indifference—massive, overwhelming indifference. It is as
axiomatic a rule as exists in politics that the lowest-ranked
television show of any given rating period will be the paid
political broadcast. This does not mean there are not cases
when the half-hour broadcast is valuable, to rally the troops,
as Reagan did, or to raise money through direct appeals, as
George McGovern and George Wallace did. But it is not an
effective way to reach the mass of voters. The politician who
would have journeyed to an encampment or picnic one
hundred years ago, or who would have toured the county
fairs fifty years ago, or who would have paid to broadcast
speeches on a radio network forty years ago, now buys time
in the middle of highly rated programs because that is where
the voter is. It costs more, by the way, to buy thirty seconds
of time on a hit network show than it does to buy thirty
minutes of time to present a political broadcast, because the
audience for the lengthy speech will be so much smaller than
for a commercial.

There is another reason why the political spot is so short.
In many if not most local markets, television stations will
not sell the longer time periods. Local stations with big audiences generally carry network television shows, which are
organized in half-hour time periods. If you want ten minutes
of time to present a carefully-laid-out argument, you cannot
buy that time on network-affiliated stations, because they
would then be forced to preempt the last few minutes of a
program, which would force them to hire security guards to

beat back the angry mobs demanding to know whether Laverne managed to drag Shirley out of the vat of beer. To be
sure, they will be glad to sell you the time at two thirty in the
morning, where you can present your political case in between commercials for tractor-trailer-truck schools and hit
records of the 1950s. But in part, you will be forced to use
the spot format because it is, by far, the easiest format to get
on the air.

But what of the essential charge? Is it really true that you
can say nothing in thirty seconds? Suppose it is 1968, and
you are running for the Senate on an antiwar platform. Here
is the text of a statement:

> I regard the war in Vietnam as the worst foreign-policy
> venture in American history. It has divided our people, it
> has bled us of our treasure, it has been waged on behalf
> of a regime that is neither just nor honest nor willing to
> defend itself. My first act as Senator will be to support
> legislation ending funds for this war—so that America
> can begin the task of healing the wounds of this disaster.

That statement can fit easily in a thirty-second commercial. And while you may disagree with its sentiment, you can
see that it offers an easily understandable, clear statement of
where the speaker stands on an issue. True, it does not include an analysis of the Geneva Accords of 1954, nor a military criticism of the search-and-destroy missions. But as a
summary, as the political equivalent of a headnote that pre-
cedes a long court decision, it informs the listener of what
the speaker believes. If a politician chooses to waffle on an
issue such as the war in Vietnam, it is not because thirty
seconds is too short a time, but because the politician
chooses not to say anything. And that same speaker would
probably choose to say nothing in a thirty-minute speech on
the war. The only difference is that there is a far greater
opportunity to shade every side of the issue in thirty minutes
than there is in thirty seconds.

Even shorter kinds of messages, loaded with visual propaganda, cannot automatically be dismissed as contentless. When conservative Democrat Mario Procaccino was running for Mayor of New York in 1969, in the midst of national student disruptions, his most frequently run advertisement was a ten-second spot featuring news footage of a campus aflame. The announcer intoned: "Violence and lawlessness *must* be stopped. Discriminating quotas *cannot* be tolerated." It did not take a lengthy address to realize that Procaccino was promising a hard line against student demonstrators, and was also promising to oppose educational policies that gave compensatory assistance to black and other minority students.

If the case against short messages is that they cannot grapple with the full complexity of an issue, then it is a meaningless argument, on the order of the splendid Pall Mall cigarette advertisement which declared: "Compare Pall Mall with any short cigarette; Pall Mall is longer." You cannot discuss the SALT II treaty in a brief statement, because issues such as verification, throw weight, and MIRV capabilities require far more time. But if the case rests on the inherent inability to be clear, coherent, and conclusive in a short message, then the argument is wrong. You can express opposition to SALT II, or support for it, in a brief summary, just the way you can show photographs of deserted city streets and argue that the real cost of crime is the fear it instills in ordinary citizens. You can point to a brief set of numbers, say, the price of gasoline in Western Europe and the lack of shortages, to argue that the marketplace is the way to set the price of fuel; or you can point to oil profits, and the fact that recent shortages are clouded over with suspicion, to demand more accountability on the part of the oil companies.

You can, in other words, do in an ad what you can do in any other form of political communication. It is your choice, *not* the form, that determines how honest, fraudulent, direct, or evasive, your message is.

Advertising is inherently manipulative and deceptive. The television advertisement is indeed an advertiser's dream, because it is the first time in history that every appeal—save those of smell and touch—can be packed into a single message. Light can glimmer off trees, music can suggest fun, romance, intrigue, danger, satisfaction; sound enables us to hear the perk of coffee, the satisfying slam of a car door, the splash of cool water in a shower. In political terms, it is possible—literally—to wrap candidates around an American flag, while patriotic music swells about them; they can be photographed striding purposefully up the steps of the Capitol, even though they have no more idea of what is inside the building than a child does; they can be surrounded by the *sense* of an issue rather than offering any ideas about it.

Not only is all this possible, it has been done. Some years ago, I wrote a satirical story about political advertising in which the world's dumbest candidate was shown listening to tough questions from voters. He never answered them; instead, the announcer simply said, "Buddy Baum *listens* to people." In the fall of 1978, Mike Curb was elected Lieutenant Governor of California. One of his most prominent ads showed young Curb chatting with hardhats, students, and housewives, as the announcer told us that "Mike Curb has talked with the people of California. . . ." We were never told whether he said "Have a nice day," or, "What's your sign?" or offered a six-point plan on air pollution.

The problem with this charge, of course, is that all political speech is manipulative, if we mean by that the idea that political speech is designed to elect support from the listeners, and that different kinds of rhetoric elect different kinds of support. It was well before the Age of Television that Adolf Hitler's Nuremberg rallies drew on skillfully manipulated images—torchlight parades, massed ranks of uniformed soldiers and youth, the dramatic entrance of Der Führer into the arena flanked by motorcycle escorts—to build a powerful emotional fervor.

Our homegrown politicians were skilled in the manipulative arts long before the Age of Television. In the 1920s,
when the Ku Klux Klan was resurgent in the South and
Midwest with attacks on blacks, Jews, and Catholics, Boston's famous James Michael Curley used to campaign at out-
door rallies, which were interrupted with remarkable
frequency by the sight of a flaming cross on a distant hill.
Curley would break off his speech, point to the burning
cross, and "spontaneously" declare: "There it burns! The
cross of hate, and not the cross of love. . . . The cross of
horror, avarice, and hate and not the cross of Christian charity."

Chicago's Mayor William "Big Bill" Thompson would
campaign by marching into halls surrounded by a flag-carry-
ing honor guard, leading the crowd in the singing of his campaign song, "America First." In his later campaigns,
Thompson would draw crowds to his rallies by staging circus
parades, a device very similar to the tactic of buying advertising time in the middle of highly rated television shows,
using them to "draw the crowds."

It is, in fact, probably true that television advertising is
less deceptive than older forms of political persuasion. No
one would dare to present a TV commercial featuring Al
Smith at the dedication of the Holland Tunnel, and claim
that this was the underground link between the United States
and the Vatican. No one would splice footage of a rival to
make it appear as if he were standing next to a prominent
American Communist, as was done in the 1950 Maryland
campaign which saw Senator Millard Tydings unseated. No
one would show a commercial featuring a look-alike of his
rival, seated in a touring car next to two cigar-smoking
blacks, as was done to an opponent of Georgia's Eugene
Talmadge in 1946.

Television commercials may have their own problems,
but they are less susceptible to this kind of crude distortion
than their political predecessors, in part because broadcasters must first screen them. And even if the Federal Com-

munications Act and its interpretation by the Federal Communications Commission permits almost any political commercial to air—at least if it includes the candidate's words or image—there is still a check on the more extreme forms of distortion that leaflets, brochures, and mailings do not contain.

There is another sharp constraint on television advertising's deceptiveness: it is seen by everyone. It has not been unknown, in days gone by, for campaigns to paint one picture of themselves in one region, or among one group, and quite another in a different part of the state or country. When Barry Goldwater ran for President in 1964, his campaign in the South stressed his opposition to the 1964 Civil Rights Act—so much so that the only states Goldwater carried outside of his home state of Arizona were five Deep South states. In the North, however, and among those few black Republicans who still harkened back to Civil War politics, Goldwater distributed leaflets with pictures of himself with important black figures; whereupon the Johnson campaign picked up as many of those leaflets as it could find, and made sure they were circulated in the South. The whole national convention system evolved as a method of mediating the inevitable, sharp splits among different regions of the country, in which political parties very much went their own way. The 1924 Democratic convention, which took 103 ballots to nominate John W. Davis, was irretrievably split between big-city, heavily Catholic, anti-Prohibitionists, and Midwest and Southern anti-Catholic, pro-Klan Prohibitionists. The 1948 Democratic convention reflected a similar fission over civil rights, and the Republican Party in 1964 broke apart over the issue of extremism.

In the past, candidates for high office preferred to paper over differences as much as possible, appealing to different sections and interests by echoing their own concerns.

Now, however, we have a political process which, thanks in good measure to television and to instant national communications, has greatly homogenized our political process.

Not only do different parts of the nation receive their information through more or less the same sources, but the words a politician speaks in Maine are heard in California and Hawaii as well.

There is, therefore, no practical way a candidate for office can speak with different voices, or even shadings, to please different regions, or different interests. The corporate executive and the steelworker both watch Walter Cronkite; the professor and the bricklayer both watch *Laverne and Shirley*. Whatever else a political commercial is, it is at least consistent. You are speaking to the entire electorate at once in a commercial. Of course you can emphasize different parts of your record or your program to different television watchers; it does not take a media consultant to realize that the audience for *Lawrence Welk* is not the audience for *The Incredible Hulk*. But what you cannot do is to conceal your agenda from disparate elements of the electorate. For purposes of honesty, or the appearance of honesty, you must assume that your ads will be seen by everybody. That assumption imposes a heavy burden of relative honesty on a campaign.

Finally, television is too polite a medium to permit the kind of outrageous charges that used to characterize our politics. It is one thing to stand in a mob and listen to a red-faced orator declare that the election of his opponent would turn the nation into a cesspool of moral decay. The frenzy of the moment excuses it. It is equally "acceptable" to read, as a journal said of Henry Clay, that "he spends his days at the gaming table and his nights in a brothel." Print is, after all, cold, and often anonymous.

But television brings a visible presence into our homes. And we expect our guests to behave in our homes. A sharp, negative attack on a candidate for office is much more treacherous on television than on any other medium. It can be done, of course (see below), but it requires a subtle, less egregious break with reality than was permitted in other times.

Advertising gives too big an advantage to candidates with money. This is, in large measure, true. With a single thirty-second spot on a local television station in New York costing upward of $8000, it is impossible to mount an effective campaign in a state such as New York unless you can spend $2 million on advertising (that applies in Illinois and California as well). And with the remarkably thickheaded "reforms" enacted by Congress in the wake of Watergate (see chapter 3), we have all but guaranteed that independent wealth will become even more important a political asset than it has been. This has meant, among other things, that wealthy individuals begin a campaign with a huge advantage over their less affluent foes, for at the very least they can afford the advertising campaign which will establish their "recognition." Sooner or later, we will have to come to grips with this blatant injustice.

But this is not the whole story. In the first place, there is plenty of evidence that wealth alone cannot buy political success. A millionaire builder in New York named Abraham Hirschfeld spent millions of dollars in 1974 and in 1977, running first for Senator and then for City Council President. Apart from his considerable ego, there was no compelling reason to believe he was exceptionally suited for these jobs. And despite his massive spending, he finished well out of the running. In California in 1974, a shipbuilder named William Matson Roth decided to run for Governor. He was impressive, articulate, intelligent, and fully prepared to spend several hundred thousand dollars of his own money. But he had no political base, no special credibility as a candidate, and finished with 11 percent of the Democratic primary vote.

Conversely, Ed Koch in 1977 was outspent on television by three other candidates for Mayor of New York, but managed to finish first in the primary, first in the runoff, and win the November election.

Moreover, there is one sense in which the free flow of advertising dollars can be seen as a kind of redress of a different kind of political injustice, the injustice which gives enormous advantages to political incumbents. As we shall see, incumbency produces a wide array of advantages. According to a 1975 Americans for Democratic Action study, an incumbent Congressman starts a reelection campaign with an advantage of almost half a million dollars, counting free mailings, trips back home, and support for district offices and staff whose work inevitably produces politically helpful fallout. For Presidents and Governors, the advantage lies in the weight of the office: favors granted, public funds spent, and the presence in office which, barring catastrophic performance, suggests by itself that the occupant is qualified for the job. In addition, the power of the office makes it a lot easier to raise funds for future campaigns, since builders, bankers, lawyers, and purveyors find the incumbent's power over the public purse an impressive demonstration of his or her worthiness.

Who can stand up to this built-in advantage? A candidate with enough money to advertise heavily. The difference between reelection ratios in the House of Representatives (96 percent since 1974) and the Senate (67 percent) can be explained in part by the fact that statewide campaigns make a major television campaign more practical than district campaigns, in which an opponent may have to broadcast to millions of voters in order to reach the few hundred thousand eligible to vote for him. Money establishes recognition quickly; money can enable the public to learn about a record that has been compiled outside the limelight of national or state capitals. Money can bring a candidate to the attention of the public outside the older transmission belts of political clubhouses; and while there is a great deal of nostalgia today for the community-based, grass-roots clubhouse system of politics, it was a system which can scarcely be said to have permitted any open competition among candidates.

While there is no question that wealth is a powerful advantage in the battle to be heard, it is also true that advertising is, at least theoretically, a potentially democratic political weapon. Assume a mass movement, or a broad protest, against a basic government policy. A few dollars from each of several hundred thousand Americans will enable a candidate espousing this dissent to mount an effective television campaign, and therefore to have a reasonable chance of winning. (This is the key to the so-called "single-issue" politics of the late 1970s in which abortion opponents, or gun-control foes, are able to help finance campaigns against their political opponents. While this form of activism has dismayed some observers, who have warned of threats to political stability, it can be seen as another method of increasing political participation. It is also at least reasonable to suppose that the criticism of "single-issue" politics is based in part on the unappetizing nature of the causes taking advantage of it.)

Unlike the lamented clubhouse politics, TV-based campaigning cannot be ruled off the screen by a hack judge, taking instructions from a ward heeler, who invalidates petitions of an independent candidate, keeping him off the ballot. TV-based campaigning cannot be drowned out by hecklers, or ignored by a politically committed newspaper editor such as the *Chicago Tribune*'s Robert McCormick or the *Manchester Union-Leader*'s William Loeb. It is a way for a political figure, however unpopular, to reach voters directly. And like it or not, that *is* one decent working definition of a healthy democracy.

Now that you are ready to approach an advertising campaign without shame or guilt, the question is what kind of advertising works best. The most general proposition you should remember is the same proposition that makes sense in speechmaking: *do not alter reality beyond credibility.* Your advertising will work best if it is rooted in facts.

I am not here talking about the kind of advertising that likes to call itself *cinéma vérité,* where a camera crew follows a candidate around for six days and edits thirty-second bites, or a half-hour documentary, out of forty hours of film. Since the ad's creators are likely to be looking for the can-

didate's best moments, as opposed to the most representative ones, and since there is nothing to prevent the creator
from matching answer B with question A, there is not all that
much *vérité* in the cinema. I am talking, instead, about a
kind of advertising that is linked to the reality of the world
and the candidate.

Let me illustrate with a case that may seem difficult for
many of you to accept: the advertising of Richard Nixon in
the 1972 campaign against McGovern. As one who was
raised by parents who threatened to send Mr. Nixon into my
room if I misbehaved, and as one who saw no reason ever to
change that assessment of Mr. Nixon throughout his public
career, I believe that there is no fond affection for the former
President which affects my judgment that the advertising in
that campaign was nothing short of brilliant. It was rooted in
two concepts which were substantially accurate: first, that
President Nixon had embarked on a series of bold foreign
policy initiatives; second, that some of George McGovern's
views were anathema to most Americans.

Instead of warm pictures of Mr. Nixon playing with puppy
dogs, the commercials showed Nixon on his visit to China,
on his visit to the Soviet Union, in Air Force One working
on those visits. Implicit in these ads was the message, *Okay,
you don't like the son of a bitch, but maybe he's so secretive
because he's planning bold moves.* As Nixon's ad director
said after the campaign, "We felt that deep down the voters
were willing to accept a President who was less than frank
with them . . . that a man as President sometimes had to do
things, in relation to his international stance . . . about
which he couldn't always be candid. . . ." In effect, we were
told that Nixon's secretive nature was the price we had to
pay for his diplomatic breakthroughs.

Second, the anti-McGovern ads were models of negative
advertising. They were done very quietly, with an announcer
who barely spoke above a whisper. They were signed by
Democrats for Nixon, because the Nixon campaign discovered that signature made the ads "far more effective" than

when the same commercials were presented by the Committee to Re-Elect the President. Why? Because, in Nixon advertising chief Peter Dailey's words, "the fact that people like John Connally, who were highly credible Democrats, were [defecting] served to reinforce their decision" to bolt the party. And what did they say? One of them showed a hardhat, perched atop a skyscraper skeleton, eating his lunch. As the camera moved steadily closer, the announcer reported that McGovern had introduced a bill in Congress which would have made every other American eligible for welfare (McGovern later was to claim he introduced this bill as a favor to welfare-rights groups, but did not really support it). And, the ad asked as the camera moved in tight on the hardhat, who would pay for this bill? "You will."

Another ad listed McGovern's changes of mind on various issues, as a photograph of McGovern flipped from left to right, like a weather vane. At the end of this litany of what McGovern said "last year" and "this year," the announcer concluded, "last year—this year—the question is, what about next year?"

These ads worked because they were based on fact. They may have been shaped to state the case more harshly than an objective journalist would have, but they were not lies, they were not smears. They were tough but more-or-less accurate statements of an opponent's position.

This is how political advertising works best: not as the fantasy of a marketing expert, not as the "creative" daydreaming of some image maven, but as an extension of the best possible case for your campaign. In this sense, your political advertising can best be compared to the work of a trial lawyer; your advertising is to make the strongest possible case for your election, based on the facts of your background and the political climate. The test is to create the kind of advertising where the reflection of reality also advances the case for your own election.

Some examples here may help. While many of them are drawn from my own experiences working with David Garth,

I mean them as examples, not as evidence of our superior work; and I will draw on cases where our opposition's advertising worked better than ours. What I hope to show is the manner in which strategic and tactical decisions were reflected in the advertising, and how that advertising was based on facts, rather than on vague notions about images.

One of the most intriguing campaigns was Tom Bradley's 1973 campaign for Mayor of Los Angeles. I've noted earlier that our principal concern was the underlying fear of white Los Angeles voters that Bradley was somehow distant from the concerns of the white middle and lower middle class; that, whatever his record he was bound by race to be sympathetic to lawbreakers, Black Panthers, and welfare recipients (and let me say again that the recognition of bigotry is not itself a sign of bigotry). Apart from the slogan ("he'll work as hard for his paycheck as you do for yours") we had to demonstrate that Bradley would understand the needs of people outside of his councilmanic district. That is a polite way of saying we had to prove he would care about white people.

The ads that went on the air stressed people who were not Bradley's constituents, people who talked about the support he had given them "even though Tom Bradley wasn't representing my district." An upper-middle-class woman from Pacific Palisades—in terms of California politics roughly six thousand miles from Watts and East Los Angeles—talked about Bradley's help in fighting beach pollution. A group of homeowners praised Bradley for saving a scenic area in their neighborhood threatened for destruction by an insensitive city agency. A former officer in the police precinct where Bradley had worked years before, who looked as if he had been sent by central casting to an ABC police series, said that Bradley had been "a tough cop, but a fair one." And a middle-aged black remembered Bradley working to turn gang members away from a life of crime. "A lot of us might not have made it if it hadn't of been for Tom Bradley," he said.

Now it should be obvious that these ads were "manipulative," in the sense that they were designed to move the viewer to a series of conclusions: that Tom Bradley could respond to middle-class needs, that his police background made him an ally of the citizen against the lawbreaker, that he would not be Mayor of Watts. But the ads worked because they were based on *reality*. Tom Bradley did not discover the police "image" in a poll. He'd been a police officer for more than twenty years. And David Garth did not rent actors to portray citizens from different Los Angeles neighborhoods. These were people who felt a debt to Tom Bradley. The advertising drew on the performance of the candidate, and presented that performance in the most favorable light.

It's important to understand that you cannot take this example and draw general advertising lessons from it. A similar use of real people talking about the candidate worked for Hugh Carey in 1974, because as a seven-term Congressman, Carey had compiled a first-rate record of service. But in 1976, when Senator John Tunney was running for reelection, his best achievements were in the legislative arena. He'd been very effective in the Senate, but his constituent service record was mediocre. We tried to develop advertising based on people talking about Tunney's service, but the ads did not work, because they were not credible. In that same campaign, S. I. Hayakawa's advertising emphasized Tunney's absence from the Senate, by showing pictures of an empty Senate desk. Tunney's attendance record was indeed a vulnerable part of his record, and the campaign "bit." Two years earlier, when New York Republican Malcolm Wilson tried the same tactic against Hugh Carey—with almost the identical images in the ads—the tactic fizzled, because Carey's record had been so clearly laid out.

Two campaigns from 1970 may also help convince you of the central place reality has to play in advertising. That year the issue of disruption was a major campaign factor: campuses were hit by turmoil, racial tension was high, Spiro

Agnew was coming down hard on dissent in general and weak-kneed liberals in particular, and the so-called "social issues" were concerning liberal Democrats. The fear was that traditional working-class "bread-and-butter" New Deal voters, horrified by militant blacks and long-haired hippies and a general breakdown of mores, would flock to more conservative candidates who reflected traditional values. In New York, Democrat Richard Ottinger had won the primary by using an expensive media campaign stressing his Congressional service. His principal opponent was Jim Buckley, running on the Conservative Party line. Buckley rode heavily on the law-and-order theme with his "isn't it about time *we* had a Senator" slogan, and by delivering some commercials wearing a trench coat, which made him look like a detective in a television series.

Was there any way to combat this appeal to the social issues? Ottinger was indeed a liberal, who was against the war in Vietnam and who did not believe in repressive measures to stop dissent. To have put him in a police car and filmed him talking tough about crime would have been senseless. All we could do was to make the case for his record as persuasive as possible. It did not work; Buckley won a narrow victory.

That same year, John Gilligan was running for Governor of Ohio. He had a similar kind of problem; he was a liberal, with a conversational speaking style that was casual, witty, almost flirtatious. It was not, in any sense, a macho impression. His record and his presence could have exposed him to attack on the issue of strength: Is Gilligan tough enough to be Governor? But John Gilligan also happened to be a war hero. We found a shipmate of Gilligan's who had been on a ship that had come under attack in World War II. In halting tones, he described how "ole John Gilligan" had performed heroically during that assault, how he'd been decorated, and how it probably would be a good thing to have that kind of toughness in the state house. That ad is by no means the principal reason Gilligan was elected in a landslide, but it did

serve to blunt any attack on his bravery. The reason it
worked was because it was a reflection of what had really
happened, an argument from a characteristic actually displayed by the candidate, not manufactured for him.

Sometimes you will even find that a heavy reliance on
reality can bear unexpected political bonuses. In the 1974
Carey campaign, one of the commercials we shot was at a
new school for the deaf in upstate New York, whose existence was due in large measure to a long Congressional fight
Carey had finally won. We wanted a teacher to talk about
the importance of the school, and Carey suggested someone
who was himself deaf. When we shot the commercial, the
teacher not only spoke words of praise for Carey, but
"signed" his remarks. We had no idea this was going to
happen, but it was how this teacher spoke, and we were not
about to interfere.

Shortly after the commercial went on the air, I got a telephone call from a reporter, who began by saying something
about what "smart sons of bitches" we were. Without dis-
puting the general observation, I asked what he meant.

"That commercial with the deaf guy," the reporter said.
"When did you figure out there were three hundred thousand
deaf people in New York State?" Suddenly I understood;
we had, completely by accident, shot the first political commercial that this neglected constituency could understand!

This, then, is the most important precept to use in planning
an advertising campaign: *do not offend reality.* It is foolish
because people will be seeing you on the news as well as in
commercials; if you have molded yourself into artificiality on
your commercials, the gap between that image and reality
will be quickly apparent when you appear in newscasts. It is
foolish because your opposition will be searching for every
misstatement in your advertising; the further you stray from
reality, the easier a target you will be. (The Carey campaign
spent days fighting a charge of distortion because the words
on a television ad said Carey "got" the Brooklyn Navy Yard
reopened, instead of that he "helped" get the yard re-

opened.) And it is foolish because there should be *something* in your public life worth praising. If this is not true, if you have done nothing in the field of business, community life, neighborhood self-help, charity, or political life worth praising, perhaps you ought to undergo a painful reassessment of your candidacy. It is, of course, possible to resort to advertising in the sense we usually think about it—martial music, patriotic images, stentorian announcers proclaiming your determination to balance the budget while wiping out the national debt while providing free health care for everybody—but it is a dangerous, self-defeating game. Sooner or later, people will find out.

Some other principles to keep in mind:

DON'T PRETEND YOU DO NOT KNOW THE CAMERA IS THERE. The *cinéma non-vérité* technique may have been effective once, but the electorate know very well, even if instinctively, that candidates know when they are on camera. A paraphrase of Bertolt Brecht's theatrical precept makes more sense: The audience is to be aware at all times that it is witnessing an act of special pleading. If you want to say something, say it to the viewers (unless you are shown in conversation with someone else, of course). Tell them, in effect: I want you to vote for me, and you know that's what I'm doing here. Now here's my case.

DON'T TELL THEM WHAT YOU WANT TO DO, SHOW THEM WHAT YOU'VE DONE. This slogan from Carey's 1974 gubernatorial campaign is a useful principle. If you've helped clean up your neighborhood, show them; take the cameras there. In the words of the famous cliché, "television is a visual medium"; it is much easier for a viewer to appreciate the dimensions of your claim if you can point to it.

LET OTHER PEOPLE DO YOUR BRAGGING FOR YOU. In an age of cynicism about politics—an age which gives every sign of lasting longer than the Pleistocene Era—you cannot blame citizens if they take politicians' claims with a grain of salt. But if an ordinary-looking, not-all-that-articulate person says, "I wouldn't have been able to live in a decent neighborhood if it weren't for the work Smithers did," that tends to be much more believable. If you've worked to clean up a river, let a fisherman praise you for that. If you've brought industry into a locality, let a worker tell the people, "I might not have a job today if it hadn't of been for Smithers." Do not hire performers to do this: After witnessing 150,000 commercials over the years, the average viewer can spot a performer in the first three frames. In the 1976 primaries, the Ford campaign tried to use actors to portray ordinary people standing outside supermarkets or carrying lunch pails, engaging in casual conversation on the order of: "Hey, Fred, did you know that the rate of inflation has been cut in half since Ford's been President?" "In *half?* Oh, boy—that's amazing!" (The ads also suffered from nonverisimilitude; the hardhats tended to blow-dry haircuts and designer jeans.) The result was an absolute disaster. Even if you can't find real-life people to say nice things about what you've done, don't use performers (given that situation a candidate might well analyze what it says about his qualifications for office as well).

USE YOUR RECORD TO MAKE A CASE, SO IT SOUNDS LESS LIKE A BOAST. Watching politicians talk about what a terrific job they have done is a distasteful experience for most people. If you want to demonstrate your achievements in a commercial, the best way is to structure the claim as a point you are making on the way to the really important issue. For example:

> YOU: They say that the ordinary citizen doesn't count these days. I think they're wrong. Here in Furburg, we took a block of dangerous abandoned buildings, and turned them into decent housing.
> ORDINARY PERSON: I looked for a decent home for two

years. Thanks to what Mr. Smithers did, we've got a good neighborhood again.

You: I'm running for Governor because I think what we did in Furburg can be done all over the state. If government begins helping people again, we can begin to make a difference.

You are not here simply boasting of what you have done. You are showing people that your beliefs about what can be done have a basis in your own experience. It goes down a lot easier that way.

NEVER ATTACK YOUR OPPONENT PERSONALLY; LET SOMEBODY ELSE DO THE JOB. There is something unappetizing about watching candidates for office invoke the names of their opponent in television advertising. It is too raw, too direct. There is, however, nothing wrong with establishing your opponent's record, using an announcer, or printed words rolling across the screen—the "crawl"—or other people complaining that "Dithers talks a lot, but we just haven't seen any results." Your opponent's record is certainly fair game, but the tougher your attack, the gentler the tone should be. In fact, it makes sense to throw in a redeeming word or two about your rival when you attack him in a commercial ("It isn't Dithers' fault that inflation went up twelve percent last year. But when he voted for ninety billion dollars in extra taxes, was he thinking of what inflation's done to you?" or, "Dithers means well. But good intentions aren't enough when it comes to fighting crime").

DON'T BE AFRAID OF LOADING YOUR COMMERCIALS WITH INFORMATION. There are three kinds of data that can be given on television at the same time. You can show a picture of something, a voice (either on- or off-camera) can say something, and words can be superimposed on the picture. In many political commercials that I worked on, all three devices were used at the same time. The candidate might be in a neighborhood he'd done something for; he, or a citizen, or the announcer, might be describing the project, while facts about the project flashed across the screen. Inevitably, the political managers who screened these spots protested violently when they first saw them. "How," they asked, "will anybody understand these commercials?" This would have been a devastating criticism—had the ads been designed to be seen once. They are, of course, supposed to be seen over and over in the course of a campaign. By giving the viewer more facts than could possibly be absorbed in a single viewing, the commercial remained intriguing far longer than the "half-life" of a typical political ad. And, not so incidentally, it seemed to us a powerful rebuttal to the argument that ideas cannot be contained in a paid ad.

It may be unsettling to you to conclude on this note, but you should be armed in advance against the idea that advertising can make of you what you are not, or can eradicate those defects in your character and record that pose a threat to your election. The way you choose to present yourself is every bit as much a reflection of your makeup as is your performance in office, or your personality. You will prove by how you choose to "sell" yourself how much you trust the voters, how straightforward or evasive you intend to be with them. Your advertising, then, will tell the people whose votes you seek what kind of leadership—or lack of it—they can expect. If your commercials make you look dishonest, or slick, or vague, do not blame the form. The fault, dear Smithers, is not in the film, but in yourself.

CHAPTER X

HOW TO DEBATE

Sooner or later in a political campaign, you will be asked to face your rivals in debate. This may happen in a school auditorium, or on prime-time television, but ever since the Kennedy-Nixon confrontations in 1960, the debate has grown into as traditional a part of campaigning as the paper cup full of cold coffee. For the voter, this is a healthy development, since any chance to see candidates in uncontrolled situations is helpful. For the candidate, the debate is a frightening development, since anything that puts you in an uncontrolled situation is a potential disaster.

A generation ago, politicians usually did not face this trauma; debates were little more than a gleam in the eye of the League of Women Voters. Lincoln and Douglas had staged their great confrontation in 1858—for the Illinois Senate seat and not during the presidential campaign two years later—and the great clashes in the United States Senate among Daniel Webster, John C. Calhoun, and Henry Clay

196

over the issues of Federalism, slavery, and states' rights were studied as models of public discussion. But our political campaigns were generally free of this kind of threat to a candidate's tranquillity. There were occasional exceptions. Harold Stassen and Thomas Dewey debated in 1948 just before the Oregon primary on whether Communists should be allowed to teach in schools, and Dewey's liberal position was credited with helping to win the primary. But until 1960, the debate was more a curiosity than anything else.

In 1960, the political landscape changed. Even before the fall, debates seemed to have come of age. John Kennedy and Hubert Humphrey held a polite exchange before the West Virginia primary, during which John Kennedy demonstrated his understanding of TV's possibilities by bringing a government-surplus food package into the studio and demanding to know whether this was sufficient help for poor families. At the Democratic convention, Kennedy and Lyndon Johnson debated before a joint Massachusetts-Texas delegate caucus. And when a pale, haggard Richard Nixon faced a tanned, confident John Kennedy in the general election campaign— a debate in which the cosmetic difference instantly established Kennedy as at least the equal in stature to Nixon—a new wrinkle had been added to our political system. How, editorialists and civic reformers demanded, could a candidate refuse to debate when the two leading candidates for President had done so? Even though the next three presidential campaigns went by without debates between the candidates, they grew into a tradition at the state and local level.

Sometimes the attempts to capitalize on the taste for debates were better suited to farce than comedy. In 1964, New York Senator Kenneth Keating challenged Robert Kennedy to debate, buying broadcast time just before the election and presenting an empty chair to "prove" that Kennedy would not debate. The only problem was that Kennedy was in the same broadcast complex, and decided to accept the "invitation." Keating's aides barred the door, and after the broadcast Keating fled Kennedy and the press.

Other times, candidates with nothing to gain from debates resorted to every excuse in the book to avoid them. Lyndon Johnson, far ahead of Barry Goldwater in 1964, chose to let the Congress get him off the hook by standing by as they refused to suspend the Federal Communications Act section —the "equal time" provision—which requires all candidates for office to be given equal time, and which therefore made major party debates difficult to arrange. His aides used the excuse that a President should never engage in political debate, lest national security secrets spill out. (Why we should ever want a President without the discretion to keep such secrets was never answered, and President Ford's eager participation in 1976 has probably rendered this excuse forever obsolete.) Richard Nixon in 1968 would not debate Humphrey with George Wallace because, Nixon said, he did not want Wallace to have the exposure, and would not debate without Wallace because Wallace would then get free time on national television.

In today's political climate you must be prepared to debate. You must be prepared to spend many nights in hotel ballrooms, school auditoria, and other centers of public life, exchanging thrusts and parries with those who want the job you want. You must be prepared to spend Sunday mornings and Wednesday evenings in television studios, arguing with your rivals in front of a panel of newspaper and broadcast reporters. You must be prepared to risk months of planning, and millions of dollars, on a careless slip of the tongue or an accidental camera angle showing you adjusting your trousers in a manner which suggests you have become unduly excited by the heat of the campaign.

This is one way to regard debates. It is understandable, given the forgivable fear most politicians have of the unexpected. But it completely misses the point. Debates are not a spontaneous form of rhetorical combat between candidates. As they have evolved today, the debate is a ritual of the most rigid sort. If you have properly grasped the fundamentals of debate strategy, there is no surprise that can catch you off guard. And there is no more chance of suffering political damage than there would be in rescuing a puppy dog from a heroin dealer on national television.

Are debates important? Except for presidential debates, which are carried on all three networks simultaneously to prevent one from winning 90 percent of the audience by offering a movie, most debates are seen by a very small percentage of the electorate, because most debates are not shown in prime time. There is some evidence that this reflects more the desire of network affiliates not to disrupt their schedules than it does the indifference of the public. In 1978, California Governor Jerry Brown debated opponent Evelle Younger in prime time. In Los Angeles, San Francisco, and San Diego, the three big California media markets, the debate placed second in the ratings, beating prime-time offerings of at least one of the networks, and the statewide audience was estimated at more than a million and a half people. As a rule, the debates are broadcast in fringe time, or on independent or public stations, and are likely to win a tiny share of the audience.

Does this mean they do not count? Hardly. Local newscasts will take "bites" from the tapes of the debates, and will feature them on their evening and late-night newscasts, which receive wide viewership, especially among the most likely voters. Newspapers cover the debates extensively, and often take their cues about electability from a candidate's performance during a debate. Dedicated supporters of a candidate, including money givers, will take heart or lose enthusiasm based on a debate performance. (After the first 1960 Kennedy-Nixon debate, Chicago Mayor Richard Daley showed up at the studio to congratulate Kennedy, and the next morning conservative Ohio Senator Frank Lausche—who had been avoiding close support of Kennedy—made sure he was to be included on Kennedy's next trip through Ohio.) Finally, debates can redefine issues in a campaign, depending on which candidate carries the argument to his or her rival. Gerald Ford never recovered from his whimsical foreign policy observation in the second 1976 debate that Eastern Europe was not under Soviet domination; it was a sudden brake on a campaign which had steadily eroded Carter's Labor Day lead. And George McGovern's campaign in 1972 was deeply hurt by the intensity of Hubert Humphrey's attack on McGovern's defense policy in the debate before the California primary.

To shape a debate properly to your own political advantage you must understand the three stages of the debate. Each of them is important. Each of them provides opportunities and dangers. Each of them requires a clear understanding of how we think about debates, and how we judge who is "winning" and "losing" not just the debate, but the skirmishes that surround the event.

The Predebate Debate

If you measure the importance of a process by the time spent on it, then the most important part of a political debate is what happens *before* it takes place. The struggles which take place trying to set up the appearance can occupy weeks of your most valuable aides' time. Why? Because most political veterans, living in another time, enjoy playing out their military fantasies by treating every telephone call, every suggestion for a debate format, as a tactical question requiring intense deliberation. Moreover, these veterans still do not realize that there is no longer any real choice about whether a candidate should participate in a debate. They are still governed by such maxims as: *The candidate who is ahead never debates.* Fifteen years ago, this probably made a lot of sense. Now, it has been replaced by a much more basic principle: *No candidate can get away with ducking debates.* With the process so much a part of major campaigns, that evasion itself becomes a big campaign issue.

It is probably true that another onetime effective strategy has gone by the boards: *When you duck a debate, always phrase your rejection in the form of an acceptance.* If, for example, you are genuinely afraid of a debate, if you believe you are running ahead and have nothing to gain from such a clash, if you believe yourself incapable of coherent speech in a tense situation, then the proper move was to take the position of an ardent advocate of debates, but to do it in a way that made the holding of them impossible. If, for example, your rival suggested a series of six debates, you would thunder that this was inadequate, a sham, a circus; only fifteen debates would really give the people of Furburg a real chance to hear the issues. If a debate was proposed on one issue, you would demand to know why the people were not entitled to hear your views on all the critical issues. If a wide-ranging debate was proposed, you would insist that this scattershot approach would deprive the people of an intelligent discussion. (In 1978, when Evelle Younger was trying to avoid debating with the glib Jerry Brown, Younger's aides at one point demanded that the confrontations only be held on public television, so that they would not be "demeaned" by commercials. Since most public stations in California are on the little-watched UHF band, they would also not be "demeaned" by viewers.)

This was an enjoyable exercise in years gone by, and gave campaign officials many hours of labor that they would otherwise have had to spend with their families, or with financial contributors. But it no longer makes sense. You must understand, however frightening it may seem at first blush, that you are going to have to debate your opponents. If you take this attitude, you gain two advantages. First, you can relax a bit, since you have no choice in the matter. Second, it puts all the pressure on your opponents, who may still be living in the past, waiting for you to thrust and parry over whether there will be a debate. Your position, at least in public, ought to be: "We want to debate, and we will agree to any reasonable format." This will throw your opposition completely on the defensive, as they struggle to figure out your ploy. The ploy is that there isn't one. You're going to debate. The question is, under what conditions?

Assuming that the initial shadowboxing has ended, the next stage of the predebate debate is over format. Although much of this byplay is rooted in the childhood conflicts of the participants, there are some concerns that must be attended to:

Is the format physically favorable to you, or at least neutral? Ever since Richard Nixon's face loomed up cadaverously on American television in 1960, political technicians have learned to check every detail of the debate set. What is the background color, and what suit will look best? Does the lighting throw shadows? Where will the camera be placed? At what angle will the candidate be shot?

This is what you pay your television adviser to worry about. In addition, your second (it is best to think of debates as duels) should have a clear sense of your own abilities, characteristics, and limits. In 1968, when Robert Kennedy and Eugene McCarthy met in a pre-California primary debate, Kennedy's advisers insisted on a sit-down, rather than a stand-up confrontation. Why? Because Kennedy was several inches shorter than McCarthy, and his aides were afraid the height difference would project badly on Kennedy's image of strength. (This is why a taller candidate always agrees to pose for pictures shaking hands with his shorter opponent.) If your candidate has coordination problems, as Gerry Ford was widely assumed to have, then you do not want a format in which that candidate must leave his seat and walk to a podium. (This is known as the "many a slip . . ." precept.) If your body language is tense, you will want a setup which hides the candidates' bodies, instead of one which seats the participants in chairs. A quick-study candidate will readily assent to a "no notes" rule, while a less secure rival will want the comfort that comes with carefully prepared cards.

You will also want a *very clear* commitment on the presentation of a televised debate. If you have a problem with nervous gestures, then you will want to rule out "reaction" shots, where the camera picks up the candidate who is listening to a rival. A picture of the Man For The Job picking at his nose is not considered politically helpful. (To recall 1960 again, during Kennedy's opening statement, the camera picked up a discomfited Nixon, twiching at the neck as he listened to Kennedy. In the third debate, as Nixon was pompously asking if Kennedy wanted to apologize for a campaign statement, the camera picked up Kennedy with an ear-to-ear, who-are-you-kidding grin.) You will never raise your objection on such trivial grounds, of course. Your point to the director is that such shots distract from the issues in a debate.

Some political types enjoy planning day-of-debate ploys to unsettle rivals. John Lindsay always arrived for his 1969 debates late, because he knew it made Mario Procaccino very nervous. A ploy that I have never seen tried, but always thought about, was to have an aide approach the candidate just before airtime, with a piece of paper that he waves frantically. He puts his mouth close to the candidate's ear, and whispers urgently, gesturing with the paper in the general direction of the rival. The candidate firmly shakes his head, rips up the paper into a hundred pieces, and says flatly, "I don't care—it's too raw—some things just aren't worth using," smiling reassuringly at his rival. I've always believed such a ploy would make a shambles out of a rival's self-assurance, but sometimes conscience does govern politics.

The Debate Debate

No matter how much energy you expend making sure that the lighting is right and the water glass will not be placed too close to your notes, you must sooner or later face the central question: *What am I going to do when it is my turn to talk?* This is a much more disturbing question in the abstract than it is in the concrete. Let us understand how unchallenging this process is.

In the first place, the debate format is almost certain to be an inquisition by a panel of newspaper reporters and broad-cast journalists. This means that there are sharp limits to the degree of aggressiveness you can expect. The questions may be stated sharply, and once in a great while a questioner will pursue a candidate effectively. Ford's "Eastern Europe" blunder was underscored when *New York Times* man Max Frankel went back to Ford's original answer, asked point-edly what Ford really meant, and got a ringing reaffirmation of Ford's unusual perception of the deployment of Soviet troops along the Polish frontier. Most journalists will not do this. They are, as one topflight political columnist said, "a collection of massive egos," and it is very rare that one will listen to a question, abandon his own, and pursue a tough line of inquiry about just how you intend to cut taxes while increasing services. As a rule, you can rely on an unrelated series of questions, which can be answered by a single clever response. While it is prudent to prepare for a follow-up ques-tion, it is an exercise much like swinging a leaded bat before a game; the real exchange is likely to be much lighter in weight.

Further, the general good behavior of the press applies with extra force in a debate situation. It simply is not part of the rules of the game for a reporter to look up at a candidate and say flatly, "Smithers, you have been evading this ques-tion now for four weeks. Are you incapable of estimating the cost of your roads program, or afraid to tell us the real ex-pense?" The reporter may write a devastating column about your tactics, but this is far less damaging than being called a four-flusher in the middle of a debate.

Since you do not have to concern yourself with an inquis-itor likely to upset the rules of the game, your next step is to put yourself through a rigorous drill designed to anticipate how these players—the reporters—will play this game. Your aides should have been following the press with consummate care throughout the campaign anyway; the debate is one arena where such care pays off. You must be prepared to clear long hours of time for briefings: skull sessions in which these aides take the roles of rivals and reporters, and pepper you with questions, the nastier the better. This has two advantages. First, it should enable you to anticipate any inquiry likely to come up during the actual debate. Second, it gives your underlings a chance to vent some of the inevitable hostility that you will have engendered during a campaign. Far safer to let them "assault" you in the persona of your opponent or a journalist than to pour out their resentments to a real-life reporter in a congenial watering hole.

This exercise will unnerve you at first, because if your aides are good at what they are doing, they will probe every weakness in your argument, every flaw in your logic; they will show you the different ways your rival might respond to your arguments. But this actually should calm you, unless you are unusually slow on your feet. For, by the time the briefing is over, you should have been forced to consider exactly how to marshal your points, and how to seize on your rival's likely strategy to strengthen your own.

What does it mean to be properly prepared for a debate? At root, it means that you have a very strong sense of what the panel will ask, of how your opponent will respond, and therefore *how you are going to make your points in a way that effectively disarms your inquisitors and unsettles your rival.* For it is on this basis that you will be judged a winner or a loser. As you have already learned, no working journalist will risk his objectivity by writing that "Smithers' proposal to rechannel the Mississippi River into Arizona is the dumbest idea since the Edsel." This is not the way they think. What they will instead judge is who controlled the debate, whose points seemed sharper, and (in the great cliché of debate coverage) *who put whom on the defensive?*

Let me make an assumption, not entirely warranted on the basis of the recent past, that you as a candidate understand your own positions, and what they imply. If your aides do their job properly, you should have a pretty good idea of how your rival has criticized you, and how the reporters have covered your campaign. Your effort, throughout the debate, must be to anticipate the criticisms and questions in your statements. If you do this throughout the debate, you will have moved to a level beyond what the other players in this drama expect.

For example: Let us assume you have decided to insist that full government services can be maintained even while a huge tax cut is passed. The obvious question is how you intend to accomplish this. You can, if you wish, draw huge Laffer curves on pieces of paper and hold them up in front of the cameras to show how excessive taxation limits productivity according to a theoretical model, but the viewers are likely to assume that you have taken leave of your senses. Instead, you will probablllllllly want to argue that the elimination of waste will provide enough money. Now the press panel, and your opponent, are all fully aware of this position. They may be ready to attack you for vagueness. Here, if you are properly trained, is how you insulate yourself from the first level of attack.

REPORTER: Mr. Smithers, you've said that you can cut taxes and maintain full government services by cutting waste. Isn't this awfully irresponsible?

You: It certainly would be—if there weren't concrete, specific indications that I'm on the right track. Two weeks ago, Mr. Jones, your newspaper began a first-rate five-part series on waste in the Department of Resource Allocation. Your colleague on the panel, Mr. Smith, was part of the broadcast investigation of Contingency Stabilization Board rulings that have cost us twenty-five million dollars in the last six months. And my opponent, Mr. Dithers, claims there's a hundred and fifty million dollars of misused funds in the Mutual Interface Agency. Now that means we've figured on close to two hundred million dollars without leaving the room. I'm not saying it's easy, and I've heard enough demagogues on taxes to be pretty careful about making promises. When Mr. Dithers says he'll get more money from Washington, I always mean to ask him if he thinks they take Master Charge down there. But every one of us *knows* where the waste is, and that's why I'm hopeful about what we can responsibly do.

The reason this approach works is that you have used *their* examples to protect *your* argument. You have evoked the concerns on the minds of the press ("demagogue," "responsible"), and often in politics the evocation of the concern is enough to suggest that you have laid that concern to rest. But most important, you have defined the argument on your terms. You have demonstrated enough specifics to make your own proposition the focal point of the debate.

Now let us suppose your opponent wishes to reply. If he is of the conventional stripe—that is, if he lacks the strategic advantage you have gained by studying this manual—he will attack you, because politicians always believe they must attack their opponents. He will begin to try to expose the weaknesses in your position.

> DITHERS: I wonder if Mr. Smithers really believes that he can cut taxes when hs own position papers call for spending five billion dollars more in tax money over the next two years. I wonder if he thinks the people will accept this new frugality when they realize that over the last five years Mr. Smithers has favored more than eighty billion dollars in tax moneys. I don't think that sets a very good example of fiscal responsibility.
>
> [*What you do here is to change the terms of the argument. And you do this by reminding the audience of the nature of the game.*]
>
> YOU [*a regretful smile*]: You know, one of the frustrating aspects of a campaign is that too often we don't take the time to really think about what we're trying to say. Of course I advocate new programs, because when the issue is whether our children will go unschooled, or whether our parents will be forced to eat dog food to survive, yes, I think we should be willing to pay taxes for that. And Mr. Dithers, when he is less pressured by the fevers of

the campaign, will agree with me, because he cosponsored five of the six proposals for which he just attacked
me. But the real point isn't whether Mr. Dithers is now
attacking his own position. He can stage a debate with
himself on that issue. What we all need to understand is
that the tax system needs to be attacked at its roots,
because it has become a self-perpetuating machine, a
sorcerer's apprentice nobody knows how to stop. I
understand why politicians like Mr. Dithers want only to
tinker with it; there's a natural fear of taking on so complicated a machine. But it simply has to be done.

What you have done is to move up one level. You have
managed to suggest that Mr. Dithers is some kind of thin-
lipped bookkeeper, while at the same time consigning him to
the ranks of political tinkerers, associating him with the idea
that he is afraid of a challenge, all the while separating yourself from the routine, business-as-usual quality of politics.

But the really admirable quality of this change-the-terms-
of-the-argument ploy is that it can work equally well in reverse. Suppose your opponent is the one who demands a
wholesale change in the tax system, who is trying to claim
the visionary high ground. Here is your response:

> YOU [*a regretful smile*]: You know, one of the frustrat-
> ing aspects of a campaign is that too often we aren't will-
> ing to come to grips with reality. The really comfortable
> part of Mr. Dithers' statement is that it's written in
> smoke; an hour later, it's gone, and we're still stuck with
> the highest taxes in history. I'll let Mr. Dithers go back to
> some university and smoke a pipe and write his Utopian
> tax plans. Meanwhile, I've got six specific programs
> which can cut every worker's tax bill by fifteen percent.
> Maybe that's not perfect, but it's a month's electric bill,
> and I'll rest my case on that.

The key to grabbing control of the argument is to tell the
viewers what you are doing. Instead of reciting facts, or
proposing plans, tell the audience what it means. Let them

know that you understand what politicians are supposed to say, and that you respect them too much to say those things. You can even praise your opponent for making sense "if you assume that the politicians are right when they say you can't fight City Hall." Grant him an honorable place in the ranks of the other guys.

There is another fundamental piece of strategy that will enable you to win the ground in almost any debate: *Answer the question you want to answer no matter what question they ask.* As a general rule, a panel member will never interrupt you in the middle of an answer to suggest that you did not answer a question, and many will not even point that fact out after you respond. To avoid those that do, you must cast your answer so that it *sounds* as if you are answering the question, while moving to whatever area you feel is important.

> REPORTER: Mr. Smithers, how would you preserve the housing stock in our central cities?
>
> YOU: I think we have to face the reason why forty years of federal housing programs haven't worked. And the reason is that the key to decent housing in our cities is an effective fight against crime—because the fear of crime is why middle-class and stable working-class citizens flee our neighborhoods and our cities. So the real question you have to answer about our housing dilemma is what to do about crime. I believe there are five practical, tough, immediate steps we can take. . . .

If a reporter wants to argue that you have not answered the question, he runs the risk of the audience wondering what he is talking about; they have heard you begin with a very clear statement about federal housing programs not working. He also runs the risk of you moving to the Eugene McCarthy–Jerry Brown tactic of coolly indicting the reporter for missing the point. ("With all deference, Mr. Jones, I believe the problem is that our entire housing policy has not answered the question, because it has not understood

the link between crime and housing decay. Do you want me
to recite the figures on Section Eight incompletions? The
abandonment records for our five biggest cities? Some proposal for redirecting HUD's rehabilitation program? It
doesn't mean anything without focusing on crime. . . .")

This is one of the ways Hubert Humphrey decimated
George McGovern in the 1972 California primary debate.
Humphrey wanted to make clear his basic disagreement with
McGovern's defense-cut ideas, which would cut "the muscle, and not just the fat" from national security needs. After
he had finished attacking McGovern, a reporter asked him
how we *could* cut a reasonable amount from defense spending. "Well I'll tell you how you *don't* do it," Humphrey
said, and proceeded to attack McGovern all over again.

It is also the easiest way to bring the debate back to your
agenda if the questions have somehow strayed from it. If
your basic argument against an incumbent is, let us say, a
lack of leadership, then no matter what you are asked, you
will probably be able to reestablish the point. If you are
asked, for example, where you disagree with the incumbent
on his inflation policies, here is what you do:

> The issue isn't policies, Bill. If Mr. Dithers were able
> to come before the people with a record of having done
> what he said he was going to do, I wouldn't be here today
> —I'd be out raising money for him. The problem is that
> the programs are sitting there on pieces of paper, not
> because Dithers doesn't want to do the good thing, but
> because he lacks the capacity to get these things done.
> It's not a crime to be ineffective, but it's not a basis on
> which to ask for another chance.

If you are asked where you differ with your opponent:

> The difference is that I believe I would be signing bills
> into law instead of issuing press releases blaming other
> people.

This tactic of answering the question you want to answer is not unknown to the press. It is, therefore, entirely possible that you will be called on it, that one of the journalists on the panel will feel constrained to break the rules of the performance just enough to ask you why you continually cite one issue no matter what question you are asked. Should you fear this? You should welcome this "challenge," because, with the right preparation, you will once again be able to alter the ground on which the debate is taking place by telling the audience that you are stepping outside the routine boundaries.

Let me show you how:

REPORTER: Mr. Smithers, you've been asked about housing, transportation, taxes, and jobs—and to each question you've given an answer about crime. Aren't the people entitled to hear what you intend to do about these other questions?

YOU: Of course they are. But I'll tell you what else they're entitled to. They're entitled to leadership that understands how ideas fit together. I don't blame Dithers or you or your colleagues for sitting here and playing the same game that's been played year after year. That's how it's been done. And that's exactly what's been wrong. How do you pretend you can bring jobs into Poorville if merchants are closing their doors every day because of crime? That's not an evasion—that's the *real* question. I don't intend to see millions of dollars wasted in more demonstration projects when the answers to your questions all intersect. If you want to accuse me of giving the same answer to your questions, fine—I'm saying that your questions come back to the same issue.

You must also keep your opponent off balance. The easiest way to win a debate is to appear better-informed, more comfortable, more at ease, than your opponent. This is part of the general principle that the press, which will interpret the debate, is much more comfortable judging appearances than substance. Reporters can see fingers drumming a table, an Adam's apple bobbing up and down, with much more certainty than they can calculate the cost of a tax abatement scheme. At all times, you should be calculating how to throw your opponent off his own game plan.

One way is to throw off his timing. Let's say that in your debate format the candidate answering the question is given a minute and a half, with a minute or so for a response. After about twenty minutes, this rhythm will have unconsciously established itself in the minds of all of the participants. So here is what you do the next time it is your turn to answer:

> REPORTER: Mr. Smithers, do you believe the growing threat of foreign competition means the United States should move away from its free trade policies of the 1960s and move toward the establishment of import quotas and high tariffs?
> YOU: No.
> MODERATOR: Now one minute for Mr. Dithers.
> DITHERS: Huh?

With any luck, you will have correctly gauged that Dithers has figured out that he has about a minute to look through his notes or cards, to find the pithy phrase that he and his advisers have concocted in answer to the imports question. By giving a one-word answer, you force the moderator to throw the question to an unsuspecting Dithers, you create the possibility of a camera shot of Dithers hastily shuffling through his notes with the general expression of a man in the act of zipping up his fly, and you increase the chances of Dithers stumbling his way through an answer. Since most debate formats allow for a comment on your opponent's answer, you can then respond, "I think what Mr. Dithers was trying to say was that the idea of quotas is tempting, and certainly we need to protect American workers from unfair competition, but quotas really will hurt us much more than they will help us.'' This enables you to escape the political costs of giving a blunt answer to a sensitive question.

Another little-used tactic to unnerve your rival is to attempt to engage him in real conversation, what legislators call a *colloquy*. Assuming that your opponent has gone through his own briefing, he is likely to be very concerned with keeping the answers lined up in his head, and with remembering the strategy to a T. Don't get this locked in. Instead, lean forward during an answer, extend an inviting hand to your rival, and see if you can coax him into beginning a conversation:

> YOU [*answering a question about Salt II*]: When you cut through the complexities—and this is an incredibly complicated treaty, wouldn't you say, Dithers? Did you see Warnke's memo on throw-weight tables?
>
> DITHERS: Well, my position—
>
> YOU: I understand, I understand, but did you expect that argument about relative destructiveness ratios to be stated in quite that way? No, it's all right, I'll yield you my time.
>
> DITHERS: Uh . . .

If you want to attack your rival's position, wait for the chance to counterpunch. One of the most important parts of any campaign is knowing when—and how—to attack your opponent. It is so important, in fact, that a whole chapter has been devoted to it (see chapter 11). In a debate format, you should remember that it is generally bad form to attack first. Even if you are behind in the polls, and need to score points fast, you run a dangerous risk in flailing out at your foe. Most voters are so ready to believe that all political rhetoric is bilge that they will likely turn off these attacks. In addition, you open yourself up for the "more in sorrow" ploy, in which your opponent looks at you sadly and says, "It really is sad that at a time when both of us have the chance to say what we intend to do with this high office, Mr. Smithers can think of nothing to offer you than a hysterical attack on someone whose worst offense is to run for the job Mr. Smithers wants. I'll let the people decide on this tactic with their votes." (The description of your opponent's "tactic" is a nice touch, because it suggests by itself something unsavory.)

Once you are attacked, however, you are in the position of a boxer whose opponent has opened himself up to attack with a wild blow. A debate always gives you the chance to hit back. And sometimes it can be done with devastating results. In 1976, Tom Hayden was waging an effective primary campaign against Senator John Tunney. Our polls—I was working for Tunney—showed that two weeks before election Hayden was closing in so fast that he actually had a chance to win. During their debate, which had been proceeding on a more-or-less even keel, Hayden was maintaining a calm demeanor, disarming for those who pictured him as a 1960s street radical.

Then, rattled by Tunney's implication that Hayden had once been less than committed to the support of Israel, Hayden turned on Tunney and spat out an accusation. Why, he demanded of Tunney, did you accept huge contributions from special interests for your campaign?

Tunney took a beat. Then, with icy coldness, he replied: "Because I don't have a wife who could give me three hundred and eighty thousand dollars."

In one sentence, Tunney had reminded the audience that Hayden's campaign was being financed, in substantial measure, by Jane Fonda, his actress-wife, who was regarded with great distaste by a substantial sector of the Democratic Party electorate. But this was not a ploy—it would have been silly, even dangerous, to have attacked Hayden for being married to a wealthy actress with half-baked political views. But Hayden had opened the door. Attacks must always be made in passing, very casually, on the way to a noble point. That way, if your rival tries to respond, it may well sound like carping.

The Postdebate Debate

Never make the mistake of assuming that once the debate is over, it is over. The real fight is just beginning: the fight to win the interpretation.

Unless we are talking about presidential debates, most debates will not be watched from beginning to end. Instead, the great majority of voters will see small excerpts from the debate on local news broadcasts, or will read accounts in the newspapers. And many of the people watching the debates will not really know what they have seen until the next-day notices tell them (Ford's Eastern Europe blunder, for example, was not understood as such by the bulk of the electorate until the commentators pointed out the foolishness of Ford's no-Soviet-domination remark). Given the arcane nature of most debate questions and answers, the audience tends to be in the position of a theatergoer attending a preview, and saying, "I can't wait to read the reviews so I'll know what I thought about this." It will do you no good to triumph in the view of six retired forensic professors who are covering the debate for the *Journal of Persuasion*. The job of your campaign is to make sure that the press and broadcast coverage of the debate reflects your triumph.

The first task is for everyone on your team to respond at the end of your debate with barely concealed glee. Just as in judging primary returns, the press will look harshly upon a campaign aide who appears just after a debate looking as if he has just suffered an attack of kidney stones. Profuse sweating, nervous whispers, hastily jotted notes, whispered expletives, tend to suggest that your seconds believe you have not carried the day.

What you need, rather, is a sense of restrained celebration, as if your campaign aides realized the bad form involved in uncorking champagne bottles on the set of a local television station. Instead, quiet congratulations, just conspicuous enough to be noticed by the press, are in order. In addition, you need a public congratulatory telephone call from someone whose endorsement you have won a day or two before, but which you are not making public. The idea is for the call to come to you on the set minutes after the debate ends, while the press is still swarming about the candidates looking for reactions. Grab the telephone nearest the press corps, right after an aide has told you that Mr. Big is on the line. The press can overhear you accepting congratulations with the modesty that befits a graceful winner: "Yes . . . yes . . . well, I'm deeply appreciative . . . no, frankly, I expect him to do much better next time . . . well, I hope to do that again. . . ."

This endorsement should be followed up early the next morning by a press conference, at which Mr. Big formally declares for you. When the press asks why, Mr. Big will say simply, "Did you see that debate last night? After that exchange, I felt I could not stay silent."

One of the most common ploys to suggest that you have won the debate is the run-it-again scenario. Just after the debate ends, your media adviser should approach the opposition, in full earshot of the press, and volunteer to pay half the cost of the debate—or all of the cost—in order to run the debate again. The chances are the other side will be so unsettled by the idea that you think you won that they will refuse the offer. If by some chance you find yourself on the receiving end of the "run-it-again" offer, don't panic. Accept—especially if your opposition has offered to pay the full cost. The managers of very few campaigns will really want to take that kind of money out of the media budget to run a debate at the expense of their own commercials. If you do not want the debate run again, accept anyway, with the proviso that it be run in prime time. That should jack up the cost high enough to dissuade any opponent.

These concerns are not abstract. In 1978, when Jerry Brown met Evelle Younger in a widely seen debate, Brown's campaign was convinced that Younger had hurt himself badly with a highly aggressive, attacking style. But the press, which had been characterizing Younger as deadly dull, had been impressed because—in the great debate phrase—he had "forced Brown on the defensive." The Brown campaign, as a top aide later said, feared that the press enthusiasm would eventually translate into a public perception that Brown had lost the debate. Consequently, the campaign made a strong effort to keep the press informed about the campaign's call-back polling, which showed that Younger had badly hurt himself, and urged the press to watch the public-opinion polls carefully before concluding that Younger had won the debate. On the other side, Younger's campaign was busily attempting to mark the campaign as a key turning point, offering to run the debate again and claiming that the debate had brought in a sudden burst of campaign contributions.

The fact is that, because of the sophistication of the press, it is no longer easy to establish yourself as the winner the way political prankster Dick Tuck tried to do for John Kennedy in 1960, when he allegedly had an old woman with a big NIXON button run up to the then Vice President and say, "Don't worry, you'll do better next time." But you must at least engage in the fight for the correct interpretation, because without it, the opposition will win by default. And there are too many opportunities to score political points in the debate format to lose the fight the morning after.

CHAPTER XI

HOW TO ATTACK YOUR OPPONENT

No campaign can really be won with a positive appeal to the voters. At least half the battle is the attempt to convince them that the other people who want your job are not as good as you are. The genuinely popular candidate can win an impressive victory; Dwight Eisenhower, probably the most beloved presidential candidate, won 55 percent of the vote in his 1956 reelection. But two far less attractive political figures, Lyndon Johnson and Richard Nixon, each won more than 60 percent of the popular vote because the electorate became convinced that their opponents were not acceptable possibilities for the Presidency. Do not ignore this lesson: If you can make your opponent seem unfit for the job you are both seeking, you can begin ordering the new stationery.

This is not to say, however, that you should begin launching searing attacks on your opponent. One of the real—as opposed to imagined—impacts of television and other forms of mass communication is that the full frontal assault on political candidates has taken on a certain unsavory aspect. The records of our past are alive with invective that would simply be too raw for the nightly news. Who today would imitate the enemies of Andrew Jackson, who charged him with being the son of a prostitute? Who would follow the tradition born in the campaign of 1844, when a false "document" accused James K. Polk of buying and branding a slave (this alleged excerpt from the journal of "Baron von Roorback" gave birth to a now-obsolete political term: the "roorback," meaning a damaging, last-minute falsehood aimed at a foe). Who would emulate the inspiring 1950 campaign of George Smathers, who unseated Senator Claude Pepper by charging that his sister was a "thespian," his brother a "practicing homo sapien," and that during college he had openly "matriculated"? Who would echo the rivals of John Quincy Adams, who charged him with pimping for the czar while serving as minister to Russia? Would the most feisty fighters charge, as Theodore Bilbo once charged a rival, thus: "Pat has taken up golf! Golf! An effete and effeminate game that is a snare of the devil, an insult to Mississippi!"? Is it imaginable that any candidate of either party would duplicate Joe McCarthy's charge that under the Democratic administrations of Roosevelt and Truman, America had undergone "twenty years of treason"?

The game is not played this way any longer. Politicians fear the stigma of "irresponsibility" more than any other label. This can cover a multitude of sins, including a political ideology which openly argues that wealthy and powerful people have a disproportionate share of wealth and power. (When Jimmy Carter said in his 1976 acceptance speech that there are some Americans who, by virtue of their power, are exempt from the painful consequences of mistaken public policies, *The New York Times* attacked him for five straight days, so frightening Mr. Carter that he probably decided then and there to hire establishmentarians Cyrus Vance and Zbigniew Brzezinski.) What it usually means, however, is that a candidate has assailed his opponent with too much enthusiasm. So any attempt to go after your rival must be planned with consummate care. You must know *what* you can attack, and *how* you can attack those points. Most important, you must know how to attack so that you seem not to be attacking at all.

One of the first politicians who understood the need for some new form of attack was Richard Nixon. This may seem absurd, given Nixon's "Tricky Dick" reputation, but consider Nixon's track record in light of the emerging television-era of politics. What Mr. Nixon helped to perfect, starting from his first famous campaigns against Jerry Voorhis and Helen Gahagan Douglas, was the bump-and-run school of political attack. This approach suggests great respect for a differing opinion or a rival political figure even as the shiv is finding flesh between the ribs. It hurls the brick surreptitiously, even as the hurler seems to be throwing his arms wide to express his fondness for the figure at whose skull he is aiming.

Perhaps its earliest national unveiling came during the "Checkers" speech, when Mr. Nixon paused in his account of his financial condition to assert: "I believe it's fine that a man like Governor Stevenson, who inherited a fortune from his father, can run for President."

But it was as President that Nixon, now attempting to play Statesman for the history books, relied most heavily on the bump-and-run school of attack. The form here was to cast an opponent, sometimes anonymous, as an adherent of a ludicrous point of view, and then solemnly defend that person's right to hold that view.

Early in the Nixon Administration, Ed Muskie—a Senator with clear presidential ambitions—opposed Nixon's plan to give a $3 billion tax break for business. Nixon commented, "Now any Senator or any critic who wants to oppose a program that is going to mean more jobs for Americans, more peacetime jobs rather than wartime jobs [*bump*] has a right to take that position [*run*]." Talking with a group of businessmen about the environmental movement, Nixon said, "I am not among those who believe that the United States would be just a wonderful place . . . if we could just get rid of all of this industrial progress that has made us the richest and strongest nation in the world." He told ABC correspondent Howard K. Smith in 1970 that "it is true of all the Presidents in this century, it is probably true that I have less, as somebody said, supporters in the press than any President [*bump*]. I understand that [*run*]." When Lyndon Johnson's Defense Secretary Clark Clifford criticized the pace of troop withdrawals from Vietnam, Nixon said that he respected Clifford's right to an opinion [*run*], but that we should remember that Mr. Clifford worked for the Administration that escalated the war [*bump*].

One of the reasons why Nixon became known as "Tricky Dick," I think, is that the very nature of his tortuous attacks on political opponents was so obviously a ploy. Older politicians went at their opponents more directly; FDR in 1940 made a joke out of the names of three prominent political enemies, with the incantation, "*Marrrrrtinnnn, Barrrrr*ton, and *Fish!*"; Senator Everett Dirksen at the 1952 Republican convention pointed a finger at Tom Dewey and bellowed, "We followed you before, and you took us down the road to defeat!" Nixon's attacks were too clever by half, too elliptical, to ring true.

The unfortunate end of Mr. Nixon's political career, however, and the relatively primitive nature of his attacks, should not invalidate the general premise. The strategy that helps in a debate is more generally applicable: *When the candidate is speaking, criticism of an opponent should be confined either to a counterpunch, or to a passing remark cited for evidence of a more noble, positive point.*

When Lyndon Johnson withdrew as a candidate for reelection in 1968 and Hubert Humphrey entered the race, the latter's announcement statement talked of "the politics of happiness, the politics of joy." It was an accurate reflection of Humphrey's energy and enthusiasm, but coming as it did in the midst of riots on campuses and in ghettos, and in the midst of the war in Vietnam, it seemed out of phase. Robert Kennedy picked up on the phrase, but instead of attacking Humphrey directly, his stump speeches would say that "I don't think you can talk about the politics of happiness—the politics of joy—at a time when two hundred Americans a week are dying in Vietnam." Often in going after President Johnson—a leader for whom Robert Kennedy was not overcome with respect and admiration—he would not state a disagreement at all, but report what the President had said and then go on to argue a fundamentally contrary point, without ever saying Johnson was wrong.

"The President says we are restless," Kennedy would say. "I believe this nation is more deeply divided than it has been since the Civil War."

Or: "The President says we have the strongest military force in the world. I'm concerned with how strong we are at home; with the strength of our schools. . . ."

More generally, attacks on rivals are more palatable when they appear to be an unhappy, but necessary, way of illustrating an important point. If you stand up and say flatly, "Dithers' position on Social Security is a half-baked, crackpot scheme that will bankrupt our children and condemn our parents to starvation," you are doing nothing more than saying what every conventional politician is likely to say about his or her opponent. It is far more convincing to say: "I don't believe anyone has all the answers to our Social Security problem, because it's been forty years in the making. Of course Dithers' proposal won't work, but that's not the real problem, because the mistakes in Dithers' ideas are so clear no one's going to take them seriously. The *real* problem is protecting the people who relied on the promise of Social Security, because sooner or later we're going to face breaking that promise or bankrupting ourselves."

If your opponent has the habit of praising his or her own

record, it is tempting to attack the accuracy of this perception. But a frontal assault is rarely effective, especially if
your opponent has invested a great deal of money in early
advertising. Once the public has seen the picture of your
adversary in front of newly opened homes and factories over
and over, that image is likely to remain pretty well in place,
no matter how indignantly you protest that it is all an exag-
geration.

There are two alternatives to the direct attack. The first is
to point to the very achievement your opponent is citing to
"prove" your point that a new approach to the problem is
necessary: "I don't think anyone can fault Dithers' intentions," you say, "but when a man running for this kind of
office points to two hundred jobs, while sixty-five thousand
manufacturing jobs have left this area in the last five years,
I think the problem with Band-Aid solutions is clear. At this
rate, Dithers will be able to bring eight hundred jobs to Furburg, while a quarter of a million will have left. Any more
'achievements' like that and the biggest employer around
here will be the food stamps office."

The second is to cast doubt on his credibility by lumping
his claim in with that of all the other political promises, to
indict your rival by evoking the ghosts of what other politicians have said: "You know," you say, "I've seen Dithers
talking about his jobs, because whenever I'm trying to watch
a football game, Dithers keeps popping up in front of a factory talking about the same two hundred jobs; maybe he
thinks we'll add them up or something. But every time I hear
Dithers promise to wipe out unemployment, I keep thinking
of all the other promises we've been given. Elect Johnson,
and there will be peace in Southeast Asia; elect Nixon, and
we'll have law and order; elect Carter, and our government
will work again. I think all of us in public life have a responsibility to be very careful about these kinds of promises."

The effect should be to raise the vague sense in the voters'
minds that Dithers is somehow part of the same crowd of
promise-breaking candidates that has let them down so often

in the past. You have not called Dithers a liar; indeed, he may well have brought those two hundred jobs to Furburg. Your effort is to make this claim sound like the thirteenth stroke of the clock, casting doubt not only on itself, but on all that has been heard before.

This approach also enables you to cite your own accomplishments while denigrating them: "I think all of us in public life have to measure what we've done—or what we *think* we've done—against the needs that have to be met. I admit I'm proud of the three hundred and fifty jobs at the Civic Center we helped to place there, but there are thousands of other people who need good jobs, too. The health care program whose funds we fought for is important, but it's not nearly enough. And we always have to ask what the cost is —whether you're accomplishing anything if the tax burden becomes impossible for our working people to meet."

The splendid quality of your record, and the dubious quality of your rival's record, always sticks better when it is absorbed, rather than being shoved down the throat of the voter.

The other tool for attack is the counterpunch, described in the chapter on debating. When a rival hits out at you, that attack invites a reply which would be too raw if you initiated it yourself. But this, too, creates a different kind of opportunity. By choosing your reply carefully, you do more than cash in on a "free ride"—an attack which must be carried by the press because they have carried the original attack on you. You also have the chance to put your rival in a clearly defensive position for even attacking you in the first place. Here are some different examples of counterpunching, in order of *increasing unconventionality:*

SO'S YOUR OLD MAN. Dithers has just accused you of being absent from your current job more than any other holder of a similar job. You say, "I hardly think the man who took fourteen trips to Las Vegas at taxpayers' expense is in a position to criticize anybody's attendance record."

This is the conventional counterpunch. He calls you names, you call him names. It is simple, easy to remember, and not very effective.

THE BRUSH-OFF. Dithers has just said that "the election of Smithers would be the greatest threat to the well-being of Furburg since the influenza epidemic of 1918." You smile, and say, "I gather this means Mr. Dithers has turned down my offer to become my finance chairman."

This has the advantage of showing that you can withstand criticism without getting nervous or suspicious, and that you retain a sense of humor about the inevitable slings and arrows of a political campaign. It works best when the charge is broad in nature, as when George McGovern assailed John Connally after Connally announced for President. Confronted with McGovern's attack, Connally simply smiled and reminded his interrogator that since Connally had led Democrats for Nixon in 1972, he wasn't exactly overcome with shock at McGovern's attack. The brush-off is decidedly ineffective when the charge against you is specific in nature. If you stand accused of bribery, or tax evasion, you cannot smile and say, "I suppose I'll have to start easing my position on white-collar crime."

THE "CONFESSION." This takes the form of an admission of what you have been charged with, but cast in a form that makes it clear your opponent, not you, has actually done wrong. One of its finest examples came in 1903, when James Michael Curley, then a rising Boston legislator, was jailed for taking a postal examination under the name of one of his supporters. While serving time in prison, Curley ran for Alderman—and won—campaigning on the basis that his act on behalf of a young father who needed to support his family proved his dedication to his constituents.

Given the changed nature of political morality, this is probably going too far. (But in the mid-1970s, Chicago Mayor Richard Daley used a similar tactic when he was accused of throwing enormous amounts of city insurance business in the direction of his son, who had only recently been admitted into the profession. Did the Mayor deny the charges? Not at all. If a father can't help out his own son, Daley demanded, then what's America coming to?) It provides a clue, however, to the general tactic of "confession." Suppose your opponent issues an attack on one of your most important accomplishments. Let us say he has found records indicating that a work-study program you spent years trying to launch has been guilty of wasting huge sums of money. It will do no good to deny that you had anything to do with the program, because the newspapers and radio and TV stations all have records of your appearance at the dedication of the program. It will do no good to brush the charge off, because wasting tax money is a serious business.

Instead, counterpunch by "confessing": "I stand here today to plead 'guilty' to the charge of trying to make life better for these young people of Furburg," you say. "I note with some interest that Mr. Dithers says this program has wasted money. Well, if teaching six hundred kids that work is better than welfare is waste, then I say, let's waste a lot more money. If bringing hundreds of people in off the streets, to make nights safer for our citizens, is waste, then let's waste a lot more money this way. I'll let Mr. Dithers explain why spending billions of dollars on prisons and hospitals for the injured and the dying is sensible while trying to get these kids out of trouble and into jobs is waste."

If this approach seems to be working, you can move to the next step: "They said that unemployment insurance was a waste, they said that Social Security was a waste, they said that medical care for the aged was a waste, they said that school lunches were a waste, and if this is the kind of tradition of which the work-study program is part, I'll let Mr. Dithers stand with the naysayers, and I'll stand with the voices of progress."

THE JOSEPH WELCH PLOY, OR "SHAME, SHAME." Without question, the single most effective counterpunch ever thrown in a political setting was Joseph Welch's indignant attack on Senator Joseph McCarthy at the 1954 Army-McCarthy hearings. After the hearings had dragged on for weeks, McCarthy suddenly hurled an attack on one of Welch's colleagues in a Boston law firm, charging the young attorney with membership in the National Lawyer's Guild, a left-wing organization.

This triggered Welch's famous reply: "Have you no sense of decency sir, at long last . . . Until this moment, I never judged your recklessness, nor your cruelty. . . ." It was an impassioned defense of his aide, accompanied by a withering denunciation of McCarthy's contemptible attack. When it was over, and the audience in the committee room had burst into sustained applause, McCarthy's political career was effectively over.

If you have the capacity to pull it off, the Welch ploy can become as effective an attack on your opponent as anything in your political arsenal. It requires some careful restraint throughout your campaign, because it is a move *that can only work once*. It requires that you have treated most attacks with the more casual, half-humorous responses, principally the brush-off; because if you respond to every charge with righteous indignation, you will greatly diminish the impact of your rebuttal—as with the boy who cried wolf. One of the reasons Welch's attack on McCarthy was so effective is that Welch was a venerable New England lawyer, with a laconic technique and a dry wit. His very lack of hot-bloodedness made his explosion so effective. It is also a move that best be made in a face-to-face encounter, such as in a debate, to emphasize your courage in taking on your rival then and there.

In form, the Welch ploy should follow the style of its originator. Wait for a particularly untrue—or particularly effective—attack from your rival. Then, take a deep breath, fix your foe with a steely stare, and begin: "Mr. Dithers, you and I have waged a long campaign. I suppose we have both said things in the heat of battle that we have later regretted. But until this moment, I do not think I really understood how desperate you are, Mr. Dithers, to win this campaign. After all that we have suffered at the hands of McCarthyism, and the Nixon Watergate years—after all we've learned about political dirty tricks—I really did not think we would hear this kind of indecent assault from you. Is the winning of a handful of votes so important that you would so casually poison the political process? Is there nothing beyond Election Day that has meaning or importance?''

The Welch ploy can also be used in a shorter, less dramatic form. A slow, regretful shake of the head, a simple ''I did not think this campaign would come to this kind of tactic; frankly, Mr. Dithers, I thought you above this, and I am sorry for having misjudged you as a man of character'' can often force your opponent back on the defensive, as he seeks to protect his integrity, while the substance of what he was saying goes ignored. It is also possible to cash in on the ''shame, shame'' move if your adversary uses clumsy body language. If, for instance, in making a charge he picks up a paper with documentation on it, remind your audience that ''in classic McCarthy fashion, Mr. Dithers waved a piece of paper in front of the television cameras a moment ago. Let me tell you what that paper doesn't say—and what that kind of mudslinging says about the desperate nature of Dithers' campaign.'' This helps make irrelevant the question of what Dithers actually had on the paper.

These are the kinds of attacks and counterattacks that will work for you personally. Always remember, however, that *the rougher kinds of attacks should always come from other people, while you stand clear.* If there is sharply negative material to deliver about your opponent, *don't do it yourself.* I am not here talking about smears, rumors, and scandal-mongering. No one in your campaign should have anything to do with these kinds of materials, for three reasons. First, it is immoral. Second, you are likely to get caught, since post-Watergate political journalism values such discoveries. Third, your opponent is likely to have made enough enemies so that this material will find its way into the bloodstream of the body politic sooner or later. We are talking, instead, of fair, but tough attacks on the public record of your rival. The distinction was well-stated by a political operative of some prominence who said: "I believe it is a smear to attack an individual on matters that have no relationship whatever to the campaign. If you attack his personal life, if you attack members of his family [that's wrong]. But it is not a smear if you point out the *record* of your opponent."

Given the fact that this distinction was authored by Murray Chotiner, the late adviser to Richard Nixon throughout his early career, you may choose to discount the advice. But it is accurate, however much its author honored it in the breach, rather than in the observance. When your campaign goes after the opposition, it must be done without your active participation. How? Here are some effective methods:

ORGANIZE MEMBERS OF THE OTHER PARTY INTO A CAMPAIGN COMMITTEE FOR YOU.   This is one of the most traditional of techniques, but also one of the most effective. It plays off the your-own-man-says-so feeling that if people in a candidate's camp are unwilling to support him, there must be a deep flaw in his character or his positions. This feeling is one reason why the 1972 Nixon campaign put the "Democrats for Nixon" imprimatur on its anti-McGovern commercials. The same arguments were more convincing coming from McGovern's camp than from the Nixon reelection committee. Even though the ties between citizens and political parties have loosened over the years, even though more people consider themselves independents than Republicans or Democrats, this framework has power.

Once you have organized Republicans and Independents for Smithers (assuming you are a Democrat), you should use this organization to launch the heaviest attacks on Dithers' campaign. The fact that the charges are coming from people usually aligned with "the other side" takes part of the partisan sting out of them, and gives them an air of credibility.

Similarly, if you have won an endorsement from a prominent member of the other party, let that endorsement be cast in a now-is-the-hour rhetoric that would be clearly inappropriate coming from you.

"I have always supported the candidate of my party," your supporter will say, "but I have also believed that there are times, as John Kennedy said, when party loyalty asks too much. This is such an occasion. I find that the positions, the record, of Mr. Dithers is simply unworthy of support. I cannot say I agree with all of Mr. Smithers' views, but he is a man of integrity, of honor, and of restraint. I must, therefore, break with my party, not to abandon it, but because I believe its candidate has abandoned those principles for which our party is supposed to stand.

USE NEGATIVE MEDIA ONLY WHEN YOUR POSITIVE MESSAGE HAS BEEN GOTTEN ACROSS.   Whatever its merits in a boxing match, it is poor political strategy to come out swinging. The electorate does not really begin to focus on a campaign until the last few weeks, if at all. In this unfocused stage, you have the opportunity to paint yourself as a fellow of achievement and integrity; but if you begin to hurl bombs at your rival, you are likely to find two reactions: first, a what's-the-yelling-all-about reaction, since your listeners are only vaguely aware that there is a campaign; second, "Who is this unpleasant fellow going around saying unpleasant things?" The voters must have a clear idea of who you are, and what the campaign is about, before indulging their natural appetite for attacks on the enemy camp.

IN YOUR ATTACKS, SPEAK SOFTLY BUT CARRY A BIG STICK.   The last thing you want is a picture of you, in the newspapers or on TV, haranguing your adversary. What you seek is the maximum exposure for your charges, with minimum exposure of yourself. In your radio and television, for example, your face or voice should appear only as much as is necessary to qualify for the lower costs of political commercials. (This is why, on radio, you will hear a familiar voice saying "paid for by Friends of Smithers." That will be you—the candidate—qualifying for the legally required discounts.) Otherwise, the voice should be calm, almost quiet. On television, the message can be delivered by a "crawl," reciting with as many dates and facts as possible the actual record, with an announcer reciting the same material.

These kinds of ads work best when no conclusion is drawn from the barrage of damaging information—missed votes, contradictory positions. The best end to such a message, rather, is one addressed to the voter: "Is this the kind of record you want here in Furburg? That's for you to decide —on Election Day." The brilliant anti-McGovern ads of Nixon's 1972 campaign did not even mention the question of voting. They just reminded the voters of McGovern's positions, having described them in deprecatory, but not extreme, fashion. The message—that McGovern's views were not those of mainstream America—stuck.

LET OTHER VOICES DO THE ATTACKING.   If your opponent has been criticized in newspaper editorials, if he has alienated many within his own party, there is no need to rewrite these sources of attack. They have far more credibility than words your speechwriters or television advisers can put in the mouths of announcers. Just throw the words right up on the screen, with an announcer saying, "You probably don't care very much about what one politician has to say about another. We don't blame you. So listen to what some newspapers are saying about the man running against Smithers." Or: "How do you judge a candidate? By what *he* says? Or by what the people he's served say about him? We do, too. So listen to what your neighbors and fellow Furburgers have to say about the man running against Smithers." Then step aside, and let the nonaffiliated voices speak. There's a fine line between talking about your opponent's record and engaging in unfair attack. This technique is one way to make sure you do not cross the line in the minds of voters.

ALWAYS BE NICER TO YOUR OPPONENT IN PRIVATE THAN
IN PUBLIC.   One of the most unattractive qualities in a politician is a sense of bitterness in private. When the last rally
of the day is over, those covering the campaign do not want
to hear a tirade about what a genuinely evil fellow your rival
is. It suggests that you do not appreciate the rules of the
game. The gap between private and public opinions is suggested by a story told about Harry Truman, who viciously
attacked Herbert Hoover in a political speech as an architect
of the Depression in spite of the fact that Hoover had rendered valuable service to Truman in the reorganization of
government. When Hoover ran into Truman, he upbraided
him for the savage words.

"You're right," said Truman. "When I got to that paragraph in the speech, I almost didn't give it."

If you find yourself in casual, after-hours conversation
with the press, do not indulge your natural inclination to
pummel your opponent. Reflect on some of Dithers' more
admirable qualities, perhaps his fine family life (this will impress those reporters who may have some knowledge about
his private habits that you do not share). Acknowledge a
point or two in his program that you think may make sense,
in a modified form, and suggest that when the election is
over, you might be calling on Dithers to see if he is willing to
help you in your new post.

A HUMOROUS TWIST TO YOUR CRITICISMS WILL MAKE
THEM PALATABLE.   A slight smile is a more appealing
expression than a face contorted with rage, especially in an
age when politicians are seen up close rather than from a
distance. The wild hand gestures and exaggerated expres-
sions are as out of place in political life as they are in an age
of talking pictures and close-ups. You no longer have the
luxury of bellowing at your political enemies; instead, the
death of a thousand cuts should be your model. This is more
than a precaution. If you can get the electorate laughing at

the opposition, it is usually a more effective weapon than to attempt to arouse their indignation. Republican presidential candidate Thomas Dewey was badly hurt in 1944 when a photographer snapped a photo of him from the side of a stage, revealing that the undersized Dewey had been standing on two milk cartons in an effort to reach the top of the rostrum.

This should always be part of your strategy: to attack with a quip instead of a brick. In one of the 1960 campaign debates, John Kennedy rose to reply to a Nixon attack. Instead of saying solemnly, "Mr. Nixon has distorted my position," he said calmly, "I always have difficulty recognizing my positions when they're described by Mr. Nixon." It is a small, but crucial, difference, suggesting composure and good nature as opposed to a thin skin. Spiro Agnew showed a similar gift for an occasional joke, when he listed a series of coming events, including the prediction that "[consumer advocate] Ralph Nader will issue a study proving that the human foot is unsafe to walk on"—a much better way of attacking the public-interest mentality than railing on about "interference with the free-enterprise system." This kind of attack is appealing because, except during genuinely grim times such as a polarized nation, domestic discord, or incipient war, the electorate enjoys listening to a politician who seems to be enjoying himself. If that enjoyment can be conveyed with a dig at the opposition, so much the better.

The other advantage of using humor against your enemy is that it increases the chance that he will blow up. In general, people can take criticism of the harshest kind, but when someone begins to mock their pretensions, thin-skinned people can get very rattled. Your fondest hope in any public appearance by your opponent is to persuade him to lose his temper. It is almost certain to hurt him badly. In 1973, when Abe Beame was running for Mayor of New York in the Democratic primary runoff against Herman Badillo, he deliberately provoked Badillo in the first moments of a debate with a charge about ethnic divisiveness. Badillo then called

Beame "a malicious little man," and all of New York was
treated to the sight of a tall Puerto Rican verbally abusing a
short, elderly Jew. There was really no need to count the
ballots after that happened. While this case did not involve a
humorous exchange, it usually happens that thin-skinned
politicians are more provoked by being laughed at than by
being attacked. It was, after all, a sarcastic account of the
comments and behavior of Senator Edmund Muskie's wife
in the *Manchester Union-Leader* that provoked Muskie into
his emotional—fatally emotional—response shortly before
the 1972 New Hampshire primary.

WHEN YOUR OPPONENT COMES UNDER ATTACK FROM AN
INDEPENDENT SOURCE, STAY OUT OF THE WAY. Earlier
I offered you Napoleon's sage advice never to interfere with
the enemy when he is in the process of destroying himself.
Remember this when your adversary is on the receiving end
of criticism from an interest group, a newspaper, or broadcast investigation. You will be tempted to jump in with both
feet, to make sure that the attacks get the widest possible
circulation. Don't do it; at least, not explicitly. If Dithers'
tax returns did not get filed, if his business interests collapse,
if a disaffected ally quits his campaign, do not try to help the
information reach a wider audience. That will only raise suspicions that the whole charge is political or, in the great
eternal phrase of besieged candidates, "a desperate last-
minute attempt to smear this campaign and divert attention
from the real issues."

If the press asks you to comment, you must curb your
justifiable sense of delight. You will be considered a spoil-
sport if you say, "I guess Dithers really's got his butt in a
sling this time," or words to that effect. Nor should you
burst into a huge grin when asked to comment on Dithers'
difficulties. Instead, move the issue aside: "I expect Mr.
Dithers to answer these allegations, and frankly, I don't
think the issue in this campaign is really Mr. Dithers' difficulty. I think the people have to decide who is speaking to

the issues, whose record speaks to these issues, and I just don't have anything else to say about these questions."

You must not approach the task of attacking your rival with any sense of guilt. Politics is about choosing, not about absolutes. It is as important to keep the wrong people out of office as it is to put the good ones in; maybe more so. Good leaders do not always accomplish their hopes, but bad ones seem unaccountably able to start wars, repress liberties, and corrupt the political process. Nor is it your job to fight your campaign with fine impartiality. That is the job of the press and the public. Remember that your opponent will be as eager to damage you as you are to damage him. And remember, too, that "mudslinging" is often an elitist code word for a vigorous campaign.

As long as you say what you believe to be true, as long as you attack those elements of your opponent's record and public performance which can arguably make a difference to the body politic, you are joining a great tradition of free-wheeling public debate. And you may also be doing your share to keep the voters awake in the last weeks of a campaign.

CHAPTER XII

HOW TO GET REELECTED

Once you have won your campaign, three questions will immediately come into your mind:

- How do I get some rest?
- What am I supposed to do?
- How do I get reelected?

The last question was once a matter of relatively little worry. Incumbents got reelected with such regularity that the late Congressman Michael Kirwan, one of the canniest political minds in the House of Representatives, wrote in 1964 that "no Congressman who gets elected and who minds his business should ever be beaten. Everything is there for him to use if he'll only keep his nose to the grindstone and use what is offered." The only examples of defeated incumbents all through the first two-thirds of this century were Presidents afflicted either with an irreconcilable intraparty

split (Taft in 1912) or with a nationwide economic depression
(Hoover in 1932). It was generally assumed that the power
of incumbency to put people into political debt, to build alliances with institutions of wealth and power, to dominate
the news with decisions made and policies shaped, gave
those in office a commanding advantage in retaining that
office.

This picture has radically changed. It is now possible to
argue seriously that incumbency has no necessary advantage
in a contest for most offices. Of our recent Presidents, Lyndon Johnson abandoned his effort at reelection in 1968 while
facing a serious possibility of defeat in the Democratic nomination battle; Richard Nixon's landslide 1972 victory was
erased by his forced resignation, due in great measure to the
cover-up launched in 1972 to avoid political damage from the
Watergate break-in; Gerald Ford lost the White House in
1976; and Jimmy Carter's entire term of office has been
plagued by such weakness and unpopularity that he is hardly
an incumbent at all.

Our Senators have faced growing vulnerability, with 33
percent of them losing their reelection efforts since 1974.
Interestingly, it has been members of the House of Representatives who have had the most success in retaining their
jobs, with 96 percent of them keeping their jobs since 1974.

Why has this happened? There are a lot of reasons, which
are all interconnected. The steady decline of party loyalty
over the last twenty-five years has eroded the sense of fealty
between voters and an elected official of their own party. No
longer is there any sense that when a Democrat has won a
Senate seat, Democratic voters feel that "their side" has
won, and that "their party's seat" must be protected.
Today, incumbents are as likely to be attacked by members
of their own party as by the political opposition; three of the
last four incumbent Presidents have been so challenged, an
event considered almost unthinkable a generation ago. Television has made it possible for an outsider to gain recognition
quickly, to "create" himself as an equal to an incumbent

through paid advertising and through appearances on debates.

There is, too, another consequence of the Television Age of politics that has made life as an incumbent more difficult. Television, as every performer and executive knows, "wears out" personalities. It is possible within the space of a few years to go from unknown, to promising newcomer, to hot performer, to superstar, to hanger-on, to has-been. The accelerated transmission of information through television can do something of the same thing to a politician. Looking back to 1976, we saw the unknown, who-he? Jimmy Carter suddenly emerge in March as the fresh face, the *Rocky* candidate, the million-to-one shot making good. Then, with the precipitous entrance of Governor Jerry Brown into the race, Brown took Carter's place as the fresh face, almost as if Carter had taken on the burden of an old-hat incumbent in the space of a few weeks. Thus, the same instrument which has made it possible to loosen the bonds of party loyalty has made it easier to establish an individual personal attraction with voters, while making it more difficult to sustain.

Finally, and perhaps most important, the nature of government has changed drastically in the last few decades. The huge expansion of programs, and the growth of government administration—the much-battered "bureaucracy"—has lessened the capacity of politicians to demonstrate dramatic, effective power over that government. A President might once have mobilized an agency to deliver some service directly to an affected state or community. Now, with the exception of floods and other disasters, that help will be administered through a slow-moving, stratified government agency. Senators and Congressmen increasingly find their offices becoming case-work centers, with aggrieved citizens asking their elected officials to find out what happened to a lost Social Security check, or a promised low-interest loan that was applied for two years earlier. The politician writes a blistering letter to the agency, gets back an abject letter expressing regret and concern, sends copies of both to the

constituent, and the price of Xerox stock takes a step upward. This does not make an elected official appear as Lo-
chinvar to the dragon named Bureaucracy in the eyes of
voters. It makes it much easier for an opponent to make a
case against an incumbent, since the steady erosion of trust
and confidence in government can be translated into distrust
of a particular incumbent. (One reason Congressmen have
not suffered as incumbents is that they are seen more as
special pleaders for their districts than as movers and shakers of the entire government. As long as the mail gets answered and the fences back home are mended, they are
somehow considered less responsible for the general confu-
sion of government.)

Because government has grown more difficult to control,
incumbents tend to be more concerned with what they appear to be doing than with what they are doing. Shortly after
Jimmy Carter's inauguration, his pollster Pat Caddell sent
him a memorandum warning him that he had to be as conscious of style as of substance, since substantive achievements
go unappreciated by the electorate if not accompanied by
symbols of concern and achievement. Perhaps coinciden-
tally, Carter launched an administration with more effort at
symbolism than in all the works of Baudelaire. Telephone
call-ins, town-hall meetings, Fireside Chats with cardigan
sweaters, blue jeans at picnics, all designed to prove that this
President was not isolated from the people, all designed to
demonstrate symbolic fidelity to the idea of the "Just Plain
Folks" anti-Imperial Presidency. The result was four years
of an administration which inspired less confidence among
citizens than any in the history of polltaking, including the
Nixon White House in the later months of the Watergate fire
storm.

It is, I suppose, useless to advise that one of the most
important elements in winning reelection is to *concentrate
on your job*. People in public life have been so conditioned
to think about the appearance of what they are doing that the
idea of just doing it must sound hopelessly muddled. If you

think about other things in your life, you will see the value
of this advice. Imagine an activity such as tennis, or dancing,
or sex. Now imagine yourself constantly thinking about how
you appear as you engage in these acts. Do you think your
performance might be affected by such self-consciousness?
Although the analogy has a touch of imprecision about it, it
does suggest the problem with an incumbent whose thoughts
are dominated by how he appears, rather than by what he is
doing. Obviously, you or your staff will be judging your policies, your programs, your schedule, by its political impact.
This is one of the jobs they are supposed to be performing. I
only offer here the idea that a certain focused concentration
on the job you were elected to do may prove helpful in your
struggle to keep your job.

At the same time, you must not be moved in the least by
criticism that you are using your office for political gain.
Every two years, reporters and civic groups discover that
people holding office are using the power of that office to
help them retain that office. This is roughly as shocking as
discovering that prostitutes can be found in the streets of our
cities, or that many professional athletes smoke cigarettes
and drink beverages containing alcohol. It has always been
done, it always will be done, and officeholders who do not
use their power to try and keep it are probably too stupid to
be trusted with the reins of power.

When President Lincoln visited Civil War battlefields in
1864, he was not indifferent to the number of servicemen
who would be voting in the coming election. When Calvin
Coolidge, a President of underwhelming energy, skipped his
summer vacation in 1924, he was probably mindful of the
need for this unelected President to appear burdened with
the heavy responsibilities of high office. When Franklin Roosevelt in 1936 heard of possible cuts in the WPA program, he
informed Treasury Secretary Henry Morgenthau, "I don't
give a goddamn where [you] get the money from, but not one
person is to be laid off on the first of October." It is likely
that President Roosevelt was aware of the proximity of Oc-

tober first to the first Tuesday after the first Monday in November. That was also a subject on his mind when he toured
defense plants in 1940, and when he embarked on a visit to
Pacific military installations in 1944. When Lyndon Johnson
called civil rights leaders to the White House in 1964, and
when they agreed, in the public interest, to call for a mora-
torium on demonstrations through Election Day, the danger
to Johnson's reelection of violent racial clashes was not far
from the minds of anyone at that meeting. Richard Nixon
was acutely conscious of the power of "peace" as a campaign issue, and the trips to Peking and Moscow in 1972
were not planned with complete indifference to the political
benefits.

What are the guides to the best use of your office as you
struggle to remain on the public payroll, in the public eye, in
a position of relative power over the lives of your fellow
citizens? Even in the Television Age, even given the lack of
party loyalty and the mob of bright, affluent young men and
women looking to replace you in office, there are ways to
help yourself by helping yourself to the perquisites of office.

**Build a network of interest groups whose members feel a di-
rect, specific debt to you.** The longtime leader of Chicago's
Democratic machine, Jacob Arvey, once said that "politics
is the art of putting people under obligation to you." The
formal nature of government benefits today has long since
made the political machine with its Christmas food baskets
and coal buckets obsolete; today it is the government computer, not the ward leader's assistant, who delivers the food
stamp, the Social Security check, the school loan. But the
delivery of government benefits, through legislation or a
change in federal or state regulations, is a venerable, thoroughly reliable way of securing support by putting an entire
group of people under debt to you. Harry McPherson, who
spent a lengthy career in Washington, and who served as a
top assistant to President Johnson, remembers his first trip
to Washington in 1950, where he met an old, Library of

Congress guard, with strong blue-collar identification, who was expressing his fondness for a Senator of extreme reactionary views. Why? Because this same Senator was sponsoring a bill for retirement rights for federal employees with thirty-five years of service.

Is this the kind of service that only impresses the less-refined, less-educated segment of our population? In September 1979 the National Education Association, the largest educational lobby-labor union in the United States, announced its enthusiastic support for Jimmy Carter in the 1980 campaign. What Carter had done was to shepherd successfully through Congress the establishment of a new Cabinet office, the Department of Education, which will presumably give the educational lobby the same special status as the defense industry has with the Department of Defense. It is almost certainly a step toward further waste in government, further growth in the federal bureaucracy, and apart from continuing the construction boom in Washington with yet another Cabinet headquarters to build, it is difficult to see any benefit from it. But by winning the fight for this new department, Carter was able to put the education establishment in his debt, and win its support for his campaign. (As McPherson said in commenting on the habits of the "higher-minded" academics, "For many distinguished scholars, the country's chief problems had to do with insufficient federal money for research in their fields, or unnecessary requirements for fellowship grants.")

It is important to distinguish between a general sense of obligation that an interest group may feel and a specific obligation. The former is all too easily voided. In 1978, Iowa's liberal Democratic Senator Dick Clark was in deep trouble in his reelection fight against conservative Republican Robert Jepson. One of the unions that had supported him in the past was the Machinists' Union, whose president, William Wimpisinger, was an ardent foe of oil deregulation. When Clark announced his support for price deregulation, Wimpisinger cut Clark's campaign off from all funds.

In contrast, California Governor Jerry Brown, who had alienated many traditional Democrats by supporting balanced budgets and fiscal restraint, had been a staunch supporter of Cesar Chavez's United Farm Workers Union in their efforts to organize in California's farm communities. He had sponsored legislation to make it much easier to organize in farmlands, and had marched with Chavez as well. Not only did Chavez's union support Brown for reelection in 1978, they supported him for President in 1976 and indicated potential support for him again in 1980. This kind of bond is far more permanent than vague support along a legislative laundry list. One government installation brought into your area is worth two hundred splendid speeches on the future of the Western alliance, and one amendment to the Internal Revenue Code to protect an important industry is better than a 98 percent voting record on the scorecard of an interest group. People do not pay off mortgages and send their children to college with voting records.

If there are people or institutions important to your voters, make sure you are identified with them. One of the best things about holding office is that you are entitled to be present at ceremonial functions of great importance to the public. For reasons that do not significantly add to the case for popular democracy, voters seem to believe that a photograph or moving picture of a politician in the presence of an admirable or powerful figure indicates that the politician is also admirable or powerful. Apparently, the voter believes that since you are standing next to the Prime Minister of Great Britain, you are somehow on a par with the Prime Minister of Great Britain, or else you would not have been able to have your picture taken with her. (This is one reason why nonincumbents go to such great lengths to have their pictures taken with people in office. It gives the impression of being admitted into the councils of power and influence. Hubert Humphrey argued during his 1960 campaign for President that an eight-hour marathon meeting with Soviet Premier Nikita

Khrushchev had given him a special insight into foreign policy.)

As an incumbent, you have the chance to cash in on these opportunities. I watched firsthand as an unpopular incumbent, John Lindsay of New York, pulled this off twice in 1969. During that campaign, Israeli Prime Minister Golda Meir came to visit the United States. While she was in New York, Lindsay followed her like a shadow. It was a time when many Jews felt that Lindsay had opposed their interests by aligning himself with some black leaders during a bitter school strike in which the heavily Jewish teachers' union fought black school activists. There was no question but that Golda Meir's acceptance of, and affection for, Mayor Lindsay helped defuse the anger of New York Jews toward their Mayor.

A more blatant example happened that same year, when the New York Mets, after years in the depths of last place, suddenly emerged as a contender for their divisional title. The city, which had been through so much unhappiness during the late 1960s, responded with the kind of enthusiasm more appropriate to a small town than a blasé big city. Now it must be said that John Lindsay was not a wildly enthusiastic baseball fan. Indeed, it might be said that his first response on hearing of the success of the New York Mets was that the opera had sold out its season. (Lindsay's connection with popular spectator sports can be suggested by the following story, which may or may not be apocryphal: In 1970, after the New York Knicks had won their first National Basketball Association championship, a reception at the Mayor's residence, Gracie Mansion, was held. An aide supposedly advised him to say farewell to three second-string Knicks who had been taken by other teams in the expansion draft. Lindsay asked the audience to pay tribute to these three young men, who would soon enter the military service.)

Nonetheless, Lindsay understood full well that the pennant and World Series would be watched by millions of New Yorkers. He attended the home games, he recited a poem of praise for the Mets, and when the Mets beat Atlanta to win the National League pennant, Lindsay appeared in the clubhouse, where he laughingly let bottles of champagne be poured over his head. Every drop was worth five hundred votes, and the ticker-tape parade and City Hall reception were worth thousands more. There was nothing immoral or unethical about this participation in a happy event. The Mayor, after all, is blamed for everything from late mail deliveries to stock market jitters; he has the right to share in a city's better moments. But it is undeniable that an incumbent has a very special opportunity to do himself a great deal of good from space shots, heroic deeds, and the visits of greatly admired visitors.

Answer your mail, answer your mail, answer your mail.   Typical citizens do not have, in Jimmy Carter's memorably foolish phrase, "a close, intimate, personal relationship" with those they elect. They are likely to skip the personal appearances and town meetings of officials, and should a President come to town, the odds against any one person being able to speak with him are great. Citizens reach out to an official when they are troubled about an issue, or when they need help. As a general rule, they write to that official.

The most important people in a politician's office are the people responding to these calls for help. If you do not answer your mail, if you do not stay in close touch with your constituents, particularly if you have been elected to a legislative job, you will be in serious trouble. No matter how impressed the reporters in the press gallery are with your speeches, no matter how skilled you may be at parliamentary infighting, the people back home will quickly conclude that you have been seduced by the bright lights and fast life of Washington or Sacramento or Helena. And once the word is out that you have lost touch with the people who put their trust in you, your chances for reelection are greatly diminished.

William Fulbright was a world figure, a scholarly, thoughtful chairman of the Senate Foreign Relations Committee. But when popular Arkansas Governor Dale Bumpers ran against Fulbright for the Senate, he defeated Fulbright in a landslide. Fulbright had lost touch. An efficient mail room is one elementary way to protect yourself against this failure.

This means more than sending computerized letters with automatically penned signatures back to your correspondents. It means setting up a sophisticated enough operation to recognize who is writing you. Here is one example of what can go wrong: In 1967, after Senator Robert Kennedy had given a major speech on Vietnam, Arthur Schlesinger, Jr., a longtime associate of the Kennedys, wrote Kennedy a note amplifying on some related ideas. Someone in the mail room, not recognizing the name, dispatched a precoded letter to Schlesinger, thanking him for his views, and enclosing a copy of an article and a speech on Vietnam—both of which Schlesinger had advised Kennedy on! That relationship was close enough for all parties to laugh the mistake off. But if an important business executive, or a key labor union supporter, is treated this way, it means trouble.

Use your power to raise a lot of money. While presidential campaigns are financed through public funds, and while matching funds and restrictive laws have changed the rules at this level, Senatorial, Congressional, and gubernatorial campaigns still heavily favor the candidate with the most money. Incumbency is a powerful magnet for money, because people with money usually want the good opinion of those who write the laws that affect taxes, zoning, business regulation, and other matters of more than passing interest. In addition, incumbents—particularly executives—have a great deal to say about government policies concerning huge development of commercial properties, transportation networks, interest rates, and matters which can directly affect the financial health of the affluent. These people do not like the idea of public officials making policies without entertaining kind thoughts about stable community influences. In order to prevent this condition, they are well disposed toward the purchase of tables at fund-raising dinners, the placing of advertisements in journals prepared to commemorate those dinners, and the contributing of funds to help the reelection of legislators and executives. (As a rule, the concern of the well heeled for the incumbent increases in direct proportion to the incumbent's power. Thus, the chairman of a congressional Maritime Affairs Subcommittee will find himself regarded with special favor by shipbuilders; the Post Office Committee senior members may find themselves invited to speak—for a generous honorarium—at a dinner sponsored by direct-mail users.)

It is not necessary to sell your soul to the devil in order to raise the funds you need to mount a vigorous fight for reelection. One of the remarkable facts about our political life is that a great deal of money exists across the ideological spectrum. If you are not enamored of giant corporations, the AFL-CIO's unions—through political action committees—can offer you great sums of money. If you have alienated public universities, then private college supporters may claim you as a champion. If you have a strong feeling that the copyright laws of the United States need strengthening against bootleggers, then music-industry officials and rock-and-roll performers may decide to throw hugely successful fund-raising concerts on your behalf.

There are enough causes to go around. It takes an incumbent of rare quality to alienate *all* of the different, and often competing, movements and interests in this country. No matter what views you come to hold, out of the most independent origin, you are likely to find some group which regards those views as the salvation of the Republic, and is willing to reward you for holding them. Even if you are famous for independence, you have a good chance of finding financial support from groups which fear that very independence, and hope to purchase a sense of goodwill.

There *are* cases of incumbents who are outspent by their rivals. In one campaign I worked in, John Tunney's 1976

reelection bid, his support for a farm workers' initiative lost
him the financial support of moderate and conservative Democrats with agricultural interests, while his opponent, S. I.
Hayakawa, raised money with the enthusiastic help of Ronald Reagan and his wealthy California supporters. In other
cases, incumbents make a political point *not* to spend a good
deal of money. Wisconsin's William Proxmire is a case in
point, relying on his campaign frugality to prove his frugality
with the taxpayers' money (on the other hand, Proxmire has
gained incalculable publicity by using his Senate staff and
position to give out his "Golden Fleece" awards detailing
examples—highly questionable, I might add—of "outrageous" government spending). But as a general rule, if you
cannot figure out how to use the leverage of your office to
raise the funds for your next campaign, you are not to be
trusted with any power at all.

Find a symbol of the status quo, and oppose it.   In 1948,
Harry Truman seemed certain to be the first incumbent President of his party to be turned out of office since Grover
Cleveland sixty years before. He had been ridiculed ever
since the death of Roosevelt put him in office. "To err is
Truman," became a national joke. And when he began his
campaign by attacking the "do-nothing Eightieth Congress,"
the press—Republican, to be sure—assured America's readers that it would be ineffective as a campaign issue. After all,
the Congress had passed significant legislation, such as the
Taft-Hartley Act. It might have been controversial, but it
was hardly a "do-nothing" Congress.

But it worked. And in an age when distrust of every institution, including government at every level and in every
branch, stands at record high levels, an incumbent must be
disassociated from things as usual to win reelection.
Whoever "they" are who are running government into the
ground, raising taxes, and wasting our money, you do not
want to be "they." You must find a target, you must do
more than prove you have governed well, you must find
someone, something to run *against*.

Fortunately, there is never any shortage of targets. It can be an opponent who has won a bitterly contested battle in the other party, and who has so divided that party that your target is extremism. Apart from the Goldwater and Mc-Govern campaigns, there are many examples on state and local levels: Mario Procaccino's capture of the New York Democratic mayoral nomination in 1969; conservative Democrat Robert Short's defeat of liberal Don Fraser in the primary in Minnesota in 1978; H. L. Richardson's run in 1974 against California's Alan Cranston. In all such cases, the incumbents could say sadly that there was no real campaign; that this time, reasonable people of both parties had no real choice. It can be an issue, such as the war in Vietnam, which John Lindsay elevated into an issue in that 1969 Mayor's race, helping keep in his corner liberals who might otherwise have stayed home. It can be a kind of "anti-incumbent" incumbency, as in 1972, when Richard Nixon positioned himself, as his adman put it later, "on the side of change," a battler against the federal bureaucracy which he did not control, despite his office.

By far the most audacious example of an incumbent running against a target was the campaign of New York Mayor Robert Wagner in 1961. Eight years earlier, he had been elected with the full support of New York's Democratic county leaders, including Tammany Hall's Carmine de Sapio. Then, in a sudden break with these leaders, Wagner announced his candidacy for a third term with a blistering attack on the "bosses," and instantly assumed command of the growing band of Democratic "reformers," who had organized in large measure against the administration he had run. The county leaders put up a candidate of their own, and Wagner soundly defeated him by making the record of his own first two terms the target. Wagner, in other words, ran against himself—and won.

This example should not be taken as literal instruction; running against yourself is a tactic of limited applicability. What it shows, rather, is the breadth of opportunity an offensive incumbent campaign offers. For example, if you have taken a hard line against utility rate increases, you can make the electric company and the telephone company your target. "Smithers has fought the big-shot gougers for four years —give him a chance to keep fighting for you." If you're a conservative with a record of fighting increased government regulation, cash in on that: "When Smithers gets mad, a thousand bureaucrats duck for cover."

If you are a legislator, one of the best ways to find a target is to head an investigation, preferably of some wrongdoing that it is impossible to defend. One thinks of Congressman Fiorello La Guardia investigating munitions manufacturers, Senator Harry Truman going after war profiteers in the early 1940s, Senator Estes Kefauver mounting a national reputation on the heels of his organized crime investigation, Senator John Kennedy going after labor racketeers in the 1950s, Senator Howard Baker looking prudent, thoughtful, and determined at the Watergate hearings in 1973 asking, "What did the President know and when did he know it?" Running an investigation proves that you are not simply up there in the capital eating steaks and planning junkets; it proves that you have discovered someone doing something wrong, and that you are determined to expose this wrongdoing, and to root it out, even if you have to do it on national television with an audience in the millions.

If you are an executive, your choice of targets must, of necessity, be different. If you are a President, you could attempt to provoke a crisis with an unappetizing but unthreatening foreign nation (Uganda under Idi Amin comes to mind) but this can produce unacceptable costs, such as the lives of any Americans who happen to be in Uganda, and our recent experience in combat against small nations is not encouraging. Congress is always a tempting opponent, since the Truman example worked, and since Congress generally makes the life of any President difficult. But even though Congress as an institution generally ranks lower than any other branch of government in public-opinion polls, its usefulness as a target is questionable—especially if the Congress and the President happen to be of the same party, and especially when a President made cooperation with Congress a key plank in his original campaign for reelection. It is probably best to find a domestic foe with the same characteristic as the foreign governments—unpleasant, but powerless. (All through his first term, President Nixon's advance men would let just enough long-haired, unkempt demonstrators into an arena so that they would be visible, as a symbol of those Nixon was fighting.)

Whoever your target, make sure that your campaign theme stresses the combative aspect of your service. You are not in an office passing or signing laws, meeting with important people, and hobnobbing with the elite. You are battling the enemies of whatever the people who voted for you are for. It was one of the great political strengths of the generations of Southern segregationist Congressmen and Senators who came to Washington that they were fighting the powers that be, struggling to preserve the Southern way of life. Every time a Northern politician or newspaper or magazine attacked them, they gained more strength from it, and their constituents never asked hard questions about what these legislators were really doing for them.

Use every conceivable tool of your office.   In his 1974 campaign, according to a *Wall Street Journal* story a year later, New York Senator Jacob Javits hired a direct-mail expert to prepare a "master plan" using 700,000 pieces of franked mail—mail sent out under a Senator's signature, rather than a stamp—with "public service messages" designed to be sent to places "where the Senator isn't strong politically." This is an egregious example of the use of incumbency, but only in degree, not in kind. The tools of office, almost half a million dollars' worth in the case of a Congressman or Senator, have not been put there by accident. They have been put there by experienced legislators who know how important stable, experienced legislators are. They have given you money for trips home. Go home, as often as you can, to meet with your constituents. They have given you telephones. Use them. Make it a point to call your political allies, and on occasion your political rivals. They have given you money for district offices. Staff them. Learn the lessons of the past. The politicians who retained popularity have been accessible to their people. New York Congressman Vito Marcantonio's constituents loved him throughout the 1940s not because he was a political radical and a Soviet apologist, but because he came home every week and sat in his storefront office for as long as it took to listen to the complaints of his people. You do not wish this for yourself? Fine. But hire someone who will meet with these people in a room with a big picture of you on the wall.

If you're a Governor, use the state planes. Let a newspaper reporter complain. Nobody cares. If you do not know how to defend yourself against such a charge—if you can't immediately fix your inquisitor with a cold glance and ask why he opposes your efforts to meet with the people of a state—you are too far gone to save in any event. For 150 years, no one has been able to figure out where government ends and where politics begins. That isn't your job. If you are sensitive, explain to the press that all the people on your staff are working full-time on state business, and using vacation time, weekends, and evenings to help out on your campaign.

Don't reorganize the government. In many ways, this is the most important piece of advice available—from me or anyone else—to an incumbent executive. It is important principally because the cry of "reorganize the government!" is always among the most fervent of all candidates for high office, it is always an obsession with these candidates once they win that office, and it is always such an astonishing waste of time that it prevents an incumbent from accumulating anything like an impressive record.

Any self-employed individual—especially a writer—can tell any President that reorganization is a fraud. Whenever writers have spent hours staring at a blank piece of paper, when deadlines are approaching and editors are jangling the phones, the first thing those writers do is to leap from their chairs, clean up their desks, sort out their files, sharpen their pencils, and set their libraries in alphabetical order. In government, reorganization performs exactly the same function. When you are meeting with your Cabinet officers on which agency gets which department for a new office, you aren't setting policy, you aren't cutting the budget, you aren't getting your legislative program through the Congress, and you aren't making life one whit better for the people who voted for you.

What has been the major policy achievement of the Carter Administration with respect to energy? It has created a new Department of Energy with a budget of some $11 billion, more than the combined profits of the six major oil companies. It has also spent so much time moving furniture back and forth that energy policy has become nonexistent. One report told of regulations stalled for months because the office responsible for issuing them has been busy moving *nineteen* times, often back and forth among the same three buildings. Now we have the government's major contribution to education: a new Department of Education, which will probably produce odd-even textbook rationing by 1985.

If you want to be a successful incumbent, make a careful note of the first aide who talks to you about government reorganization and dispatch him on a permanent mission to Guam. Take the government exactly as it is, because reorganization will help neither you, nor the country; and by leaving the structure alone, it will force your top aides to concentrate on policy instead of form. That just might help you build a record on which you can successfully make a case for your reelection.

CHAPTER XIII

THE SECRET OF WINNING CAMPAIGNS—POLITICAL JUJITSU

There is no single secret to winning campaigns. As I said at the outset, the brilliant stroke of one year is the fatal blunder of the next. The rhetoric of an optimistic age rings hollow in an age of broken promises and lowered expectations. But I do believe there *is* one approach to campaigning that can serve as an infallible model. I do not mean that it will guarantee you an electoral victory, because some campaigns cannot be won and others hinge on fate. But I do believe that this approach will make you the strongest possible candidate you can be, and it will shift every marginal battle within that campaign to your advantage. It works in large measure because it runs exactly against the most fundamental instincts that grip candidates and campaign workers alike. I have seen it work in circumstances where all seemed lost, and I have seen an opponent use it to neutralize one of our most prized issues.

I call this approach *political jujitsu.*

It is so named because, like its martial arts equivalent, it uses the strength and power of an adversary to turn an attack into a strategic advantage for your own campaign. It recognizes the inherent futility of the conventional political posture of resistance and defensiveness. It takes all of the usual approaches to political conflict and stands them upside down.

You have already seen political jujitsu in action; you have seen it, in historical example and in strategic suggestions, throughout this book. Now I've given it a name. It is what knits together many of the disparate suggestions I have made, suggestions which come not from any wondrous insights that I have created, but from experience in winning, and losing, campaigns, and from the lessons of our political past.

When S. I. Hayakawa told a questioner "I don't give a goddamn about dog racing," that was political jujitsu in action. Instead of bluffing an answer about something he knew nothing about, Hayakawa took the aggressive question and attacked it as unworthy. The effect was very much like running full tilt toward a closed door in an attempt to knock it down, only to have it flung open at the point of impact. It is the lack of resistance that sends the attacker completely off balance.

When a debater answers a complicated question with a simple yes or no, that, too, is a kind of political jujitsu, as is the invitation to an opponent to engage in a dialogue during a debate. Usually when candidates meet face-to-face, they feel sufficiently threatened by their opponent to build a barrier separating one from the other. The very invitation to respond, the breaking of the rhythm of formal replies, is what can put an opponent off his rhythm.

Perhaps the most compelling use of political jujitsu is to advertise, highlight, emphasize, and otherwise stress the

very element of your campaign that your opponent is counting on to be your biggest weakness. The first Reagan campaign in 1966 was a perfect example of the approach. Except
for his years of after-dinner speeches for General Electric,
and his nationally televised address for Goldwater in 1964,
Reagan was an amateur; he had held no office other than an
executive position in the Screen Actors' Guild, and was
known as an actor. Both his primary opponent, San Francisco Mayor George Christopher, and incumbent Governor
Pat Brown, were sure this would be a fatal drawback;
Brown, in fact, celebrated Reagan's primary victory, assuming he would be easier to beat.

Reagan's campaign consulting firm, Spencer-Roberts,
knew full well that experience would be the key issue against
Reagan. And as adviser William Roberts explained the plan:
"Our answer was to be very candid and honest about it, and
indicate that Governor Reagan was not a professional politician. He was a citizen-politician. Therefore, we had an automatic defense. He didn't have to know all the answers.
. . . A citizen-politician is not expected to know all of the
answers to all of the issues. As a matter of fact, before the
end of the campaign, he hit it so well and so hard that Governor Brown was on the defensive for being a professional
politician."

Jimmy Carter did exactly the same thing in 1976. In another year, he would have been assailed as an amateur, out
of his league in attempting to compete with "the big boys"
for the Presidential nomination; Democratic elder statesman
Averell Harriman's revealing observation—"he can't be
nominated; I don't know him, and I don't know anyone who
does"—would have been accurate as well as arrogant. But
Carter, reading the political winds shrewdly, made his in-
experience the centerpiece of his campaign, with his "I'm
not a lawyer, I'm not from Washington, I haven't served in
the Congress" litany.

And in 1980, reacting to the sense that Jimmy Carter's
Presidency was an Administration of amateurs, John Con-

nally proudly boasted to audiences that he was indeed a "wheeler-dealer." A conventional politician might have resisted this characterization, especially since it was aimed at a wealthy Texan with warm feelings toward corporate giants, multinational corporations, environmental permissiveness, and who had been indicted and tried (albeit acquitted) on charges of high-level bribery.

But Connally recognized, as Carter and Reagan did before, this central principle of political jujitsu: *the very openness with which one faces and discusses a weakness acts as powerful evidence that there is in fact no weakness at all.* In a political campaign, the ventilation of a charge by the accused is frequently, in and of itself, an effective rebuttal of that charge. As you move through the campaign life, you should picture your electorate as a nervous audience, listening to a speaker whose reputation has been thrown into question by a scandalous charge. The speaker stands up, and promptly makes a joke about that charge. Invariably, the audience breathes a sigh of relief; the tension has been eased by the speaker's recognition of the unspoken issue. Is Reaagan *really* an ignorant amateur? Is Carter *really* the white sheep of the Snopes family? Is Connally *really* the candidate of corrupt oil barons? The open discussion seems to disprove the charge, on the theory that politicians are so given to evasion that they would not possibly talk openly about something that bothered them.

This was also the underpinning of John Lindsay's I-made-mistakes commercial in 1969. Even though he "admitted" nothing worse than shared responsibility for the school strike, and for guessing wrong about the winter weather, it was the sense of Lindsay admitting a mistake—something no politician likes to do, much less a mayor with a reputation for arrogance—that softened the hostility to him (which is why this commercial was nicknamed the "Lindsay eats shit" ad). The ad took the skeptical viewer with it on the way to making the point that the Mayor had "the second toughest job in America." Instead of saying, in effect, "You're wrong about what you think,'' Lindsay said to the voter, ''You're *right* that I've screwed some things up, and here's why.''

A commercial created for Tom Bradley in his 1973 Mayor's race in Los Angeles offers an even more unusual example of jujitsu. As I've discussed, the Bradley campaign faced the clear fact that racial prejudice was underlying many of the doubts of Los Angeles voters. They knew that Mayor Sam Yorty had become a national joke; they knew that Bradley was a moderate, rather than an agitator. But he had lost in 1969, in the midst of campus and street turmoil, because many voters believed he would somehow be sympathetic to extremists of his own race. The slogan, which emphasized hard work, was designed to answer part of the racial stereotype. But midway through the campaign, Bradley went on the air with a commercial aimed squarely at the race issue.

''The last time I ran for Mayor, I lost,'' Bradley said, ''probably because a lot of people weren't sure what I stood for. Maybe you were one of them. Maybe you wondered whether I'd treat all the people fairly, or whether I'd only listen to the problems of the blacks. Frankly, I couldn't win this election with one bloc of voters.''

The whole attempt of this statement was to dissipate the unspoken issue in the campaign, the issue that had cost Bradley the race in 1969, when he had campaigned as a mainstream Democrat, with no reference at all to the fact that he was black. Having raised the issue of color, and—more fundamentally—having raised, and then disposed of, the fear of bloc voting and government by racial favoritism, Bradley had cleared the air of a hidden issue. Could it really be a danger if Bradley was addressing it so clearly?

Political jujitsu works because of the nature of most political disputes, and most political rhetoric. The unacknowledged premise lurks behind the average statement by public figures; the hidden agenda is as prevalent as the press release. Suppose there is a fight over a public policy, such as the presence of police officers in a big-city transit system, or the staffing of the public schools. Do you ever hear the leader of the police or the teachers' union acknowledge that one of the reasons for their concern is that they want their members working—and paying dues to the union? Do you ever hear a municipal official make a gesture toward the fact that these facilities are used mostly by the poor, and the less powerful, and that these people can inflict less damage on public officials than people with a great deal of money or influence? For that matter, do you expect a government official to speak in English, or in a language vaguely resembling that tongue?

You do not. We have made a kind of calculation when we listen to a politician; we have already discounted for evasions, half-truths, and opaque language when we settle down to listen to a politician. When we hear a candidate for office speak in clear English, when we listen to an office seeker acknowledge *our* doubts, *our* uncertainties, when we listen to the language of a "private face in a public place," the effect is startling. What might be regarded as a reasonable observation by a friend or colleague becomes a revelation coming from a supposed practitioner of sophistry.

This element of political jujitsu can be summed up with a single idea: Instead of thinking, It's not so! think, Of course it is. Instead of bracing yourself for a battle, listen to the charge for any element of truth, and embrace it. Enjoy the process of turning an attacker into a victim.

Are you charged with having failed to win the support of the political mainstream? Remember the gleeful response of Fiorello La Guardia. "Isn't it *grand?*" he exulted. "Not a single county leader—of either political party—is endorsing me. Well, as Al Smith used to say, 'I could run on a laundry ticket and beat those political bums.' "

Has someone found out that you violated a provision of the campaign law in a previous campaign? Remember the lesson of Hugh Carey, who told a hard-pressing reporter at his press conference announcing for Governor: "It happened

once. It shouldn't have happened. It will not happen again."
What is the shrewd follow-up question to that answer? It is
like confronting a friend who has wronged you, and being
told as you open your mouth, "I know I hurt you, and I only
hope you can forgive me, because your friendship means too
much to me to lose."

Did you go to jail for taking the Post Office examination
for a political ally? Remember Curley of Boston: Don't deny
it—cite it as proof of your devotion to those who support
you. You can hear the exchange: *Candidate X:* "I charge
Mr. Curley with serving a prison term for falsely taking a
civil service examination!" *Curley:* "Of course I did; what
have *you* done for the people whose votes you want?" *Candidate X:* "Uh . . ."

There is, of course, a limit to this use of the cheerful ac-
knowledgment (I mention it only to meet in advance the
objections of critics who believe they discovered a fatal flaw
in an argument because you have not made clear that your
case is weakened if a meteor strikes the earth). If you have
been living under an assumed identity for fifteen years, and
you are found to be an escaped convict, a willing acknowl-
edgment of this condition will not help. It is also important
to sense what *kinds* of deeds will be supported by your constituency. Adam Clayton Powell, the late Congressman from
Harlem, thrived despite the many stories of his high living
and womanizing. There was a sense that the more Powell
outraged his colleagues, the more his constituents got vicar-
ious enjoyment out of watching Adam stick it to the white
Establishment. But when Powell fled New York for the island of Bimini in the Bahamas to escape a court order, the
love affair waned, and Powell wound up being soundly defeated in a Democratic primary.

In 1979, in the wake of a billion-dollar sewer scandal, Suffolk County (New York) executive John Klein decided to
take a page out of John Lindsay's book, and bear responsibility for the oversight. Perhaps he was thinking, sensibly
enough, of the forgiving nature of the New York electorate,

or the fact that when John Kennedy took full responsibility for the Bay of Pigs disaster, his poll ratings went up. So Klein went public with his apology, and a few months later he lost his fight for renomination by the Republican Party by a 2–1 margin.

When you move from the defensive to the offensive political position, the lessons of political jujitsu can serve you well. The key is to move beyond the normal strategy of attack, and to strike where the opposition least expects it. If this seems obvious, it is something that is rarely practiced in politics. If one candidate is a legislator running for executive, the opponent attacks him for lacking managerial experience. If a candidate is a veteran incumbent, he is attacked for losing touch with the people. If he is from upstate, he is criticized for not being in sympathy with downstate.

The problem is that this is what the public expects. The "discount" factor in political rhetoric applies every bit as much, if not more, to attacks than to other kinds of speech. That is why the lesson of the tactic of pursuing a totally unexpected line of attack, while not always possible, can be very rewarding.

During John Tunney's 1976 battle against Tom Hayden, one of the prevailing questions was when and if Tunney would go after Hayden for the more extreme positions the latter had held in the 1960s—not so much his antiwar opposition, but his flirtation with the idea of armed insurrection in the ghettos, and his romantic attachment to such groups as the National Liberation Front of South Vietnam. As Hayden moved up in the polls, many of Tunney's supporters were urging this course on the campaign, and Hayden's own campaign was constantly warning its supporters and the press to expect a last-minute "McCarthyite" smear.

There were two problems with this tactic. First, it was unappetizing. Even doing nothing but citing Hayden's own statements left a bad taste in our mouths, given the attempts of the Nixon Administration to repress dissent, and given the fact that Hayden in particular had been among the more earnest, less theatrical, proponents of the New Left. Second, it could backfire. With the memory of Nixon and Agnew fresh in everyone's mind, the labeling of a political opponent as a radical, even if an accurate label, would have seemed very much the act of a desperate incumbent—especially in a Democratic primary in a state with a great number of liberals. So while Hayden had been free with his personal attacks (at one point he had called Tunney "a Chappaquiddick waiting to happen") Tunney was unable to hit Hayden where he seemed to be vulnerable.

What the campaign did, instead, was to attack Hayden in the most surprising way possible. Actor Gregory Peck cut a commercial (designed to offset Henry Fonda's commercial for son-in-law Hayden) in which he accused Hayden of using the tactics of McCarthy and Nixon in smearing Tunney, and in distorting his record. "After Watergate," Peck concluded, "haven't we had enough of this kind of politics?" The Hayden campaign, which had been so primed for the "radical" attack that they had cut a radio commercial deploring the onslaught that never came, had no way to respond to this comparison with odious right-wing politicians.

This little-used strategy was actually conceived by the late British satirist Stephen Potter, as part of his classic "Gamesmanship" series. In his advice on taking examinations, Potter suggests going after literary giants by attacking their greatest strengths—thus, accusing D. H. Lawrence of a certain squeamishness in matters of sex, or attacking Wordsworth for his stark realism. It suggests great advantages, provided you have the capacity to play a high-stakes game, and provided you do not violate the principle of reality (Adlai Stevenson going after Dwight Eisenhower for his lack of military skill would be an example of such a violation). If you have the support of the regular party's organization in a state where a reform movement in your party is strong, you should waste no time assailing your opponent for his link to the "old, discredited political system." This is what Jerry

Brown did in 1976 in Maryland, when he entered as the candidate of the New Age with the fervent support of every moss-backed political boss in the state, who were hoping that Brown would stall Jimmy Carter long enough to get Hubert Humphrey into the race. If you have had no experience in any executive position, while your opponent has done nothing but administer departments of government, attack him for "not knowing how the process works," and point to anything in your record that remotely resembles an administrative achievement, even if it is keeping the size of your legislative staff below the legal limit.

In formulating this kind of attack, it is critical to keep in mind that voters do not like candidates to surprise them with defects. It was acceptable for Richard Nixon to be devious, humorless, charming in the manner of Uriah Heep. This was part of the package. When it turned out that he was *not* a practitioner of traditional virtues, that he cheated on his taxes, enriched himself at government expense, and used a vocabulary out of the sewer, many of his most fervent supporters broke away. A similar example comes to mind from a 1968 California Senate campaign. Max Rafferty, a far-right political figure who had served as Superintendent of Public Instruction for the state, had made something of a national reputation as a shrill advocate against the permissive, radical education of our time. Tapping into the conservative heart of the Republican Party, he had won a primary, unseating liberal Republican Thomas Kuchel. To have attacked Rafferty as a reactionary, as a heartless demagogue, would have done no good to Democratic nominee Alan Cranston. Rafferty had been elected to statewide office with these characteristics in full view.

Then, during the campaign, it was discovered that Rafferty had applied for a draft exemption during World War II, appearing with a cane when he went for his examination. Shortly after the war ended, so did Rafferty's reliance on the cane. This revelation went to the heart of Rafferty's stature as a defender of the American Way of Life, a firm critic of long-haired, cowardly draft dodgers. Thousands of miniature canes began appearing all over the state of California, and Rafferty's political base melted away. He not only lost the Senate race to Cranston, but lost his state superintendent post two years later to the first black ever elected to state-wide office in California.

This is why political jujitsu is so valuable; if you hit the mark, you will aim not at the part your opponent assumes is vulnerable, but at that element of his character and record on which he is most heavily relying. Does it make sense, for example, to attack Jerry Brown as a "flake" or a "weirdo" when everyone understands that he speaks a language that is far removed from those of us landlocked on planet Earth? There is, I suggest, much more profit in looking through Brown's record as Governor and going after him enthusiastically as a Governor mired in the ways of the past, using twenty-first-century rhetoric to disguise nineteenth-century government philosophy. When everyone knows that Ronald Reagan brags about himself as a "citizen-politician," do you think it makes a great deal of sense to rake up the actors-aren't-qualified attack? Or would it make more sense to count up the number of races which Reagan has entered since 1966—a total of five, including three runs for the Presidency—and ask what happened to the citizen since he became a professional politician? Is Ted Kennedy more vulnerable on the liberalism issue—positions which have failed to hurt his standing in the poll—or on the question of leadership on which he bases his political future? Can Ted Kennedy point to any concrete accomplishment since he entered the Senate seventeen years ago?

It is even possible, if you are clever enough, to attack one candidate in a race by ostensibly attacking another. Nowhere was this done more brilliantly than in New York in 1970, in a three-way race among a liberal Republican (Charles Goodell), a liberal Democrat (Richard Ottinger), and a conservative (James Buckley). The Nixon White House wanted a Buckley victory, but did not want explicitly to endorse a third-party candidate. They also knew that Goodell, who was running a poor third in the race, had to win enough liberal votes to keep Ottinger from beating Buckley. In the middle of the campaign, Vice-President Spiro Agnew came to New York for a speech. His attacks on the press and on "radical-liberals" had made him a hero on the Right and a villain on the Left.

In his speech, Agnew attacked Goodell, and proclaimed, "I will not support a radical-liberal of either party." This made Goodell a hero to a segment of liberals in New York, and probably guaranteed him the endorsement of *The New York Times,* which may have meant the difference between victory and defeat for Ottinger. What Agnew had done was to win votes for Goodell by attacking him—and in the process ensure victory for the real candidate of his choice. While this has more in common with cushion billiards than with jujitsu, the principle applies.

There is one final virtue in this approach to politics. It is liberating to you, and to those who support you, because it presumes that one of the most surprising elements in any political campaign is candor. Saying more or less what you mean—about issues, controversies, even personalities—will keep opponents and the press alike constantly off-balance, because they simply do not know how to respond to it. Watching Ed Koch run for Mayor of New York in 1977 was an eye-opening experience, as he attacked municipal unions in the strongest of union towns, as he told the mother of a police officer, "Your son does not have the right to strike," as he stood on a street corner telling two cops why they did not have the right to take two days off when they donated a pint of blood. Apart from separating Koch from the rest of the candidates, it made the grueling campaign much easier for him than for other candidates, since he never had to remember which group he was speaking to, and what promises he had made.

By speaking with one voice, Koch protected his campaign against charges of inconsistency; by saying the same thing everywhere, he sufficiently impressed the press to win the endorsement of two of the three city dailies. In this sense, Koch's entire campaign was an exercise in jujitsu, since it played upon the most essential assumption of the electorate: that a politician is incapable of running for office by saying exactly what he means. It may not, as Koch's own experience has shown, be the way to govern, since outspokenness is not that far removed from insensitivity. But it does demonstrate that the element of surprise can be a potent tool in campaigns, and nothing appears more surprising in our time than the willingness of a candidate to say what he means.

CHAPTER XIV:

HOW TO MAKE THINGS BETTER

It is not quite illegal to write a book about politics without suggesting how to improve the state of the art, but it might as well be. If *The Prince* were published for the first time today, some assistant professor of political science would whimper that Machiavelli failed to offer a six-point program to make the Medici more democratic.

I am about to offer, therefore, a three-point program to make things better. These ideas may seem too farfetched to be implemented immediately, but that is because they have been cast in deliberately visionary terms, so as to appeal to the people who write newspaper columns with wide circulation. They combine a clear-eyed view of the political process with concrete, hard-nosed solutions to some of our most perplexing ills. If the people who wield power today lack the foresight to appreciate these remedies, that is their problem, not mine. I should also point out that each of these reforms,

however bold they may seem, is rooted in historical experience, and in pragmatic possibility.

Rent-a-Celebrant and Other Devices to Win the Presidential Battle of Expectations

It is by now a grade-school lesson in the science of presidential politics that primaries are won not by counting the votes,
but by measuring votes against the expectations. If you did
better than you were supposed to, you won; if you did worse
than you were supposed to, you lost.

This new tradition in our system had its genesis in 1960,
when John Kennedy proposed to demonstrate his drawing
power by winning the nomination through the primary process, thus convincing the leaders of big-state delegations that
his youth and Catholicism were not real barriers to his electability. Since he had no real opposition in New Hampshire,
his first test was in Wisconsin, where a 40 percent Catholic
population was counted in his favor, while its proximity to
Hubert Humphrey's Minnesota was counted as an obstacle.
Traveling reporters really had no sense of who the favorite
should be, until then Wisconsin Governor Gaylord Nelson's
press secretary told the press that John Kennedy should be
expected to win all ten Congressional districts in the primary. As a result, his victory in six of the ten districts—and
a substantial statewide margin—was counted as unimpressive.

The Kennedy people learned their lesson. In West Virginia, with a 4 percent Catholic population, they constantly
bombarded the press with data showing Kennedy in trouble,
with polls showing an early lead for Humphrey, with "background" briefings reminding the press of the strong anti-
Catholic sentiment in that state. By primary day, the reporters had become convinced that this was a do-or-die state for
Kennedy. When the combination of Kennedy charm, Kennedy money, and a vicious attack on Humphrey from the
son of Franklin D. Roosevelt all combined to produce a 60

percent Kennedy landslide, his path to the nomination was all but strewn with roses. The Kennedy people also applied this lesson very well during the 1960 convention. According to Pierre Salinger, JFK's press secretary, the Kennedy forces were hoping for as many as sixty-five delegates from California. But the state, whose delegates were longing for Adlai Stevenson, only gave him thirty-seven votes. But— and this is the key—the Kennedy forces did not claim any votes at all in the preballot handicapping. "Because we had never claimed as much as one vote in California," Salinger observed, "our behind-the-scenes defeat in the California delegation actually appeared as a victory."

In 1968, Eugene McCarthy's peace campaign against Lyndon Johnson benefited from the same phenomenon. When the campaign began in the fall of 1967—with no professional support, almost no money, and no backing from important political leaders—the guesses were confined to the 10 percent category. New Hampshire Governor John King and Senator Thomas McIntyre, both supporting Johnson, wrote the McCarthy campaign off as an aberration. But with the war news worsening, particularly in the wake of the Tet Offensive in early 1968, and with money coming in from disaffected Democrats, the McCarthy campaign took root. What actually happened in the primary was that President Johnson *defeated* Eugene McCarthy on a write-in (McCarthy was the only Democrat on the ballot). But because McCarthy came within a few thousand votes of defeating the President, and because he had done two or three times better than anyone expected him to do, he scored a huge victory in the press perception of the campaign. I suspect that one of the easiest barroom bets to win is to ask a friend if he remembers who won the New Hampshire Democratic primary in 1968.

Just as Eugene McCarthy won by losing, Ed Muskie lost by winning four years later. The clear front-runner ever since his 1970 election eve speech, Muskie was running in a state neighboring his own Maine, and everybody knew he would

win. So the question became "how big a win?" Dick Stew-
art, Muskie's press secretary, recalled the dilemma after the
election:

"Muskie kept playing a game with the press . . . the question was constantly, 'How much do you feel you have to win
by here, since it's a neighboring state, to be a viable candidate after New Hampshire?' Muskie always said, 'I've been
in politics all my life, and I've always felt that the guy who
got one vote more than anybody else won the primary.' Unfortunately, however, one of our coordinators in New
Hampshire said, 'If he doesn't get fifty percent of the vote,
I'll blow my brains out,' or words to that effect. From that
moment on, fifty percent stuck. Despite whatever Muskie
said, that comment by that woman stuck and fifty percent
became the target which he was held accountable for."

So when Muskie won the primary with 46 percent of the
vote, and George McGovern came in second with 37 percent
of the vote, Muskie had "lost"—because he had failed to
meet the prediction of 50 percent—and McGovern had
"won" because he had pulled a "surprisingly strong" showing and had come within ten percentage points of Muskie.

By 1976, the reporters were fully aware of the expectation
game, and so were the candidates. But that did not prevent
the same kinds of accidental benchmarks from occurring.
When Reagan challenged Ford in New Hampshire, no one
had a fair way to "expect" the primary to go. A Republican
incumbent hadn't been seriously challenged for renomination since Theodore Roosevelt took on William Howard Taft
in 1912, so that was an obstacle for Reagan. On the other
hand, Ford was an unelected President with no national political base. Could this be a primary in which the winner was
whoever got the most votes?

No—not after New Hampshire Governor Meldrim Thom-
son, a figure out of H. L. Mencken by way of Nathanael
West, declared that he expected Reagan to win with 55 percent of the vote. Using the "your own man says so" rule of
politics, the press held Reagan to this figure; so when he

came within a thousand votes of outpolling Ford, the press treated it as a major Ford victory, and the Reagan campaign stalled for two months, until a string of Southern primary victories almost gave him the nomination.

In the Democratic campaign, Henry Jackson, who had been stripped of his front-runner status after New Hampshire, was fighting for the nomination on the premise that Carter could not appeal to traditional Democrats in large, big-city states which were critical to the party's hopes in November. Jackson had won a smashing victory in Massachusetts, but no one had cared, because the press was still trying to discover how to get to Plains, Georgia, for background material on the winner of the New Hampshire primary. So the next test for Jackson was New York.

A substantial Jackson victory—over Carter, Morris Udall, and uncommitted delegates waiting for Humphrey to enter the race—would reestablish the Senator as the candidate of traditional Democrats. But during his New York campaign, in a careless moment, Jackson expressed his confidence that he would win a "landslide" victory in New York. Well, the press wanted to know, what were the dimensions of a "landslide"? At least 50 percent of the vote, or a majority of delegates, right? Jackson was stuck. On primary day, he won a substantial plurality of the delegates, some 38 percent in all—but *not* 50 percent. In his victory address, Jackson explained lamely, "We got our landslide, but we just missed our majority." The press didn't buy it—and the next day more coverage was given Carter's hairbreadth win over Udall in Wisconsin than to Jackson's win in the second-biggest state in the union.

If you have any plans to run for President, or to help plot a presidential campaign, you must be prepared to meet and master the challenge not just of outpolling your rivals, but of outexpecting them. Fortunately a little-noticed device, used only once in the 1976 Democratic campaign, provides a breakthrough of staggering possibilities for political professionals.

In the preprimary season of 1976, a caucus of liberal Democrats convened in Massachusetts to decide which candidate for President would win their support. Among the not-yet-declared candidates was Senator Frank Church of Idaho, whose supporters came to this caucus fully knowledgeable of the expectation game, and absolutely determined to win a psychological victory from the balloting.

Before the votes were cast, they had printed a press release which exulted: "The Senator's achievement in winning ———— percent of the vote here today was termed remarkable by his supporters, who went into the caucus with little hope of any kind of victory." Following the vote, Church's overjoyed followers scribbled in the correct number (about 23.7 percent) and distributed the prepackaged expression of glee to the press.

At first, this appeared to be nothing if not dangerous. Had all of Church's supporters been kept from voting (by a felonious violation of the laws of probability or by tainted chicken salad at the prepsychological victory lunch), it would have left the statement a shade limp ("The Senator's achievement in winning *one-tenth of one percent* of the vote here today was termed remarkable . . ."). It also raised some exquisite philosophical questions. Can something be proclaimed as remarkable before it happens? Indeed, is not an expectation of remarkability a self-contradiction? The preparation of those releases meant that nothing Senator Church might have done —not even winning every single vote and proving Fermat's Last Theorem (a mathematical proposition incapable of proof or disproof) correct—would have been really remarkable.

But on sober second thought, it became apparent that this was indeed an instrument of such cunning as to remake the political landscape of our time. As we have seen, in the crucial battle of expectations, the mortal enemy of any campaign is spontaneity—that uncontrollable, unresearched, unbudgeted, unadvanced outburst by someone which blasts all the carefully controlled strategy of a campaign completely out of the water. You may have labored for months to convince the press corps that you would be ecstatic with 32 percent of the vote—five points less than your latest polls show you receiving—only to have a receptionist in South Lozenge blurt out, "If Smithers doesn't get forty-five percent, I'll hurl my twins off Furburg's Peak!" and you are finished.

Using the Church formula, this danger is done. All you need do is to print up a victory statement, which is usable in every primary, and which declares: "Senator Smithers today scored a surprisingly strong (x) percent of the vote in the ———— primary, surpassing the highest expectations of his supporters, who would have been happy with (x–10) percent of the vote, and dealing a devastating blow to his rivals, who had been hoping to hold Smithers to (x–20) percent of the vote."

This will keep you in the expectation ball game as long as the reporters do not react with cynicism to this innovation, and begin to fill in the blank spaces with unprintable comments. It is not, however, the whole answer. You must also convince the press by the responses of the campaign inner circle that you believe you have scored that all-important psychological victory. One of Ronald Reagan's fatal mistakes was to appear disappointed by his showing. On the postprimary flight out of New Hampshire, his staff—playing the game well—popped open a celebratory bottle of champagne. But Reagan was overheard grumbling to an aide about the results of the campaign, and in any event the Ford campaign was practically throwing a New Year's Eve party.

There are specific steps you can take to avoid this fate:

Rent-a-celebrant. At the beginning of a primary campaign find the most dour, pessimistic, out-of-work political pro in the state and put him on your payroll. His job will be to sit in Holiday Inn coffee shops and bars whenever the press is in town. He will have reams of computer printouts, which he will reluctantly discuss with the press on an off-the-record basis. ("Off-the-record" means that it will be printed in a story which says, "Privately, the Smithers campaign is concerned about . . .") His job, further, is to "reveal" to the press his doubts about Smithers' strength in precisely those districts where Smithers is running strongest. He should never be so pessimistic as to doubt Smithers' "viability"— this can produce the kind of negative stories that chip away at your momentum—but just indicate all of the difficulties facing Smithers. ("They're outspending us three to one in Smithville." "The local editor in Glenplains hates Presbyterians. . . .")

On primary night, this prophet of gloom suddenly will blossom into a full-fledged celebrant. From the moment the first returns come in, your celebrant will be racing through the pressroom, showing how Smithers has exceeded the greatest expectations of his supporters in whatever community he has managed to do well in. He should be carrying a bottle of very expensive champagne, and on occasion borrow a press phone to call some prearranged supporter in another state, during which call he will carefully let the reporters overhear him saying, "Honest to God, I never thought we could pull this off. . . . Six Malibu millionaires called Smithers in the last hour. It's fantastic!"

Express concern at the achievement.   On the day after the primary, the campaign manager should draft a highly confidential memo (its "status" will assure better placement for the newspaper stories that will be written about it). The memo should warn all members of the staff not to take excessive comfort from "our remarkable success in the recent primary. No matter what rumors you may have heard about forthcoming developments, I urge you not to give way to complacency. There is still much to do before victory is assured." Other campaign strategists should begin to examine the records of potential new candidates who they "expect" may be entering the race after all of your present rivals withdraw.

Start looking for a running mate. Press secretaries and other campaign officials should casually ask reporters what they know about prominent Senators and Governors. "Have you ever met Trelbaum's family? Are they attractive? Anything in his background that could hurt him? What's your sense of O'Hanrahan? Has he got the stuff to make tough decisions?" Never tell the reporters why you want to know this information. If they aren't smart enough to figure it out, then they aren't worth misleading.

Preplant a defection. In the pre-Watergate days, campaigns routinely attempted to put operatives in other campaigns for the purpose of obtaining information. On purely pragmatic grounds, this would be a terrible mistake. If any confidential material ever wound up in your offices, the campaign would be over, and you would find yourself a footnote in the history books ("Smithers: See Smithersgate"). What does make sense is to encourage one of your supporters to work in a rival campaign. As soon as the first key primary is over, this supporter can "defect" to your side with an open letter to his former campaign. It should be cast in the most generous possible light: "I joined the Trelbaum campaign because I believed that Trelbaum could lead America toward a new direction. The results of the primary, however, are clear. Smithers clearly has the momentum to carry him forward to victory. It is crucial that those who believe as we do must unite behind Smithers to achieve the victory for reform and progressivism [or conservatism] that we need. Further division can only divide us further."

None of these moves will work if a candidate has gone down to crushing defeat; none are necessary if you have won 65 percent of the vote. But where the outcome is uncertain, where the interpretation of results is everything, these moves may just make the difference between lunch at the White House mess in a few months, or another Whopper with fries on a park bench.

Move Your Supporters to New Hampshire for Presidential Primaries

Even in an era of political apathy, there are always more people who want to participate in political campaigns than there are things for participants to do. Sometimes, clever political technicians can hit upon useful—or apparently useful—tasks for these well-meaning citizens. Larry O'Brien, a longtime worker for John Kennedy, hit upon a now-legendary solution to this problem in 1958, when Kennedy was running for reelection to the United States Senate, and when his supporters were looking for a margin impressive enough to establish his credentials as a potential presidential nominee. O'Brien put these 1800 excess volunteers to work drafting thank-you letters to the 250,000 Massachusetts citizens who had signed John Kennedy's nominating petitions. It was a step which could only produce goodwill toward Kennedy, and it offered to the would-be volunteers "the illusion of service," as O'Brien put it later.

With the growth of presidential primaries, volunteers took on greater importance. The legions of Barry Goldwater supporters within the Republican Party gave him the resources to compete with Nelson Rockefeller's limitless wealth in the caucuses and primaries of 1964; indeed, in many nonprimary states, the sheer numbers of Goldwater supporters guaranteed him hundreds of delegates without meaningful opposition. It was this core of support which ensured Goldwater's nomination after his victory in the California primary. The thousands of (mostly youthful) supporters of Eugene McCarthy made his impressive showings possible in the New Hampshire and Wisconsin primaries, which effectively drove Lyndon Johnson out of the 1968 race. And George McGovern in 1972 survived the year-long drought of money and support in 1971 because his antiwar position ensured him an intense, loyal, and large following.

These are impressive uses of volunteers. But they are still

severely limited, in comparison to a political move which, in all modesty, holds out the possibility for completely revolutionizing American politics.

To understand the basis for this proposal, it is necessary to understand how irrationally important the New Hampshire primary is in the American political system. Beginning in 1952, when the first-in-the-nation primary began to be contested, this small, unrepresentative state has exercised influence out of all proportion to its size and significance. Eisenhower's 1952 write-in victory over Robert Taft—a victory achieved without his formal declaration of candidacy— was the event that brought Ike into the race, while Kefauver's Democratic primary win drove Truman from it. Ever since 1952, armies of reporters have descended on New Hampshire, battling with each other for the right to seize typical New England folks, and demand anecdotes, insights, and epiphanies from these ordinary, unpretentious Americans. (One vicious rumor has it that New Hampshire citizens will soon adopt minimum price regulations to prevent citizens from undercutting each other: $15 for an insight, $25 for a prediction, $50 for a quote worthy of a Sunday magazine lead.)

Because the press needs something concrete to report in its ever-more pervasive coverage of our system, the New Hampshire primary has become a crucial weeding-out process. A favorite who fails to win in New Hampshire—or to win by enough, as Ed Muskie and Lyndon Johnson found out—is discredited. An unknown who wins, or who does better than expected, as George McGovern and Jimmy Carter proved, quickly becomes the front-runner. His picture is on the cover of *Time* and *Newsweek*. He is interviewed on the late-night network special programs, on the next day's *Today* show and *Good Morning, America* and *Morning*. He is interviewed—personally—by Walter Cronkite, John Chancellor, and Frank Reynolds. Money suddenly starts flowing into the campaign. This victory is, by itself, more than enough to give a candidate credibility.

The absurdity of this importance can be shown by a few numbers from the 1976 campaign. In the Republican primary, Ronald Reagan came within less than a thousand votes of defeating incumbent President Ford (see the section Rent-a-Celebrant and Other Devices to Win the Presidential Battle of Expectations for an examination of the expectation dilemma and how to solve it). A shift of 500 votes would have given Reagan the victory, and might well have finished off Ford right then and there. In the Democratic primary, Jimmy Carter won with 26,000 votes—some 5000 votes more than second-place finisher Morris Udall. So a shift of 2500 votes from Carter to Udall would have given Udall the covers of the newsmagazines and the blitz of interviews. By contrast, a week later Henry Jackson won the Massachusetts primary with 146,000 votes, with Jimmy Carter finishing a distant fourth, some 65,000 votes behind. Yet, despite the greater size and electoral strength of Massachusetts, despite the fact that Carter's first foray into a big, industrialized Democratic state was a disaster, the glow of New Hampshire surrounded Carter long enough to carry him through the Florida primary, where his victory over Wallace brought him renewed strength.

So mystical is the power of the New Hampshire primary that it has produced its own political rule: No one has been elected President without winning the New Hampshire primary since 1952. It is possible to win the primary and not win the Presidency (Estes Kefauver, Henry Cabot Lodge, Ed Muskie), it is possible to lose New Hampshire and win your party's nomination (Barry Goldwater, Hubert Humphrey), but you cannot, this rule says, win the White House without winning New Hampshire. Since this is a rule, and not an eternal principle, there is no reason to believe this will hold true for every election. But a good campaign knows how to exploit the misconceptions of the political hype machine. Rick Stearns, who was McGovern's chief delegate hunter in 1972, said after the election that "it was our assumption that . . . the primaries that had been significant in sixty-eight would loom important to the press in 1972. That assumption proved to be true. Otherwise, there was no reason that Wisconsin should have been the watershed for the McGovern campaign that it was; the Wisconsin primary fundamentally was not that important." Had George McGovern not gotten a "surprisingly impressive" 37 percent of the New Hampshire primary vote, he might never have made it to Wisconsin at all.

All a genuinely creative political campaign needs to do is put these two notions together:

- There are usually more volunteers than can be creatively used.
- Each vote in a New Hampshire primary is worth five to fifty times as much as a vote in the later primaries.

The solution, of course, is to gather up as many volunteer supporters as you can find, and move them to New Hampshire sometime in the late fall—not just as campaign workers, but as citizens.

The rules for establishing voting residency in a state are not that difficult. All a voter needs is an address, and a willingness to file a declaration of residency in conformity with New Hampshire law—right now, ninety days before the primary is required, meaning that volunteers could be moved after Thanksgiving and still be eligible to vote in the primary. For college students, the move would be simple: relocate in New Hampshire, file a declaration of residency, and then go right back to school. (This could pose a hardship for students taking advantage of in-state tuition rates at public universities, but there is nothing wrong with young people learning the meaning of sacrifice.) For ski bums and other part-time workers looking for light labor to combine with a winter vacation, the mobile-voter plan is perfect. In return for a few hours a week of canvassing, envelope stuffing, and brochure distribution, a campaign would provide room and board through the winter season. For those with independent incomes, or those with understanding parents, the New Hampshire lodging could be provided without cost to the campaign.

Applying a cost-benefit analysis, we find that this mobile-voter plan is by far the most effective possible expenditure of funds available to a presidential campaign. Assume you rent a farmhouse in Franconia, or a cottage outside of Manchester, for $250 a month, and assume that five people can live there. Assume further that food and other necessary expenses will cost $10 a day—roughly $300 a month. Adding this all together, we find that a mobile voter can be supported through the three-month residency period in New Hampshire for a unit cost of about $1000. Given the fact that the great majority of your mobile voters will actually be working at jobs, or attending schools out of state, this would bring the cost of these extra voters down to, let us say, $300. Thus, by spending an extra million dollars in the weeks before the New Hampshire primary, your campaign virtually guarantees itself 3000 solid voters in that primary—and in the Democratic primary, fewer than 100,000 votes are cast in all. Those 3000 votes all but ensure you of a "credible" showing in the New Hampshire primary—and in anything like a close race, it should guarantee you a victory, the covers of *Time* and *Newsweek,* and all the other benefits.

Never, I venture to say, has money been spent as creatively, with as sure a certainty of an effective return, as would be spent under this mobile-voter plan. The people of New Hampshire, so anxious for increased tourism, would welcome these new arrivals. After a short training course, these mobile voters could don plaid shirts and woolen hats, and give out taciturn interviews to visiting reporters, explaining in simple New England phrases that " 'pears tuh me that this fella Smithers kinda speaks what's on our minds," further exciting the political community with yet another man of the people. Of course, William Loeb would turn the *Manchester Union-Leader* inside out with his attacks on outside agitators, but his credibility is something less than overwhelming.

In some future election, the New Hampshire primary may be reduced to sensible proportions. Until that happens, potential Presidents overlook the power of the moving van at their peril.

Allow Us to Sell Our Votes to Each Other

Whatever the danger of political predictions—just ask George Gallup about the fortunes of President Dewey—but one thing can be said with unhappy certainty about how Americans will vote this November, the next, and the next: they will vote less.

The ever-shrinking faith, or interest, in our political process has been proven at the polls. Since 1948, our national elections have drawn a more-or-less steadily dwindling percentage of eligible voters. Even as we enfranchise once voteless Americans—Southern blacks with the 1965 Civil Rights Act, eighteen-year-olds with the Twenty-sixth Amendment —more Americans each year seem to vote with their backsides.

So far, none of the suggestions for increasing voter turnout seem practical. Some have proposed changing Election Day to Sunday instead of Tuesday. This is absurd. Sunday voting would interfere with professional football telecasts. Not only would the average voters refuse to move from their television sets, but the networks might well react to this economic threat by refusing to cover campaigns at all.

Others have suggested postcard registration, even postcard balloting. Given the condition of the United States mails, it would be spring before the votes could be counted. Switzerland has been held up as an example to us; that nation fines its nonvoters, and turnouts regularly exceed 90 percent. This is not only unconstitutional, it is poor public policy. Staying at home—out of disgust, indifference, or satisfaction—is as legitimate a political statement as is frenzied

political participation. Recent studies have shown that the
nonvoter is as fully informed as the voter. (Given the quality
of recent political leadership, nonvoters may well be better
informed, or reflecting the attitude of a senior citizen of New
Hampshire who once said, "I never vote—it only encour-
ages them.")

Is there anything that can be done? Yes there is: a very
simple, administratively easy, eminently American solution
which can, at one stroke, bring out millions of new voters
while violating none of our cherished principles of freedom:
*We can allow the American people to sell our votes to each
other.*

I realize, of course, that this idea will strike fear and loath-
ing into the heart of every good government organization
from Common Cause to the League of Women Voters. It
conjures up scenes of skid-row bums, lined up outside of
polling places while cigar-smoking thugs hand out pints of
whiskey and five-dollar bills in exchange for votes; or perhaps the image of big-city ward heelers dropping off Christmas turkeys to unread slum dwellers who pull the levers for
candidates whose names they cannot pronounce.

Now, in the first place, it is by no means certain that this
old-fashioned vote buying was as evil as we have assumed.
If, as one political scientist said, politics is the study of "who
gets what, and why," then these transactions seem perfectly
fair. "One drink, one vote" may never be carved in marble,
but to those whose lives are shaped by access to whiskey, it
seems fair enough. Further, it seems much less costly to the
economy to exchange votes for turkeys than it does to exchange votes for cargo preference bills, beef and sugar quotas, higher minimum wage levels, and other concessions to
interest groups which inflate the currency and swell the def-
icit. There is no logical reason why wholesale vote selling
should be admirable, while the much-less-expensive retail
vote selling should be treated as a crime.

Even if you do not accept this perfectly reasonable argument, consider this approach. Americans are always told

that with the right to vote they possess a pearl of great price, purchased with the blood of our forefathers, envied by more than half the world. But what is it worth in hard, practical terms? Less than a Green Stamp, less than a cigarette coupon. It is redeemable only by granting increasingly bigger chunks of our lives over to increasingly small-minded people. In a society where wealth seems the only real measure of worth, it is no wonder that Americans take the franchise so lightly.

Now, suppose we changed the mechanics of voting this way. Suppose the Board of Elections sent to every voter—using a computerized check of Social Security numbers, utility bills, and other means of verification—a packet full of tickets, each good for one vote for every office and proposition on the ballot. (If we do not trust the government with this task, we can contract the work out to the firms that run *Reader's Digest* and Publisher's Clearing House sweepstakes. These organizations clearly have the ability to reach every household in America with their mailings.) Any American citizen who wanted to vote would simply show up at the polls on Election Day, and exchange his tickets for the right to vote.

Now suppose a citizen doesn't want to exercise his right to vote. He would be perfectly free to exchange any, or all, of his tickets with anybody else, for whatever price they agreed to. (If we wanted to limit institutional power, we could pass a law providing prison terms for any corporation, labor union, or other organization from engaging in this exchange, while leaving individuals free to buy and sell at will.)

Imagine the advantages of this process over politics as usual. Suppose you cared passionately about a campaign for Congress, and didn't give a rat's whisker about any other contest. You could trade your State Assembly ticket for a Congressional ticket—maybe throwing in a City Council ticket as well. You could collect other Congressional tickets by a simple cash-and-carry proposition—say, $5 a ticket—or with a combination of cash and exchange ($2 plus a Civil

Judge ticket). Then you might swap your Governor ticket for a Congressional ticket and $5, then give that $5 away for yet another Congressional ticket. Suddenly, you could vote five times for the one office you cared about, without actually gaining or losing any money at all, while others would be casting your discarded votes for the candidates *they* most wanted to win.

It is almost impossible to list the different advantages such a system would have over our present method of voting:

IT WOULD INSTANTLY INCREASE THE ENTHUSIASM QUOTIENT ON ELECTION DAY. No longer would campaign workers bang on doors, dragging apathetic voters out into the November chill, prodding them with free transportation, meals, and money to cast their votes reluctantly. Instead, the only people at the polling places would be enthusiastic holders of five, ten, fifty legitimate votes.

IT WOULD MAKE EACH VOTE A MORE GENUINE EXPRESSION OF CITIZEN INTEREST. One of the more expensive costs of representative democracy is that it counts the votes of the apathetic and the committed alike. One voter may believe that the election of his candidate is the most important issue of the decade; another may pull a lever because the candidate has the same last name as a good friend. Under the sell-your-vote proposal, the influence of the unconcerned is greatly lessened. If a voter doesn't really care about a campaign, all he has to do is sell the franchise to somebody who does. In this way, each vote cast has the power of commitment behind it.

IT WOULD RESTORE A SENSE OF EXCITEMENT ABOUT POLITICS. The Age of Television, despite its vast reach and pervasive coverage of campaigns, has produced a sense of numbness at election time. We have little left of the tradition of torchlight parades, mass rallies, and the other participatory elements of politics. Vote swapping would, I am convinced, trigger a renewed sense of excitement about campaigns, because it would get the ordinary citizen involved. Remember your schoolyard days, when bubble-gum cards and marbles were traded with all the fervor of a commodities market? Our factories, offices, bars, and beauty parlors would be abuzz with the chatter of newly motivated citizens, who would begin to care about political contests with the same excitement that now greets the appearance of the football pools.

"Give you ten bucks for your President!" the cry would resound. "Swap you my Senator and judge for your Governor!" the shout would echo. The long-elusive goal of citizen participation in the process would be no longer a dream, but a reality.

IT WOULD REDUCE INFLATION. Most economists now agree that the money supply is a key factor in producing inflation: the more money in circulation, the more likely we are to have too much money chasing too few goods, and the more likely we are to produce inflation. The legalization of vote selling would introduce a potential source of lessening the money supply. Small shopkeepers and other entrepreneurs might well begin accepting votes in exchange for goods; lawyers might offer small bits of legal advice at the cost of vote tickets. If this habit spread, the money supply would shrink and inflation might, at long last, be brought under a measure of control.

IT WOULD RENEW RESPECT FOR THE FREE-ENTERPRISE SYSTEM. Politicians never tire of telling us that we have come to expect too much from government. Generally, these are the same politicians who remain in office for decades by voting for increases in federal spending, and by turning their offices into service centers for constituents who believe themselves entitled to more benefits and privileges from the government from which we have come to expect too much.

The problem, of course, is that few of us ever experience

directly the joys and sorrows of the free-enterprise system. Either we work for huge organizations in the private sector, or we work for the government, or we work for public utilities, or we work for educational institutions, or we don't work at all. Vote swapping would, in effect, give every American a small supply of capital, and the chance to compete in an open marketplace. It would be a kind of gigantic Junior Achievement, in which we would be able to see the results of our exercises.

Since politicians have been buying votes with their promises—and with our tax money—vote selling is nothing new. The only real difference is that it would eliminate the middleman, permitting us to buy and sell in the deepest tradition of the American Way of Life.